D1530151

THE TURIN SHROUD

The Illustrated Evidence

THE TURIN SHROUD

The Illustrated Evidence

Ian Wilson
and Barrie Schwortz

This edition published by Barnes & Noble, Inc.,
by arrangement with
Michael O'Mara Books Limited
2000 Barnes & Noble Books

A CIP catalogue record for this book is available from the British Library

ISBN 0-7607-2245-5

M 10 9 8 7 6 5 4 3 2 1

Designed and typeset by Martin Bristow

Printed and bound in Singapore by Tien Wah Press

FRONTISPIECE: *Present home of the Shroud in Turin Cathedral. On display is a photograph. The cloth itself lies in a specially designed conservation case behind the curtaining. Visible behind is a* trompe l'oeil *painting of the altar and Chapel in which the Shroud was kept between 1694 and 1993. This painting, on a huge steel wall, screens the damage this altar and Chapel sustained in a major fire the night of 11 April 1997.*

ACKNOWLEDGEMENTS

Abbreviations: (*u*) upper; (*b*) below; (*r*) right; (*l*) left; (*c*) centre

Most photographs are by Barrie Schwortz except those and other illustrations listed as follows, whose copyright is gratefully acknowledged:

Aegyptisches Museum, Berlin: p. 43 (*ul*); Professor Nicholas Allen: pp. 124–5 (*all*); A.E.R.E. Harwell: p. 96 (*u*); University of Arizona: p. 8 (*ul and b*); Dr August Accetta: pp. 130 (*u*), 131 (*all*); Dr Leo H. Bazant: p. 74 (*b*); British Museum: pp. 54, 96 (*b*), 117 (*u*), 153 (*u*); Centro Español de Sindologia: p. 78 (*all*); Commissione Ostensione Sindone, Torino: pp. 138–9, 156 (*b*); Prof. Avinoam Danin: pp. 86, 87 (*bl and br*), 90–1; Edizioni San Paolo S.r.l.: p. 57 (*u and bl*); Giuseppe Enrie: pp. 28, 140–1; Mark Evans: pp. 73 (*r*), 75, 100 (*b*), 137 (*u*); Dr Leonardo Ferri: p. 47 (*r*); Dr Max Frei: p. 82; Ed Galda p. 8 (*ur*); Dr Leoncio Garza-Valdes: p. 99 (*ur*); Aldo Guerreschi: *Frontispiece*, pp. 22 (*u*), 37 (*bc*), 154 (*u*); Holy Monasteries of Meteora: p. 113 (*l*); The Holy See: pp. 12, 13; IS&T: The Society for Imaging Science and Technology, sole copyright owners of *The Journal of Imaging Science and Technology*: pp. 122 (*u and b*), 123 (*ul*); St Joseph's Hospice Association: p. 118 (*all*); The Manchester Museum, The University of Manchester: pp. 98–9 (*u*); Monastery of Klosterneuberg, near Vienna: p. 115 (*br*); Dr Walter McCrone: p. 120 (*b*); Lennox Manton: p. 109; Emanuela Marinelli: pp. 22 (*u*), 154 (*u*); Prof. Luigi Mattei: p. 53; Prof. Stephen Mattingly: pp. 126–7; Vernon Miller: pp. 47 (*l*), 76 (*u*), 77, 113 (*r*); Mario Moroni: pp. 107 (*r*), 151 (*b*); William Mottern: p. 26; Museum of Art & Archaeology, University of Missouri-Columbia (Gift of Leonard Epstein): p. 43; National Széchenyi Library, Budapest: p. 115 (*l*); Dr Eugenia Nitowski: p. 76 (*b*); Fr Francis O'Leary, St Joseph's Hospice Association: p. 119; Dr Deirdre O'Sullivan, University of Leicester: p. 43 (*ur*); Roel Oostra, CTC: p. 15 (*u*); *Osservatore Romano Servizio Fotografico*, p. 13; Oxford Research Laboratory for Archaeology and the History of Art: p. 97 (*ur*); Maurizio Paolicchi: p. 16 (*b*); Dame Isabel Piczek; pp. 38–9, 48, 49; Z. Radovan, Jerusalem: p. 60 (*u*); The Royal Collection © 2000, Her Majesty Queen Elizabeth II: p. 104; University of Texas Health Science Center: pp. 99 (*b*), 102–3; Telegraph Group Ltd, London: pp. 9, 133, 155 (*b*); Leo Vala: p. 34; Vatican Press Office: p. 156 (*c*); Dr Paul Vignon: p. 56; Dr Jean Volckringer: pp. 84, 85 (*r*); Dr Alan Whanger: pp. 39 (*ul and ur*), 83 (*b*), 85 (*u*), 87 (*ul and ur*), 91; Robert Wilcox: pp. 15 (*l*), 155 (*u*); Dr David Willis: pp. 17 (*b*), 29, 63 (*ur*); Ian Wilson: pp. 24, 44 (*br*), 51 (*br*), 52 (*br*), 62 (*b*), 63 (*br*), 110 (*c*), 111, 112, 120 (*u*), 151 (*c*), 152 (*c*), 153 (*b*); collection of: pp. 43 (*b*), 101 (*b*), 108 (*all*), 110 (*b*), 116, 117 (*b*), 128 (u), 129 (*b*), 152 (*u and b*); Judith Wilson: pp. 46 (*u and b*), 50 (*u and b*), 51 (*l*), 52 (*bl*), 65 (*u and b*), 78, 88, 89 (*all*), 123 (*ur*); Joe Zias: p. 60 (*b*); Dr Frederick T. Zugibe: pp. 58 (*b*), 59 (*bl and br*), 62 (*u*).

Every effort has been made to trace copyright holders of illustrations, but should any have been inadvertently missed, please contact Michael O'Mara Books.

CONTENTS

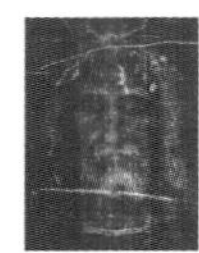

AUTHORS' PREFACE

As co-authors of a book on a cloth that is claimed to have wrapped the dead body of Jesus, Barrie Schwortz and I could hardly have more different or more unlikely backgrounds. Barrie was born and raised as an Orthodox Jew in Pittsburgh, Pennsylvania. He spent four years in the US Navy, was trained as a photographer at the Brooks Institute of Photography in Santa Barbara, California, and has long had his own photographic studio in Los Angeles. Having early lapsed from attending Jewish religious services, to this day he is not a practising adherent of any specific faith. I was born in south London. My mother, although nominally Anglican, never attended any regular church. My father had not even been baptised. I grew up highly agnostic, with religious relics very definitely beyond the pale.

Yet the subject on which Barrie's life and mine have come together, now for rather more years than we care to remember, is the Turin Shroud. Barrie's association with this began back in the 1970s when he was invited to be an official photographer for the STURP team that directly examined the Shroud in 1978. Today organizations as diverse as the BBC and the *Encyclopaedia Britannica* have recognized his web-site *www.shroud.com* to be not only the best available on the subject but also one of the finest examples of good usage of this medium.

My first exposure to the subject was a Leonard Cheshire *Picture Post* article in 1955. A deeper interest began to develop three years after I graduated in history at Oxford University, with some serious 'hobby' historical researches that significantly influenced my becoming a liberal-minded Roman Catholic in 1972. The same researches led to my being invited to examine the Shroud during a very privileged special showing the next year, and in turn to the cloth becoming the subject of my first-ever book, published in 1978.

Yet, although numerous other Shroud books, including one relatively recently by myself, have been published in the years since, none has so far presented the subject with colour photographs of the scale, quantity and quality that such a visual subject deserves. This is the deficiency that our book is intended to remedy, as well as to update on the quite remarkable developments that the subject has undergone even during the last two years. In the case of the photographs, as befits a photographer co-author, most of these are Barrie's, except where otherwise indicated. In the case of the text, although 'I' mostly means Ian Wilson, all content and opinions have been agreed by both of us as representing a fair-minded assessment of the available facts.

As Barrie and I are deeply conscious, this book would not have been possible without some very special help from individuals, some of whom, like ourselves, have given rather more hours to the Shroud than common sense and family life would consider reasonable. Barrie singles out for special mention Don Lynn 'for profound advice many years ago that ultimately helped me find the true perspective of my involvement with the Shroud', also 'my son David for his love and patience with me, particularly over these last four years since the web-site went on line'. Our thanks also go to, in alphabetical order: Dr August Accetta for making available his very recent medical research; Dr Alan Adler for advice and discussion on the Shroud's chemistry; Professor Leo Bazant; Professor Avinoam Danin of the Hebrew University, Jerusalem, for making available his latest botanical findings; Mark Evans; Professor Leonardo Ferri of Rome for books and photographs on his father Lorenzo's anatomical researches; Dr Mechthild Flury-Lemberg for making available her very recent textile analysis discovery; Aldo Guerreschi of Studio Scoffone, Turin; Mark Guscin for his exhaustive knowledge and help concerning the sudarium of Oviedo; Dr John Jackson and his wife Rebecca; Lennox Manton; Professoressa Emanuela Marinelli and Maurizio Paolicchi; Professor Stephen Mattingly for his help on microbiological matters; Sandra Milano, Vernon Miller; William Mottern; Dr Eugenia Nitowski of the Ariel Museum of Biblical Archaeology; Fr Francis O'Leary of Jospice International for his help with the Les Hunter mattress imprint; Richard Orareo for making available his superb collection of Shroud exposition prints and engravings; Isabel Piczek, for her many favours, but in particular for arranging my Shroud pose experiment; Archbishop Severino Poletto of Turin, Monsignor Giuseppe Ghiberti, and Professors Piero Savarino and Silvano Scannerini for arranging my most recent visit to Turin and second close-up viewing of the Shroud; Zev Radovan; Dr Alan Whanger and his wife Mary for their patience arguing over 'flower image' issues; Dr Fred Zugibe for much helpful discussion and for checking this book's medical aspects; and last but not least, my wife Judith who, as the photo acknowledgements reveal, can now add deputising for Barrie among her many duties and talents.

Barrie and I also particularly appreciate the kind help of those whose views on the Shroud may differ markedly from ours, yet with whom we can remain on friendly terms: Professor Nicholas Allen of Port Elizabeth, South Africa; Dr Emily Craig, Frankfort, Kentucky; Dr Timothy Jull of the University of Arizona; Dr Walter McCrone, the McCrone Institute, Chicago; Joe Zias, formerly of the Israel Antiquities Authority, Jerusalem.

Finally our very special thanks to Michael and Lesley O'Mara for speedily taking up the book idea, and to editor Jacquie Wines and her team for so ably steering the project to completion, including not least making light of the communications logistics of one of her authors being in Los Angeles, USA and the other in Brisbane, Australia.

Ian Wilson
and Barrie Schwortz

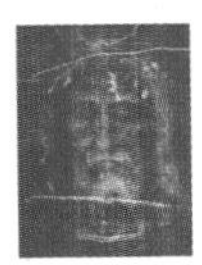

INTRODUCTION

The Shroud: 'a challenge to our intelligence'

(Pope John Paul II, 24 May 1998)

FACING PAGE: *(Above left) Photographed prior to radiocarbon dating, during which it was destroyed, a subsection of one of two samples of the Shroud received by the Arizona laboratory. Viewed here larger than life-size (the scale is in centimetres), this has been photographed from the underside, the side unseen when the Shroud is displayed.*

(Above right): The University of Arizona, where the first radiocarbon dating of the Shroud was carried out, 6 May 1988.

(Below left): A technician making adjustments to some of the radiocarbon dating apparatus used at Arizona.

RIGHT: *Announcement of the results of the radiocarbon dating, at the British Museum, 13 October 1988. On the left is Professor Edward Hall of the Oxford laboratory, at the centre Professor Michael Tite of the British Museum, and at the right Dr Robert Hedges of the Oxford laboratory.*

It was 9.50 a.m. on the morning of 6 May 1988. The location was the University of Arizona's high-tech radiocarbon-dating laboratory at Tucson, Arizona, amidst the cactus-dotted landscape of the Sonora Desert. In a huddle around a computer screen a group of physicists waited anxiously for the appearance of a crucial set of numbers. Veteran Professor Harry Gove, invited from New York State to be present because of his invention of the technology being used, jocularly likened the moment to the opening of Tutankhamun's tomb. As the numbers appeared, deputy laboratory chief Professor Doug Donahue, a Roman Catholic, made some momentary interpretative calculations, then went 'instantly drawn and pale'.[1] Gove, too, though an agnostic, later described himself as disappointed.

For the Arizona laboratory's computer had just shown that the Shroud of Turin, world famous for its enigmatic 'photographic' imprint, thought to be of the crucified Jesus, dated from around the year 1350. From their work on the tiny Shroud sample that Donahue and laboratory head Paul Damon, a Quaker, had collected from Turin just two weeks before, they had become the first scientists in the world to learn that, according to carbon dating, the Shroud was a medieval fake – seemingly just like so many other of the Roman Catholic Church's notorious 'relics'. Five months later, after the Arizona scientists' colleagues at similar laboratories in Oxford,

England, and Zurich, Switzerland, had reached similar conclusions, the news was released to the world. From the samples that each had been given, the laboratories collectively claimed a 95 per cent probability that the Shroud dated from between 1260 and 1390, with the odds against its dating from the first century being 'astronomical'.

As Professor Edward Hall of the Oxford laboratory pointed out during the British Museum press conference at which the announcement was made, such results were only to be expected. Even back in 1389, when there was much more gullibility about religious relics, a French bishop had told the then Pope that the Shroud was 'cunningly painted'.[2] Radiocarbon dating had, therefore, merely confirmed the truth of this allegation and eliminated any remaining mystery surrounding the Shroud. With characteristic forcefulness Hall concluded: 'There was a multi-million-pound business in making forgeries during the fourteenth century. Someone just got a bit of linen, faked it up, and flogged it.'

The next day, Friday, 14 October 1988, the news media around the world duly carried the story. The Shroud's legal owner is Pope John Paul II, the cloth having only five years earlier been bequeathed to him by the former owner, ex-King Umberto II of Italy, whose ancestors, the Dukes of Savoy, had owned it for five centuries. However, because the Archbishop of Turin is its executive custodian, it fell to Turin's then Archbishop, man-of-the-people Cardinal Anastasio Ballestrero to comment publicly on behalf of the Church, which he did almost simultaneously with the scientific press conference in London. Insisting that the Church had nothing to fear from the truth, Ballestrero formally accepted the scientific findings, simply adding that 'The problems about the origin of the [Shroud's] image and its preservation still remain to a large extent unresolved.' This Britain's *Daily Telegraph* newspaper translated into the headline: 'Turin shroud is a forgery, says Catholic Church'.

It might well have been thought, therefore, that from that moment on any further serious interest in the Shroud simply *had* to be over. Three internationally respected laboratories, two European and one American, all using the very latest, state-of-the-art radiocarbon-dating technology, had reached near identical findings that the Shroud's linen dated from no earlier than the late thirteenth century.[3] Furthermore, it all readily checked out with what was known – and not known – concerning the Shroud's history.

Thus it could be considered well documented all the way back to the mid-fourteenth century, the late sixteenth and seventeenth centuries having been its apogee, when its owners the Dukes of Savoy held big public expositions before huge crowds in Turin's Piazza Castello. In the early sixteenth century they kept it mostly in their former capital Chambéry, where it was nearly destroyed in a chapel fire. Fourteen fifty-three was the year that the Savoys acquired the cloth from its previous owner, widow Margaret de Charny, whose domains included the postage-stamp-size

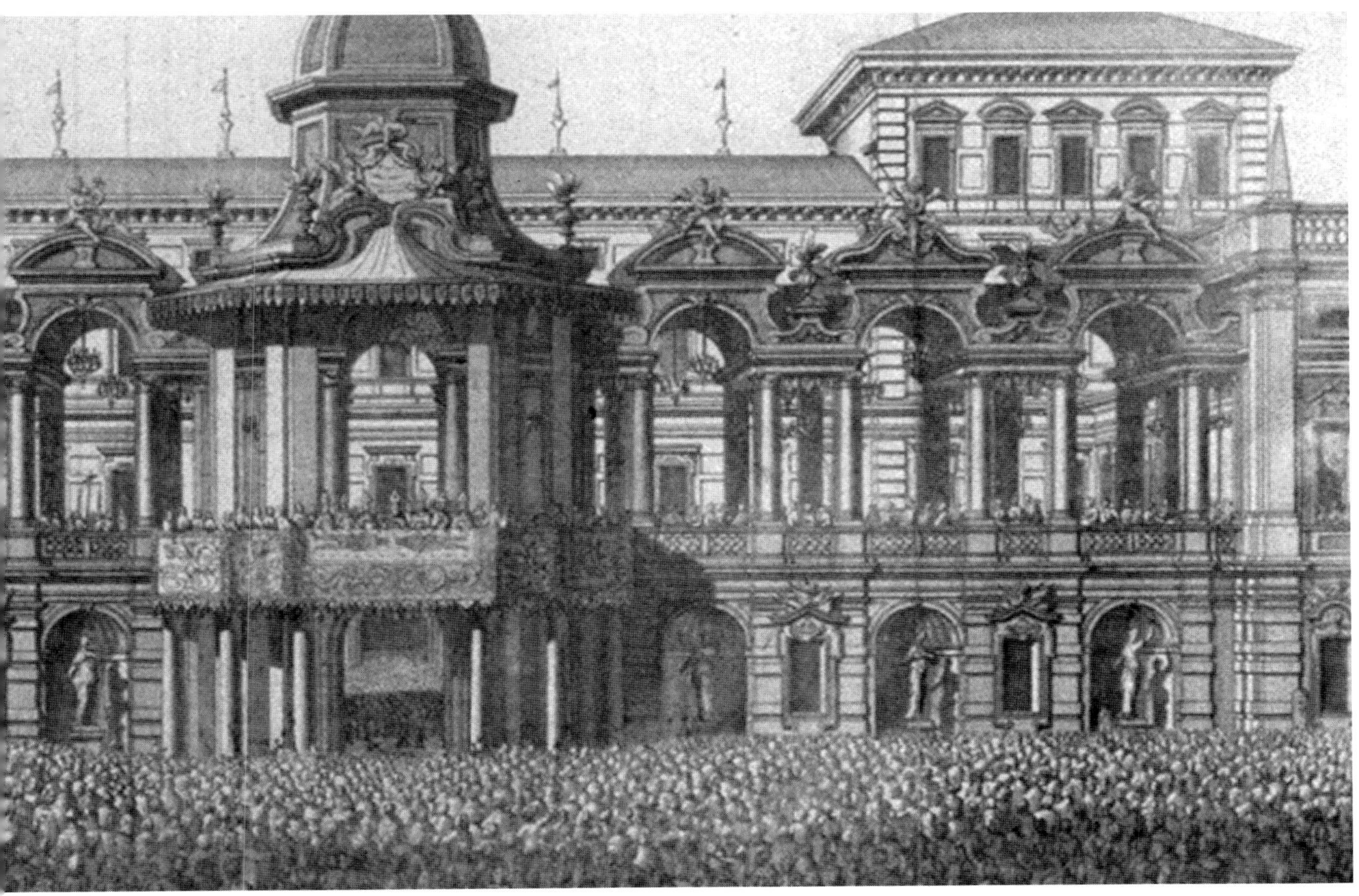

ABOVE: *Grand exposition of the Shroud held in Turin in 1737 to mark the marriage of Duke Charles Emmanuel of Savoy, whose family owned the Shroud from 1453 to 1983. The magnificent Pavilion seen here, specially built for Shroud expositions, was destroyed by fire in 1811.*

LEFT: *In marked contrast, the church in the tiny French village of Lirey. It was here, in a wooden predecessor of this church, that the first known European showings of the Shroud began back in the mid-fourteenth century.*

French village of Lirey, where Europe's first known Shroud expositions are recorded to have been held.

But during the generation immediately preceding 1389 the Shroud was the subject of serious forgery charges on the part of no less than two French bishops. It is true that the cloth's first known owner, Margaret's grandfather Geoffrey I de Charny, who died in 1356, was a war hero noted for his piety. But his very minor status in the French hierarchy made him most unconvincing, even in the Middle Ages, as the legitimate owner of a relic that, if genuine, would have been worth several kings' ransoms. And there was no clear record of where the Shroud might legitimately have come from before it surfaced in the 1350s. Effectively, therefore, the evidence of the Shroud's falsity seemed overwhelming.

Yet, though the Shroud might have seemed finished in the light of these findings, twelve years on something really very strange has happened. Between 18 April and 14 June 1998 it was publicly exhibited in Turin Cathedral. Throughout this period it received world-wide publicity, including being the cover story of America's *Time* magazine and the subject of CBS TV's *Public Eye* programme, and was mostly treated as seriously as if the carbon dating had never happened. In Turin itself it was accorded the tightest security measures and was viewed by nearly 3 million visiting pilgrims and tourists. Particularly curious was the way it was being presented to these – certainly not as any discredited example of medieval religious fraudulence, nor even as an interesting example of medieval religious painting. Instead, though the Church was careful not to spell it out in so many words, it was presented with all the solemnity and reverence that would be accorded to the real thing.

Nor was this all. Because, only the previous year, the Shroud had come very close to destruction in a cathedral fire, Italy's giant Italgas corporation funded the building of a state-of-the-art new bullet-proof showcase for it, complete with air-conditioning, climate control, fibre optic lighting and elaborate security devices, to the tune of 300 million lire. What right-thinking corporation spends 300 million lire for the display and conservation of a proven fake?

Further, on 24 May 1998 none other than Pope John Paul II, the Shroud's legal owner, paid an official visit to Turin during the period that the expositions were in progress. Yet instead of merely passing the Shroud by with the studied disdain that the Roman Catholic Church's highest dignitary might be expected to accord an object scientifically condemned as having been created to deceive his flock's most gullible, what did he do? In the company of a distinguished clerical entourage arrayed in its fullest finery, he spent several minutes on his knees before the subtly illuminated Shroud, his back to the high altar and his head bowed before it, clearly in the most intense prayer and meditation. After listening to a Gospel reading describing the discovery of the true shroud – whatever this might have been – in Jesus' empty tomb, he then delivered his longest-ever known sermon on this 'fake' object.

While in keeping with Church policy on all relics Pope John Paul stopped short of *ex cathedra* pronouncing the Shroud genuine (in his words, it is 'not a matter of faith' and 'the Church has no specific competence to pronounce on these questions'), none the less he made very obvious what he believed in his heart. Expressing the profoundest thanks for this 'unique gift', he described the Shroud as 'a mirror of the Gospel', which no sensitive person could fail to be inwardly touched by. Defining it as an image which 'everyone sees and no one at present can explain', he declared it 'a challenge to our intelligence'. He 'urged' that it be studied without 'pre-established positions', and with 'a free-thinking mind' conscientiously respecting both scientific methodology and religious sensitivities.[4]

It is with that advice in mind, and in the light of recent highly reputable scientific findings, which are most strongly contra-indicative of the radiocarbon-dating verdict, that my co-author and I have combined to put together this present book. It is a partnership that we believe to be both balanced and authoritative, not only because of our very different back-

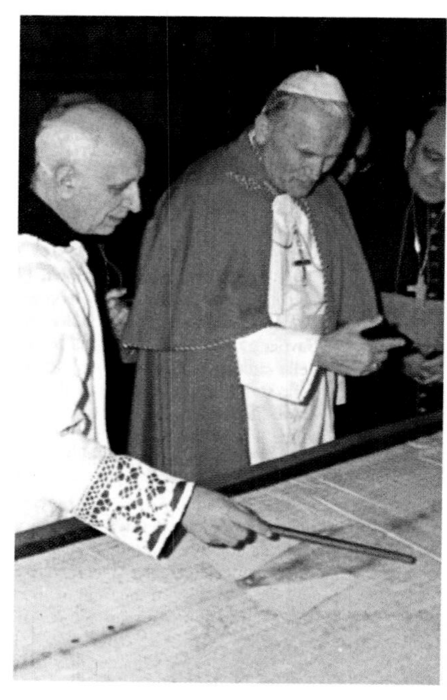

ABOVE: *Pope John Paul II's special close-up viewing of the Shroud, 13 April 1980. He describes the Shroud as 'a mirror of the Gospel', which no sensitive person could fail to be touched by.*

grounds and fields of expertise, but also because we share with Pope John Paul II one rather rare and special privilege.

On 13 April 1980, just over a year after the start of his pontificate, the Pope had a lengthy private viewing of the Shroud, in which the cloth was laid out before him so that he could study it at closest hand, and without any covering glass, an experience that with little doubt greatly affected his personal opinion of its genuineness. Barrie had the same privilege over no less than five days between 8 and 13 October 1978, immediately following a six-week period of 'traditional' expositions, the first such since 1933. As one of the two official photographers among a team of some twenty-four American scientists – the Shroud of Turin Research Project, or STURP – he spent five days photographically documenting both the Shroud itself and the exhaustive round-the-clock scientific work being carried out on it. When he was first invited to join the project he had been somewhat hesitant about accepting, questioning whether he, a Jew, might have any rightful place on such a Christian venture. In the event, the impressions gained from this close encounter with the Shroud so profoundly affected him that not only has he kept up his interest throughout the years since, but he has

BELOW: *Pope John Paul II at prayer before the Shroud on his visit to Turin, 24 May 1998.*

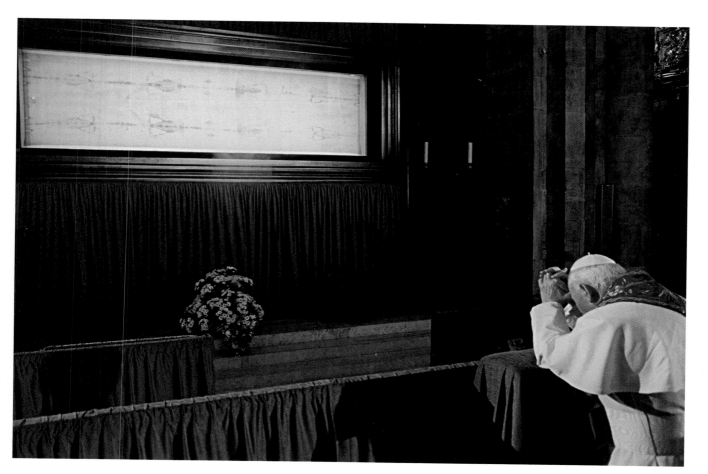

also created, to well-deserved international acclaim, by far the most authoritative and encyclopaedic Internet site on the subject, *www.shroud.com.*

In my case I have been doubly privileged, with two prolonged close-up encounters, albeit more than a quarter of a century apart. The first was between 22 and 24 November 1973, when it was brought out for its first-ever television appearance. At that time it had not been shown publicly in forty years, and uniquely on this occasion it was hung vertically rather than horizontally. Having been urged by a New York friend, the late Fr Peter Rinaldi, to attend this showing, I found, to my astonishment, that I was allowed to approach to within touching distance of the cloth, which was unprotected by any glass. This enabled me to examine its enigmatic image at a variety of angles and in very close detail over a period of three days, impressions that subsequently became recorded in my first ever book *The Turin Shroud.*

Although I subsequently attended the public expositions of 1978 and 1998, during which the Shroud was exhibited behind bullet-proof glass, my second truly 'direct' encounter was almost as unexpected as the first. While this book was in production the Turin ecclesiastical authorities arranged for me and over thirty international specialists to travel to Turin for a 'behind closed doors' symposium to discuss what directions future

BELOW: *Barrie Schwortz as he is today, and (lower picture) as he was in 1978, with the Shroud displayed before him on the special test-frame on which he and others spent five days studying and photographing it.*

BELOW: *Ian Wilson today, and (ringed in lower picture) examining the Shroud in close-up, 22 November 1973. Uniquely the Shroud was displayed upright on this occasion.*

studies of the Shroud might take. This convention was held from 2 to 6 March 2000 at the historic Villa Gualino, situated high on Turin's eastern outskirts, with breathtaking views towards the snow-capped Alps. On the second morning, that of Friday 3 March, we were driven to Turin Cathedral and conducted by Turin's new Archbishop, Severino Poletto, into its surprisingly light and airy sacristy. Specially brought out for us, and mounted horizontally at a slant, as if on a very long easel, was the Shroud, again completely unprotected by glass. Although a simple rope barrier kept us slightly back, this was no more than token. For more than two hours I and a unique gathering of specialists – Italian, English, American, French, German and Russian, including chemists, physicists, forensic pathologists, botanists, microbiologists, historians, radiocarbon-dating experts, textile experts and New Testament scholars – were able to point out to each other and discuss detail after convincing detail, our fingers sometimes less than an inch from the cloth's surface.

Reinforced in virtually all minds, both on the part of those already familiar with the Shroud and those viewing it for the first time, was that this cloth was simply far too subtle for any facile dismissal of the 'Someone just faked it up' variety. As was quite clear, a whole new chapter of fresh approaches to the Shroud was about to begin . . .

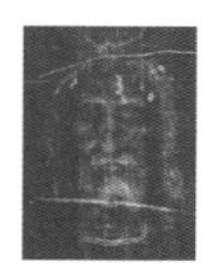

CHAPTER 1

A virtual tour of the Shroud and its features

APART FROM RARE INTERLUDES OF WAR, the Shroud has been kept in the Piedmontese capital Turin, in its late fifteenth-century Cathedral, or *Duomo*, since its traditional owners, the Dukes of Savoy, brought it there from Chambéry in 1578. Towards the end of the seventeenth century the acclaimed Italian architect Guarino Guarini was commissioned to build a magnificently domed upper floor chapel for it, the Cappella della S. Sindone, approached by stairs on either side of the Cathedral's eastern end.[1] Reserved for the Savoy family's private worship, this chapel was the Shroud's home for three centuries, during which time, except for special occasions, it was locked away inside a grilled reliquary shrine set atop an exotic, wedding-cake-tiered marble altar designed by Antonio Bertola.

When in 1993 crumbling stonework made major restoration work necessary in the chapel, the Shroud, rolled up as normal inside its traditional silvered casket, was moved to a temporary display case down in the main body of the Cathedral, behind the high altar. This was most providential, as events proved, for on the night of 11 April 1997 the all-but-completely restored chapel was gutted by fire. Had the Shroud been inside at the time, it would undoubtedly have been reduced to ashes. As it was, Turin's fire brigade, fearing imminent structural collapse at the Cathedral's entire eastern end, had to smash open its armoured-glass display case in order to whisk it to safety.

Today the Guarini chapel, so badly damaged that repairs may take decades, remains indefinitely closed. Its ruination and the currently vigorous efforts to restore it are cleverly screened from Cathedral visitors by a vast *trompe l'oeil* steel wall painted by scenery designer Gianpaolo Lanza to look as it and its Shroud altar formerly looked from the Cathedral nave.[2] For the Shroud itself, thanks to the munificence of Italgas, a new, high-tech bullet-proof-glass conservation case has been created by Turin's Bodini workshop. This is specially designed to be dual-purpose, both for public exposition times, when it can be mechanically tilted upright, and for the long periods when it is off display, when it lies flat, and Cathedral visitors have to be content with a lifesize photograph in lieu of the original. Luxuriously curtained, this case stands centrally in the Cathedral, behind the high altar, and immediately in front of the *trompe l'oeil* wall. Measuring 464 cm long by 138 cm wide and weighing 3 tons, it is air-conditioned, its

FACING PAGE: *(Above) Turin Cathedral photographed at the time of the 1978 expositions. Guarini's Cappella della S. Sindone can be seen at top right, with (this page, above) how the same scene looked at the height of the chapel fire on the night of 11 April 1997. (Below) Interior of the Cappella della S. Sindone as it looked before the fire of April 1997. The Shroud altar is in the centre. Today the whole Chapel is a blackened ruin.*

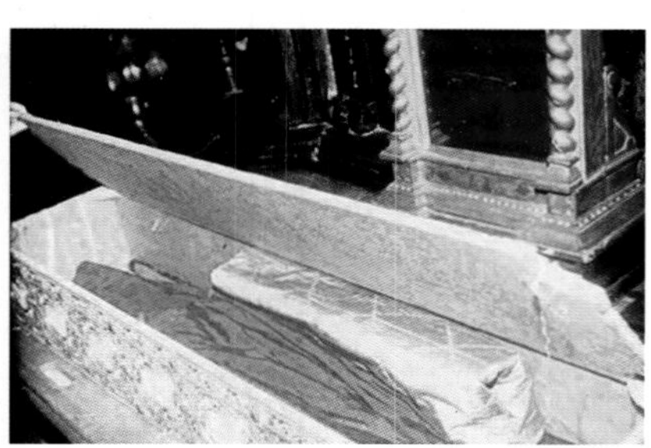

ABOVE: *The silvered reliquary in which the Shroud reposed, rolled around a velvet-covered staff, throughout most of its time in Turin. In 1998 it was transferred to its present repository, the elaborate conservation case commissioned by the Italian gas corporation, Italgas.*

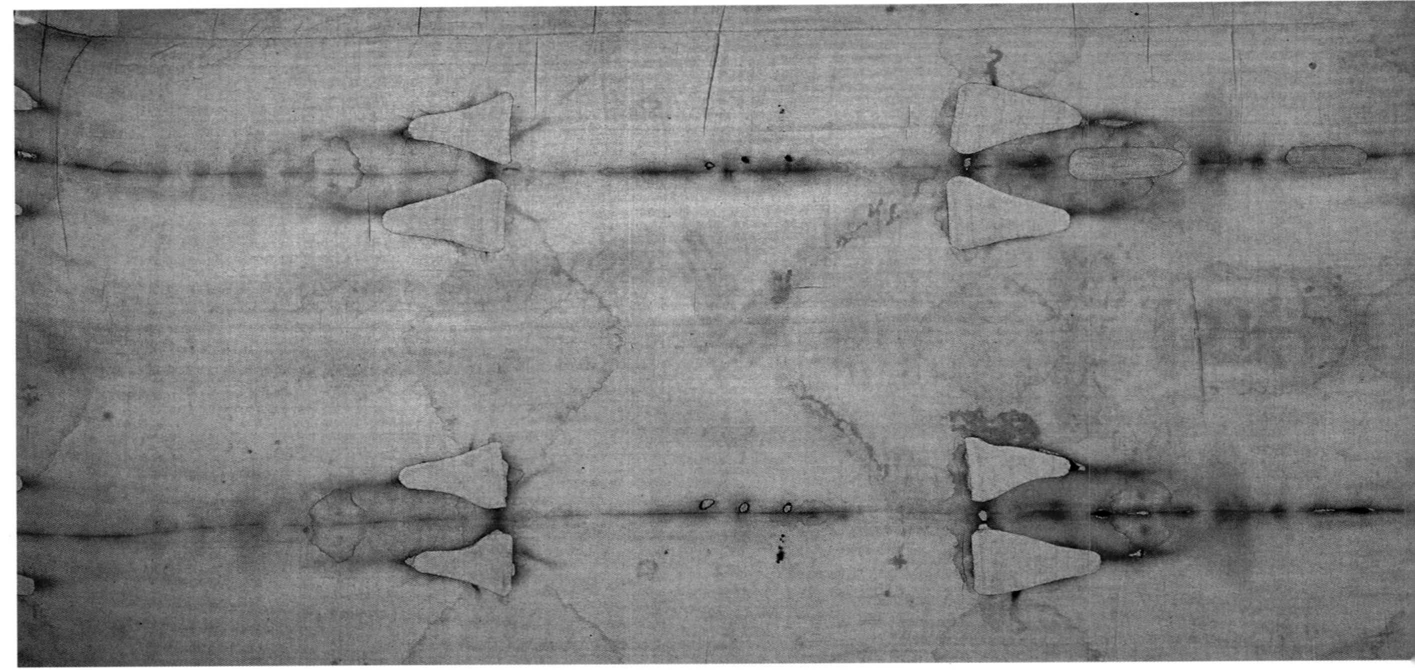

temperature is controlled to around 18°C, and its atmosphere is scientifically formulated to be chiefly of nitrogen and the inert gas argon, the oxygen level being kept to no greater than 0.01 per cent. Inside, the cloth lies stretched flat and full length; conservation-wise this is an important advance on its former mode, rolled up around a velvet-covered staff, which caused creases and wrinkles which multiplied with each and every unrolling.

The occasion of the Shroud being housed in this new case, immediately prior to the expositions of 1998, also saw the removal by Swiss textile conservator Dr Mechthild Flury-Lemberg, assisted by Sister Maria Clara Antonini, of a blue satin frame-type surround that had been sewn onto the Shroud in the nineteenth century, and its replacement by a new white cloth. This removal enabled the original cloth's dimensions to be measured rather more precisely than had been possible before, at 437 cm long by 111 cm wide.[3] In describing its most salient features, we shall use terms such as 'left', 'right', 'top' and 'bottom' to refer to the mode in which it was displayed in 1998, that is landscape-wise, with the imprint of the front half of the 'Christ' body ranged to the left, and the back half imprint ranged to the right, as in the photograph on this page. This has the virtue that it is also the mode in which it has most commonly been displayed since as early as the 1350s, up to and including my own second viewing in March 2000.

When the Shroud is viewed in this 'landscape' way the two 'Christ body' imprints appear somewhat incongruously head to head. Yet, as was deduced by artist-copyists nearly four centuries ago, this is actually very readily explained. Whether the Shroud is authentic or a forgery, the theory behind the imprints' origination is that the 'Christ' body was laid on the half of the cloth that now bears the 'back' imprint, the other half of the cloth then being brought over the head and down to the feet, thereby creating the 'front' imprint.

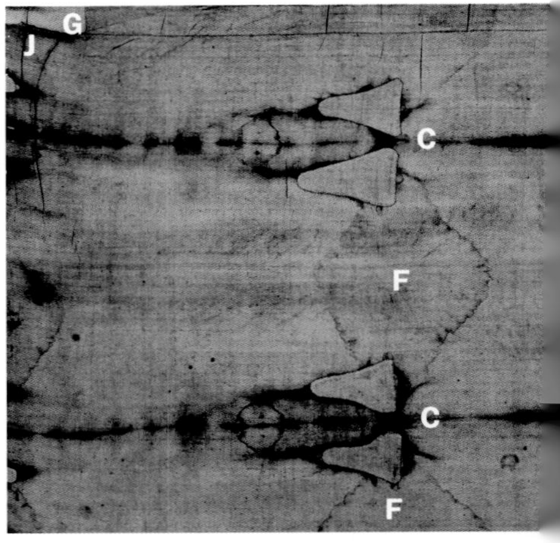

ABOVE: *The full-length Shroud, natural colour, with a plan of its main elements: (A) the front-of-body imprint, (B) the back-of-body imprint; (C) patches sewn on by Poor Clare nuns; (D) scorch marks from the 1532 fire; (E) so-called 'poker' holes; (F) water stains from water used to extinguish the fire; (G) missing portions removed at some unknown period; (H) the so-called side-strip; (J) the area from which the carbon-dating sample was removed.*

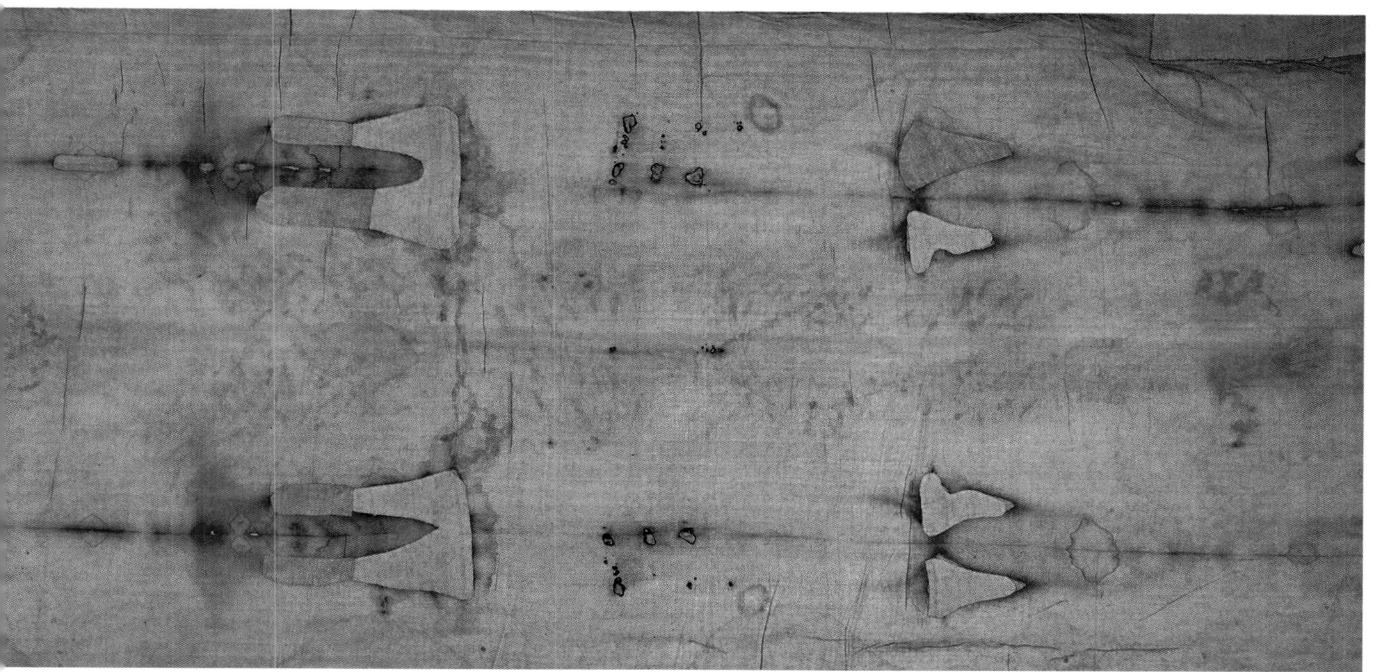

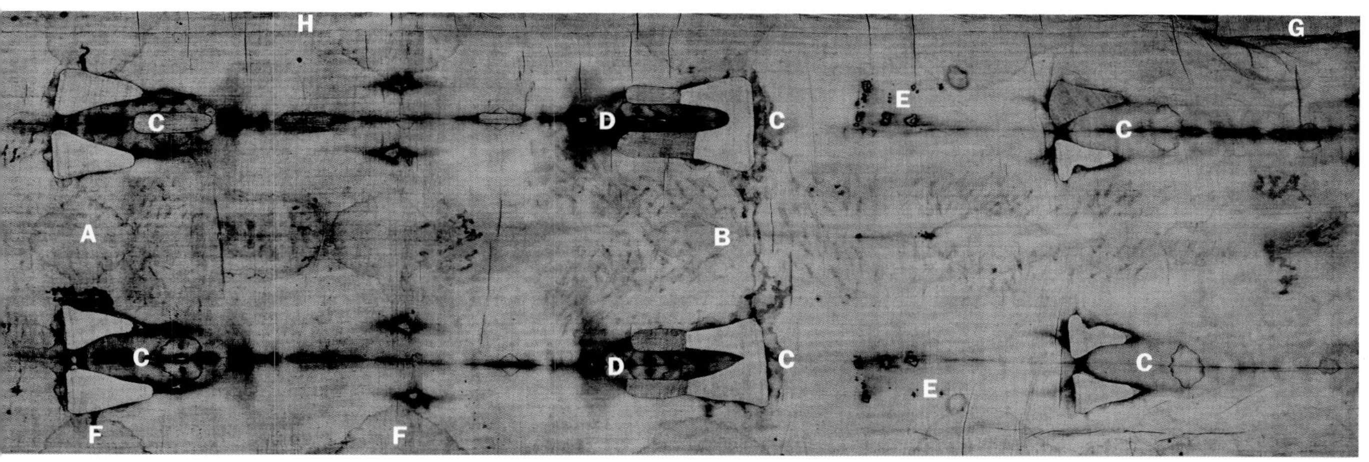

BELOW: *The theory of how the imprint on the Shroud was created by the body laid in it, as envisaged by the seventeenth-century Italian artist Gian Battista della Rovere.*

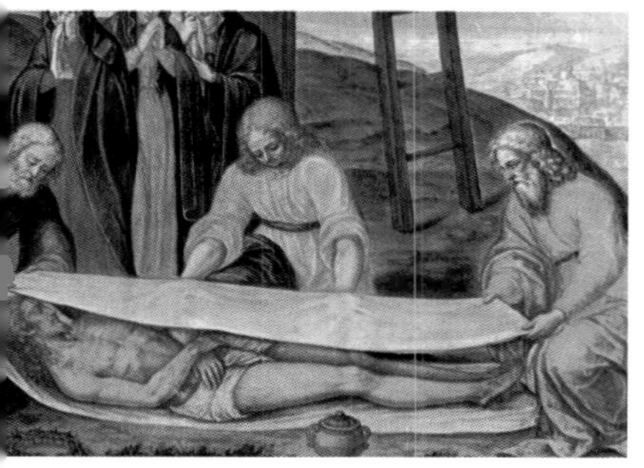

Inevitably the more impressive of these two imprints is the left, or 'front-of-the-body' half, on which can be discerned a ghost-like front-facing face, complete with hair, nose, beard, moustache and eyebrows. The coloration of this and all related so-called 'body' imprinting is so subtle and evanescent that it is extremely difficult to describe. 'Sepia' was the term that I adopted following my 1973 viewing, but 'straw-yellow' was preferred by the STURP scientists of 1978 – while a somewhat greyer cast was the impression that I came away with from my March 2000 viewing. Self-evidently, different lighting conditions all too easily affect how the coloration is perceived. But in any event the body image's prime characteristics are its lack of apparent substance (as from any pigment), also its failure to exhibit optically meaningful contours, and its imperceptible fading into the background colour of the natural cloth itself, without any defined edges.

All around the forehead of the face can be discerned overlying trickles in a distinctively redder colour. Although the only logical interpretation of

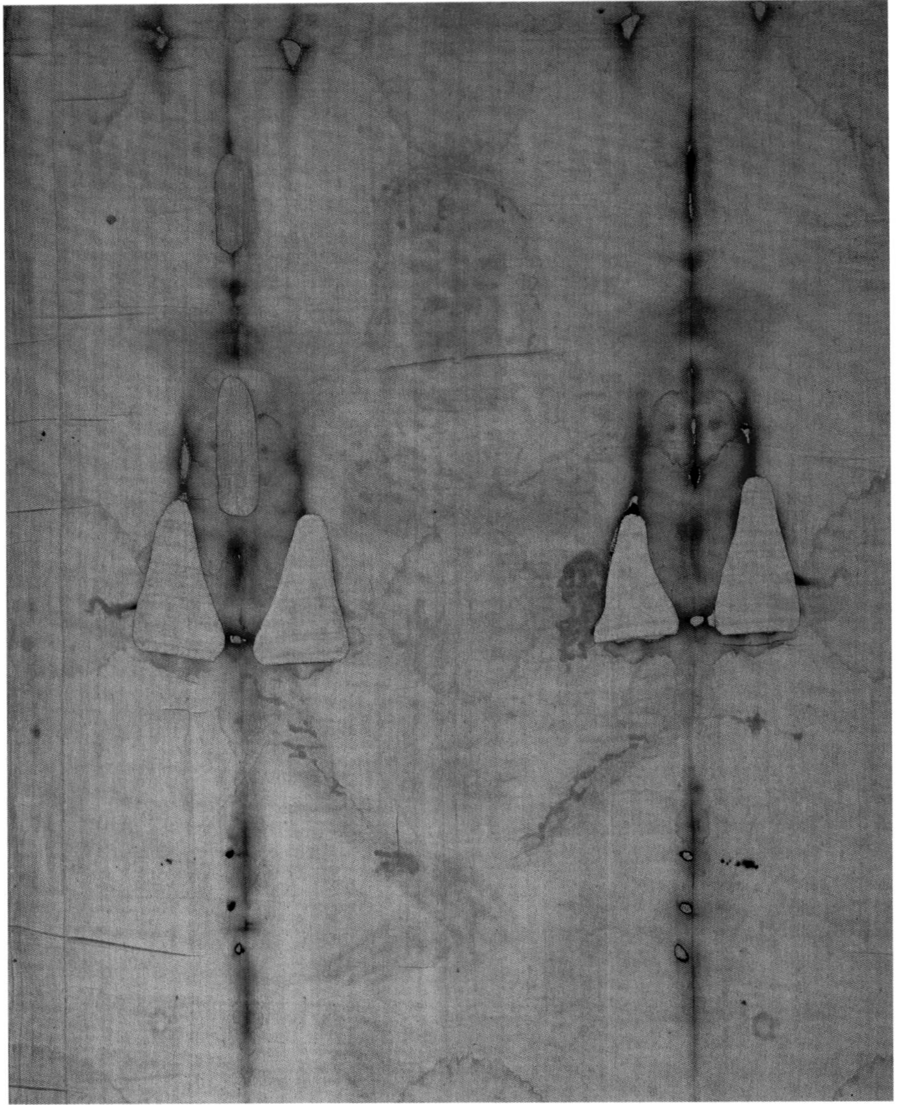

Detail of the Shroud's front-of-the-body image.

these trickles is as blood stains, their colour under artificial lighting is more magenta than is normally associated with blood which is even a day old, let alone twenty centuries. In room interior daylight, as in my March 2000 viewing, they can appear more maroon, deepening in places where the trickling of droplets has terminated. In this same colour there is also a large 'blood' flow overlying the right-hand side of the figure's chest. More, similar-coloured 'blood' trickles down the figure's forearms, one larger, distinctively V-shaped stain at the one visible wrist seemingly indicating the source of this. In the 'body' image colour, bony-looking hands are very clearly discernible crossed over the genitals region. And yet more 'blood' is apparent at the cloth's far left end, where the figure's feet might be construed to have been.

Detail of the Shroud's back-of-the-body image.

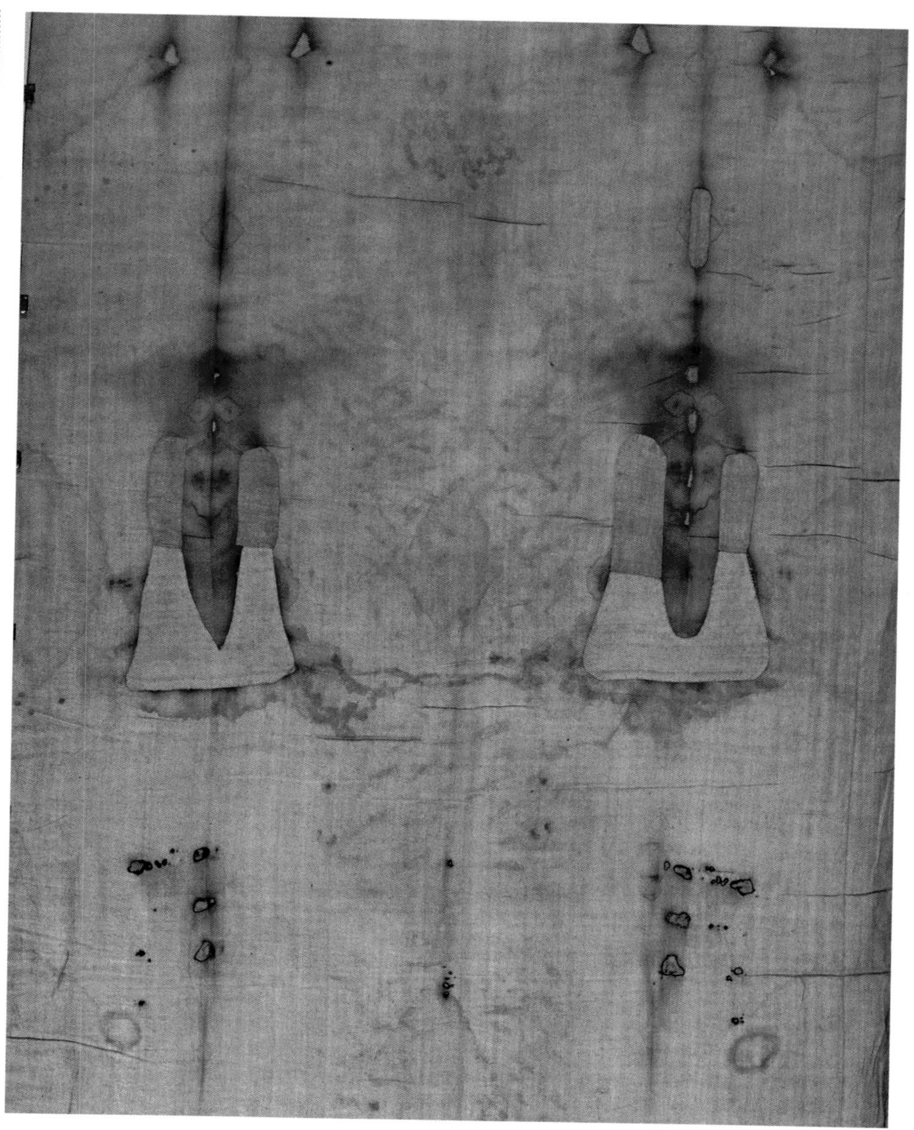

When we turn our attention to the right-hand half of the cloth there are several more 'blood' trickles in the back-of-the-head area, resembling those earlier noted on the forehead. These trickles overlie a head-shaped 'body' image suggestive of long hair, together with what seemed, in my 1973 viewing, to be an unbound pigtail lying in parallel with the spine, though from the closer view afforded to me by the March 2000 viewing I am now less sure of this interpretation.[4] Again in the 'body' image coloration, there is the impression of shoulders that became peppered with faint but distinctively regular-size marks, each having a characteristic dumb-bell shape. In the 'blood' colour a chain-like complex of rivulets runs across what would appear to be the small of the figure's back, while a scattering of more 'body'-coloured dumb-bells can be discerned on faintly indicated buttocks. Limbs are similarly vaguely indicated in the 'body' image colour, the back of the figure's upper or left-hand leg seemingly slightly more strongly imprinted than its partner. At the cloth's far right we can make out the surprisingly well-defined sole of a foot, with its 'body' image colour almost completely covered over with heel-to-toe 'blood'. From the heel/ankle area a rill of more 'blood' seems to have spilled sideways directly onto the cloth, arguably as the figure was laid in it, while a complex of further 'bloodstains', as from a second foot, is also evident, though rather less clearly delineated.

Yet, although this enigmatic 'body and blood' imprint is the Shroud's very *raison d'être*, specialist multi-disciplinary assessments of which will occupy us for most of the rest of this book, it is by no means its most conspicuous feature. That most doubtful 'honour' must instead go to two lines of brownish marks and add-on patches that each run the length of the cloth transversely, only just beyond the sides of the two head-to-head figure imprints, thereby effectively framing these.

These brownish marks are scorches from a fire in December 1532, when the Shroud was being kept in the Savoys' then capital of Chambéry, high in what are now the French Alps. As the cloth lay in an ornate silver casket, secure behind a multi-locked iron grille, the Savoys' Sainte Chapelle burst into flames, leaving no time for the clergy to obtain the keys from the various worthies holding them. Although a hastily summoned blacksmith managed to prise the grille open in the nick of time, the Shroud's casket was found to have melted in the heat. Inside the cloth had been stored away folded up in forty-eight folds, and upon its being opened up a drop of molten silver fell on one corner, causing it to burst into flame, and necessitating a hurried dousing with water. Although the Shroud had not been destroyed, as some rumoured at the time, it was undeniably seriously scarred and blemished with a sorry patchwork of burn-holes, scorch-marks and water-stains.

Accordingly, in April 1534 a group of Poor Clare nuns from Chambéry's local convent were entrusted with doing what they could to stabilize its condition and to disguise the worst of its damage. Joining together pieces of strong linen Holland cloth to form a single, Shroud-size backing, they first sewed the Shroud onto this, then cut an altar cloth into triangular patches which they stitched over the worst of its holes, sewing these through to the backing for maximum stability. The convent's abbess, Louise de Vargin, left a memoir detailing the conditions and manner in which they had worked.[5] Either on this or on later occasions the edges of several small holes were darned to stop them becoming any worse, and in 1694, the year that the Shroud was installed in its now ruined Guarini chapel, further patches, mostly oval-shaped and in a browner cloth, were added in order to cover and stabilize other burn-damaged areas that were showing signs of deterioration.

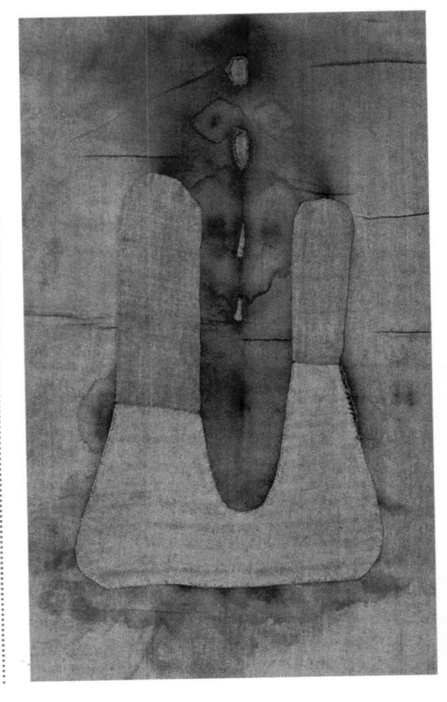

FACING PAGE: *(Above) The Sainte Chapelle, Chambéry, as it looks today, with (centre) the once grille-guarded niche in the apse wall from which the Shroud was rescued from the fire of 1532. (Below) One of the patches with which Poor Clare nuns covered the worst of the fire damage.*

BELOW: *Modern-day Poor Clare nuns unstitching some of their predecessors' handiwork for the 1978 scientific examination.*

These various repairs gradually came to be depicted in the many souvenir engravings of Shroud expositions which were popular from the late sixteenth century on,[6] and they may be regarded as an integral part of the Shroud's history. Likewise the lozenge-shaped stains from the water used to quench the fire, one of which can be seen between the two head imprints, another in the front-of-body imprint's diaphragm region, and a third at the knees, in each instance flanked by mirror-image versions.

But the 1532 Chambéry fire is not the only historical incident of this character to which the Shroud's fabric bears witness. Running along the same transverse lines as the 1532 fire marks are four further damage areas, two on either side of the crossed hands and two on either side of the buttocks, taking the form of holes with markedly blacker charring at the edges than any of the visible burns from the 1532 damage. Careful scrutiny of

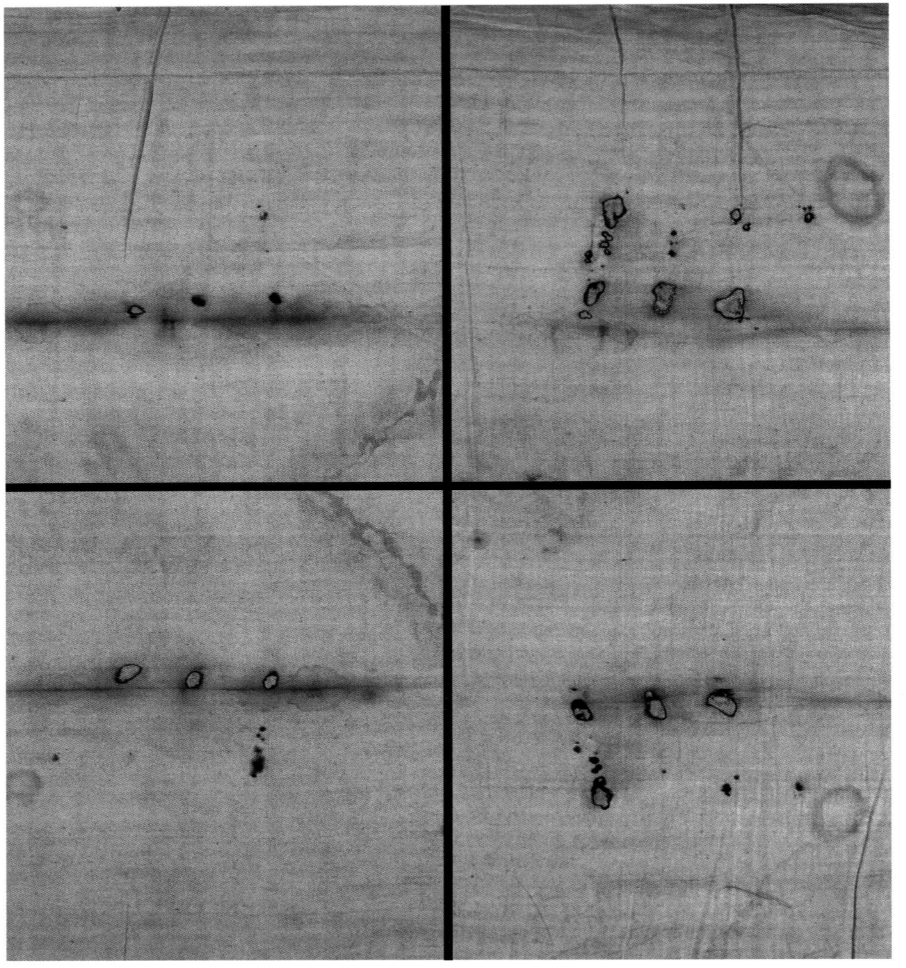

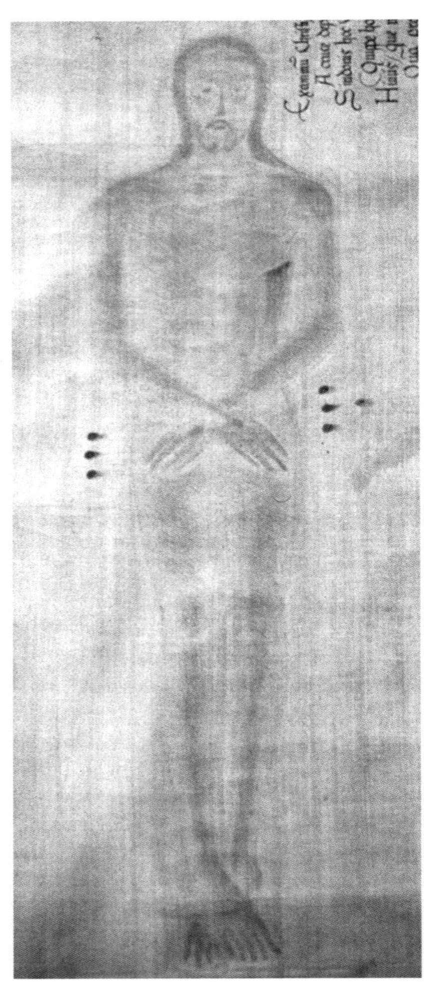

ABOVE: *The four sets of holes on the Shroud (left), thought to have been created, possibly by an oil-soaked poker having been thrust into the cloth three times. These certainly pre-date the 1532 fire, as they can be clearly seen on a copy of the Shroud dated 1516 (right), preserved in the church of St Gommaire, Belgium.*

these damage areas reveals that all four are mirror images of each other, suggestive of the Shroud having been at the time folded not in the forty-eight folds of 1532 but in just four. In this mode it suffered three or more penetrations from something resembling a sputtering, red-hot poker that had been dipped in pitch or oil. This may be inferred from the sets of holes being in a relatively neat row at the centre of the folding arrangement, and demonstrably in descending order of penetration. Topmost would have been the top right-hand set in the buttocks region, where the holes are largest and exhibit much irregular, ancillary spark damage. Next would have been its opposite number vertically, at bottom right, then the one at bottom left and finally the one seen at top left, which would actually have been the lowest of the four layers. It is from this latter that the apparent root of the damage can clearly be seen as three small, imperfectly aligned burn holes with very black edges.

We can be sure that this damage occurred before the 1532 fire, since the holes are clearly depicted in a copy of the Shroud painted in 1516. They are also somewhat less clearly indicated in a mid-fourteenth-century pilgrim's medallion, and we will see later evidence for their having been made even earlier than this. The appearance is of damage with a red-hot poker, the holes' centrality to the folding arrangement suggesting this was done deliberately. Barrie and others have postulated an accident with an incense burner, while Dr Mechthild Flury-Lemberg, speaking at the March 2000 Symposium,[7] suggested some spilt liquid which chemically reacted with the linen to create a burn-like effect. Whatever the cause, Barrie stresses the need to appreciate that these holes would have been the Shroud's most prominent feature before 1532, more distinctive at first glance than the imprints of the body. But of exactly when and why the Shroud might have suffered this particular violation there is no known historical record.

Likewise nothing is known of when and why two substantial portions of the cloth were removed, one from the top left-hand corner, the other, somewhat larger, from the top right-hand one. Since in all expositions in and before 1842 the Shroud was always held up at these corners, one possibility is that they were cut away because of considerable wear and soiling, though another rather more likely possibility is that they were given to visiting dignitaries as souvenirs.

On the Shroud's fabric itself, a question I am often asked is how, if it is genuinely two thousand years old, it has not fallen apart long ago. However, this is one of the very least of the difficulties it poses. A profusion of linens survive from ancient Egypt, dating from a thousand years and more before the time of Jesus, some astonishingly intact and, as observed of one example found in Tutankhamun's tomb, 'so strong that it might have come fresh from the loom'.[8] Because linen is unpalatable to moths, providing it is preserved in the right conditions it can survive

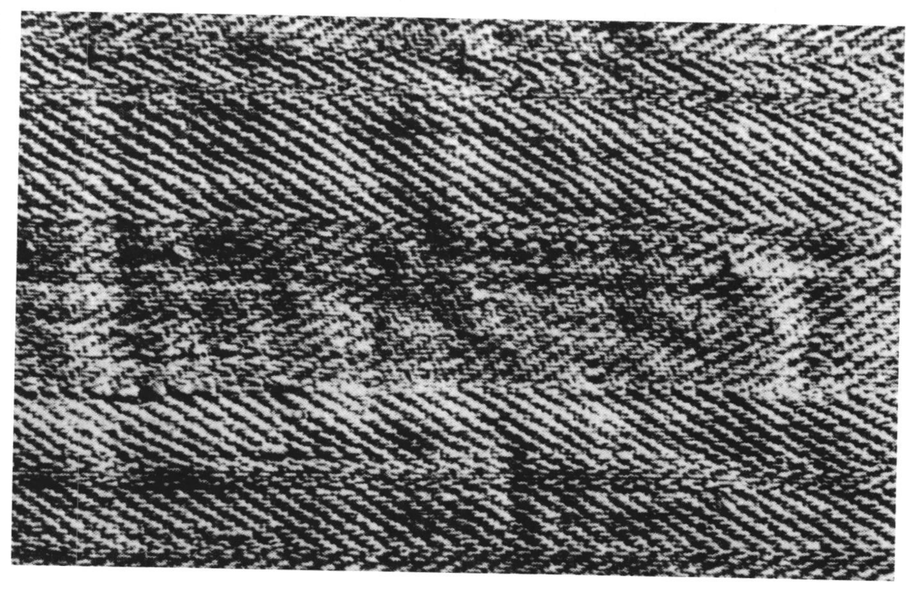

RIGHT: *Close-up of the Shroud's weave, showing its distinctive herringbone pattern. Although examples of this type of weave are rare both in antiquity and in medieval times, most surviving specimens being of a plain weave, some are known in silk and wool which date even from several centuries before the time of Christ.*

indefinitely, and certainly the Shroud is still surprisingly robust and supple.

Whoever originally spun the threads from which the Shroud's linen was made did so with a Z twist, meaning that when they held the original spindle they rotated this clockwise. It was woven on a loom in a single piece, and the weave is of no little interest because, as adjudged by textile specialists, it is a three-to-one herringbone twill. That is, it was woven by each weft thread being passed alternately under three warp threads then over one, producing diagonal lines, the direction being reversed at regular intervals. Though very uncommon compared to the plain weave of the many surviving ancient Egyptian linens and the small scattering of ancient Jewish examples, it was undoubtedly known in antiquity (from which period the vast majority of fabrics have perished), since there survive examples of ancient silks with this same weave. Also worthy of note is that this particular type of weave is almost equally rare during the Middle Ages, European examples properly emerging only from the late sixteenth century on.

Another noteworthy feature of the cloth is a seam line running its entire length, approximately 8.1 cm from its 'top' edge, which is now confirmed, thanks to Dr Flury-Lemberg's removal of the blue surround, as bearing selvedge, as does the bottom edge. Since the weft-run can be seen to be the same on both sides of this seam line, the impression is that the cloth was originally wider and was cut and joined along the seam in order to conform to a particular measurement standard. This impression is

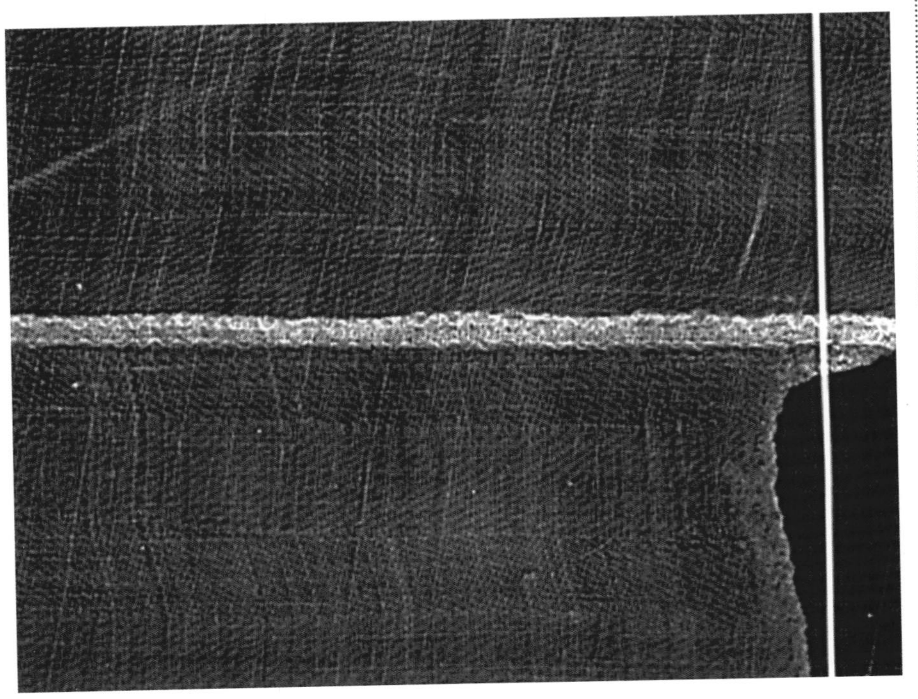

LEFT: *Seam of the side-strip, seen via X-ray, showing how the strip belongs to the same original piece of cloth, which was cut along its length, then the pieces rejoined.*

RIGHT: *Close-up of the removal of a thread from the Shroud, showing how the cloth remains surprisingly supple.*

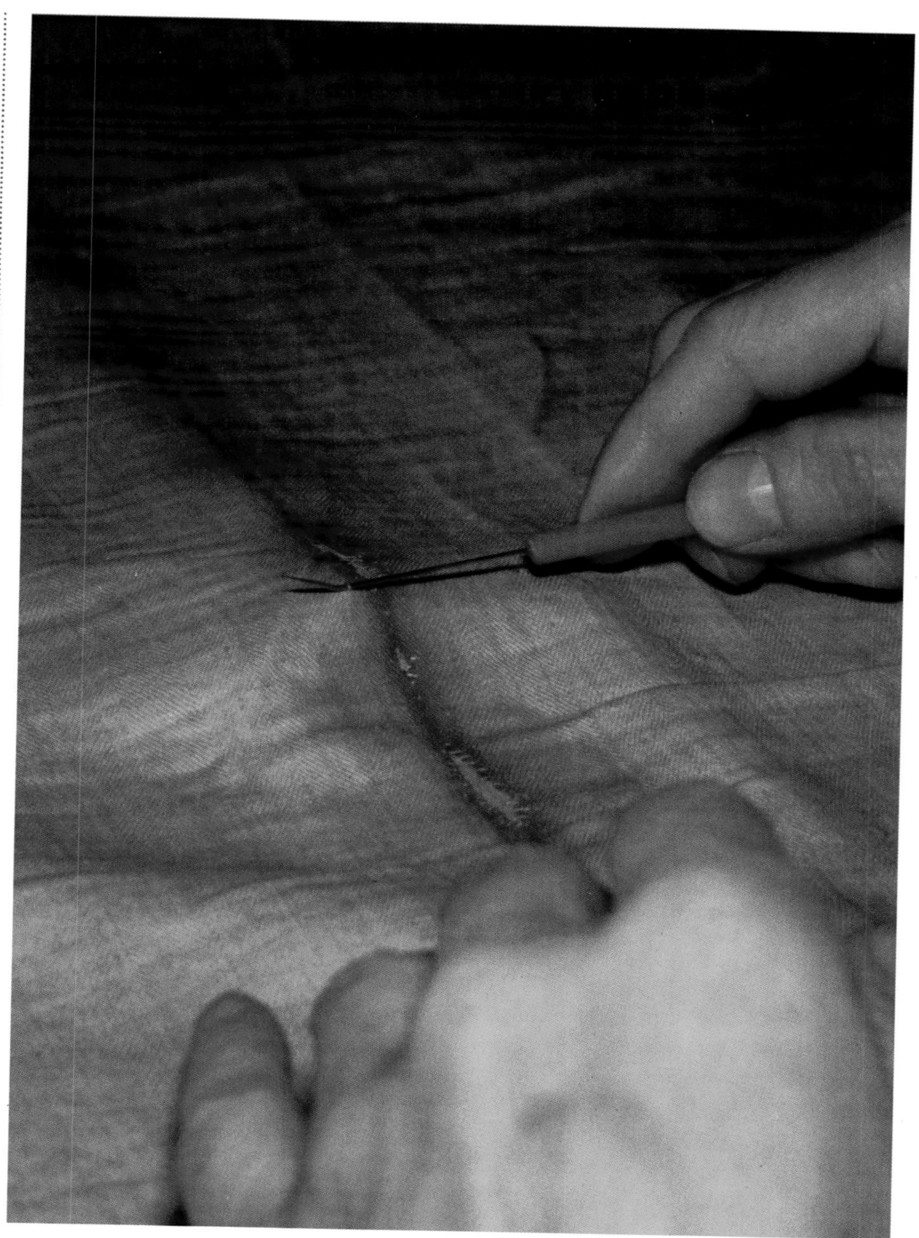

further reinforced by Dr Flury-Lemberg's finding, following her removal of the surround, that the Shroud's left and right sides both originally had raw cut edges that were then carefully hemmed to finish them by the very same hand that was responsible for the lengthwise seam.

These, then, are the Shroud's most readily visible features, and thanks to more than a century of photographs, we can mostly study them at leisure in some detail, even without direct access to the cloth. But as we are about to discover, the same science of photography has also revealed quite literally far more of the Shroud than initially meets the eye.

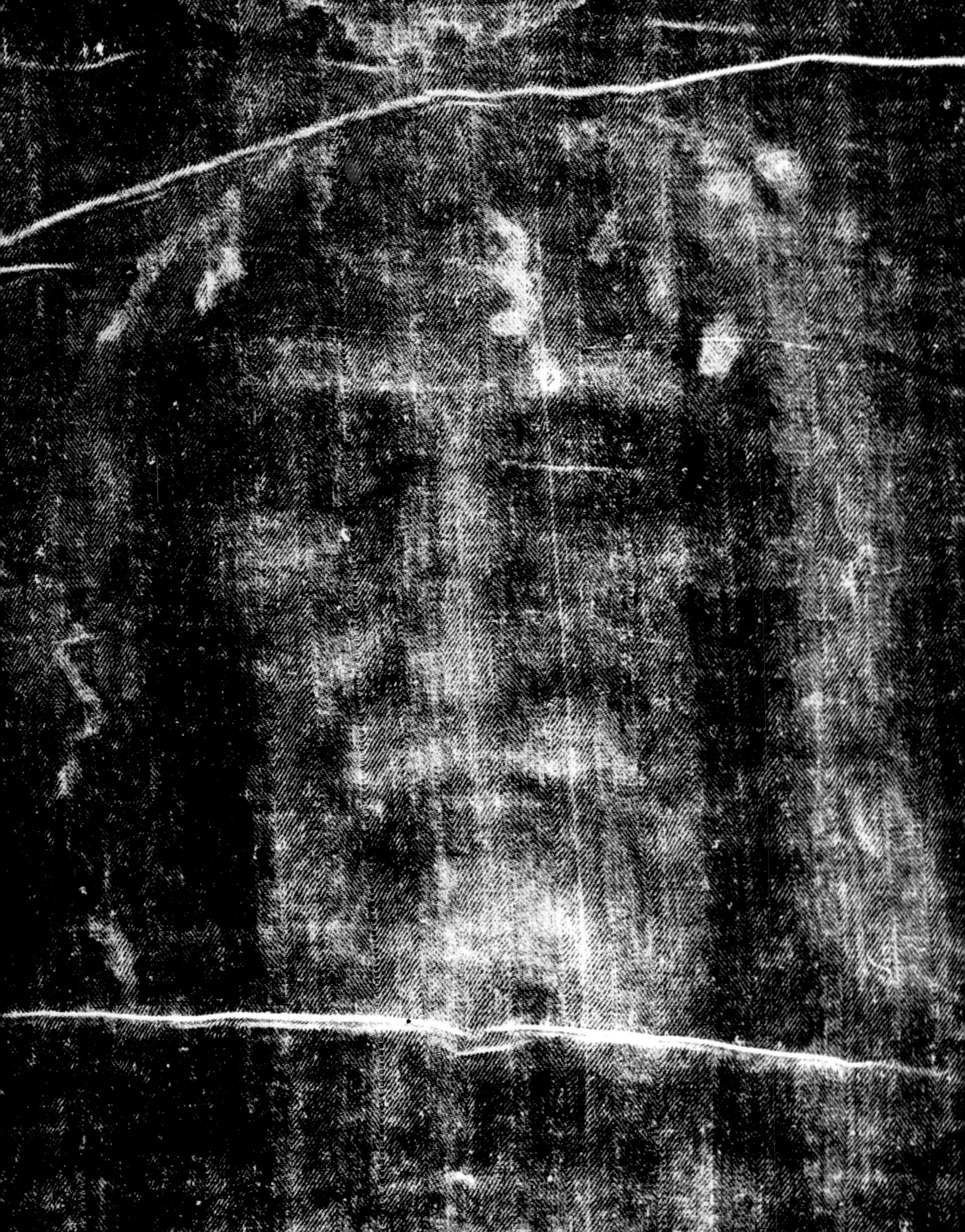

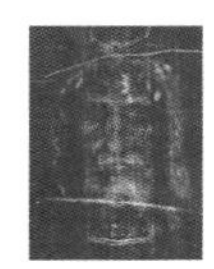

CHAPTER 2

'No one could have faked that image!'

(Photographer Leo Vala)

FACING PAGE: *The Enrie negative of the Shroud face, as produced on life-size black-and-white plates in 1931. This proved that the effect first discovered by Pia was no accident or fakery.*

HAD PHOTOGRAPHY never been invented, it is most unlikely that the Shroud would ever have been considered of serious scientific interest. At the end of the last century even Roman Catholic historians were well aware of the fourteenth-century forgery allegations and, with so many of the Church's so-called 'relics' being of doubtful authenticity, it had to rank among the most doubtful.

But, as is now part of Shroud folklore, such attitudes received a serious jolt on the night of 28 May 1898. It was the third day of an eight-day period of public expositions of the Shroud in Turin Cathedral, the first such to be held for thirty years. As part of the celebrations of the fiftieth anniversary of the Italian Constitution, the Shroud had been brought down from its normal repository in the elevated Guarini chapel and set up on the Cathedral's high altar in a brand-new display frame. It was, therefore, one of the very first occasions for it to be displayed in static mode, rather than hand-held by bishops, as had previously been the norm. And, with the science of black-and-white photography now well established, the Shroud's then owner, King Umberto I of Italy, at long last granted permission for the first ever official photograph of the cloth to be taken. The man appointed for this was the well-respected local councillor and proficient amateur photographer Secondo Pia.[1]

BELOW: *The original camera used by Pia in 1898, preserved in Turin's Museum della Sindone.*

Pia's allotted time for carrying out his task was after Turin Cathedral's doors had been closed to the general public for the night. His first obstacle was overcoming the fluctuating electrical voltages in the Cathedral that caused his lights to flicker and vary from moment to moment. Mounting his heavy box camera on a temporary platform matching the height of the displayed Shroud, he carefully focused his Voigtlander lens on the cloth, loaded a large glass photographic plate and gave it a twelve-minute exposure, followed by another for fourteen minutes, doing much the same with several smaller plates. Then he hurried back to his darkroom to develop these as the negatives from which prints would be made.

Given that the Shroud's imprint is so shadowy and ephemeral, Pia had little if any expectation that its negative would prove any more meaningful – but he received the shock of his life. Under the developer there began to appear an image so extraordinarily lifelike that it was as if the Shroud itself was a negative, so that photography produced a 'positive' photograph from it. To all appearances the Shroud man's face and body were 'lit' with natural light and shade, with the blood-flows as from crucifixion and the wound in the chest showing up in white. This immediately raised the question of how any forger back in the Middle Ages could produce an image like that, without any means of checking his work, and without anyone properly able to appreciate it for another five hundred years. Pia, as he would later attest with no little emotion, felt himself to be the first man since the days of the apostles to gaze on the body of Jesus, as this had appeared in death nearly nineteen centuries before.

When Pia's photographs were released, the initial flurry of excitement that they aroused quickly gave way to scepticism, with even prominent Roman Catholic exegetes such as France's Canon Ulysse Chevalier and England's Jesuit Herbert Thurston pointedly remarking on the medieval 'cunning painting' accusations. Every variety of scientific explanation was offered, among them over-exposure and transparency, the most hurtful to Pia being suggestions that his negatives were some kind of trick or fraud.

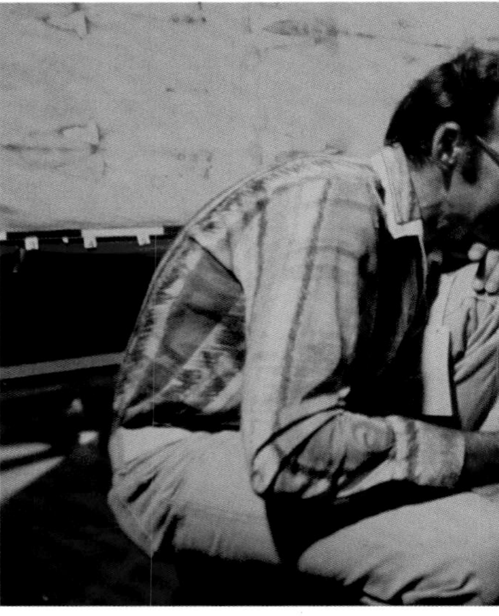

ABOVE: *The STURP photographic team discuss their next 'shoot'. Barrie Schwortz is pictured on the right.*

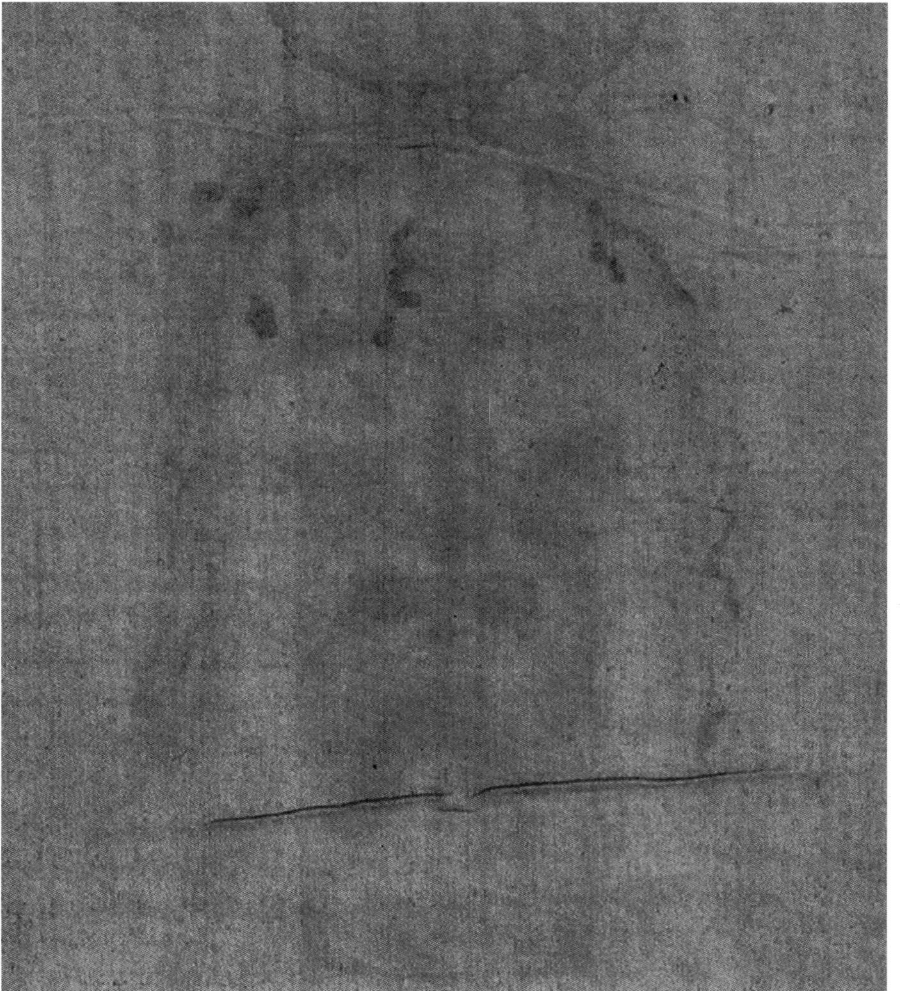

LEFT AND FACING PAGE: *The Shroud as photographed in colour, and in black-and-white negative by Barrie Schwortz.*

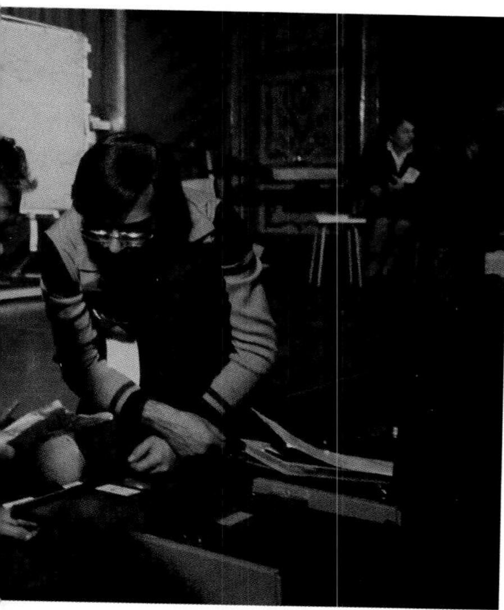

But thankfully Pia was still alive, though by then a septuagenarian, when a fresh, twenty-one-day round of Shroud expositions was held in May 1931, during which a new set of black-and-white photographs was taken, this time by a professional photographer, Giuseppe Enrie. Enrie had an immediate advantage over Pia in that he was allowed to work with the Shroud uncovered by any protective glass. He also benefited because it was displayed genuinely full length, unlike in 1898 when the frame had been made too short and part of the cloth had had to be tucked away out of sight. Improved photographic technology also enabled him to take life-sized views of details such as the face, the crossed hands and the chest wound.

It was duly revealed that, far from any trick or fraud, the hidden 'photograph' is quite unmistakably there whenever the Shroud's light values are reversed by the camera. The considerably improved definition obtained by Enrie showed this up yet more clearly. His original life-sized glass negative of the face, which I have held in my own hands, is particularly stunning in

its detail, the countenance unmistakably photograph-like and lacking in any artist's style. To this day Enrie's 1931 plates, although beginning to deteriorate, have such clarity and pinpoint focus that they continue to provide a rich hunting ground for Shroud researchers. Also, because photographing a yellow or sepia image with the orthochromatic, or less red-sensitive, film that Enrie used has the effect of dramatically enhancing what has previously been only faintly visible, they are very valuable even in their positive form.

But the Shroud's photographic revelations were far from over in 1931. Following the gradual introduction of colour photography, in 1969 the first-ever colour photographs of the Shroud were taken, by Giovanni Battista Judica-Cordiglia, as part of a preliminary scientific examination of the Shroud called for by Turin's then Archbishop, Cardinal Michele Pellegrino. He was followed nine years later, at a time of celebrations of the four hundredth anniversary of the Shroud's arrival in Turin, by my co-author Barrie Schwortz, participating as one of the two official photographers among the twenty-five-strong STURP team that conducted the most exhaustive scientific examination that the Shroud had ever, and, to date, still has ever received. Barrie remarks of this:

> During the five days and nights that we examined the Shroud, I photographed it first in natural colour, as it appears to the eye in normal light. Unable to back away far enough to include the full cloth on a single sheet of 4in x 5in film, I photographed the ventral and dorsal halves on separate sheets of colour and black-and-white film. Later the panels of the examination table were removed and I photographed the cloth with light transmitted *through* it, allowing us to visualize the stains and scorches that penetrated deep into the fibres while the image proved invisible.
>
> Our team also photographed the cloth using special films, lights and filters to determine ultra-violet fluorescence properties that might be important. We also made detailed close-up photographs microscopically with the aid of a Wild M400 Photomakroscope.
>
> I also photographically documented the work done by other team members as they performed their own experiments on the cloth. One of my primary responsibilities was to document the specific areas on the Shroud where each researcher took his data. This was ultimately accomplished by placing magnets on the cloth at each data point, which I then photographed. From these I reconstructed photographic data maps for each experiment.
>
> Of the 120 continuous hours given to our team to examine the Shroud, I spent 102 in the room, exposed eighty rolls of 35mm film and a hundred sheets in 4in x 5in film, and assisted Vernon Miller in producing a number of 8in x 10in colour transparencies and Polaroids.

ABOVE: *STURP scientific photographer Vernon Miller sets up equipment for another of the team's photographic experiments with fellow team members Sam Pellicori and Don Devan.*

RIGHT: *The Shroud front-of-the-body image in colour, with, (far right), the extraordinary 'photographic' effect when this same image is viewed in black-and-white negative.*

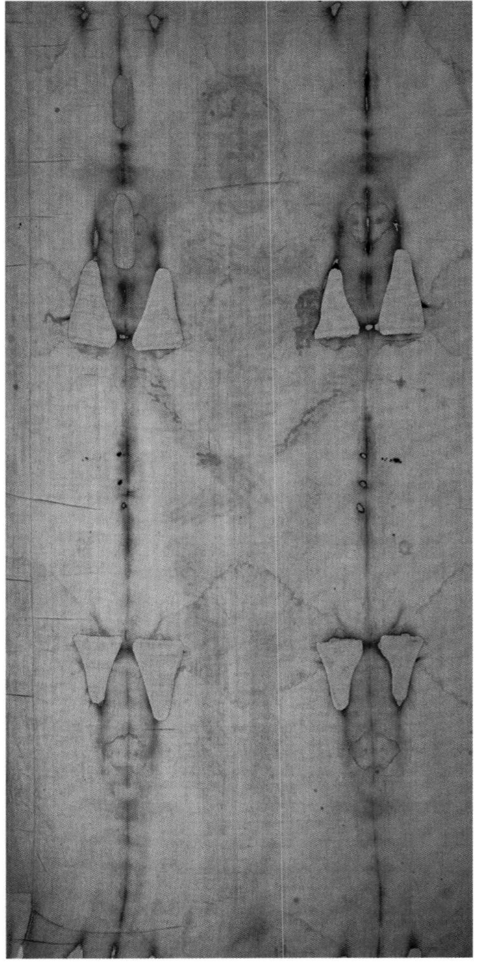

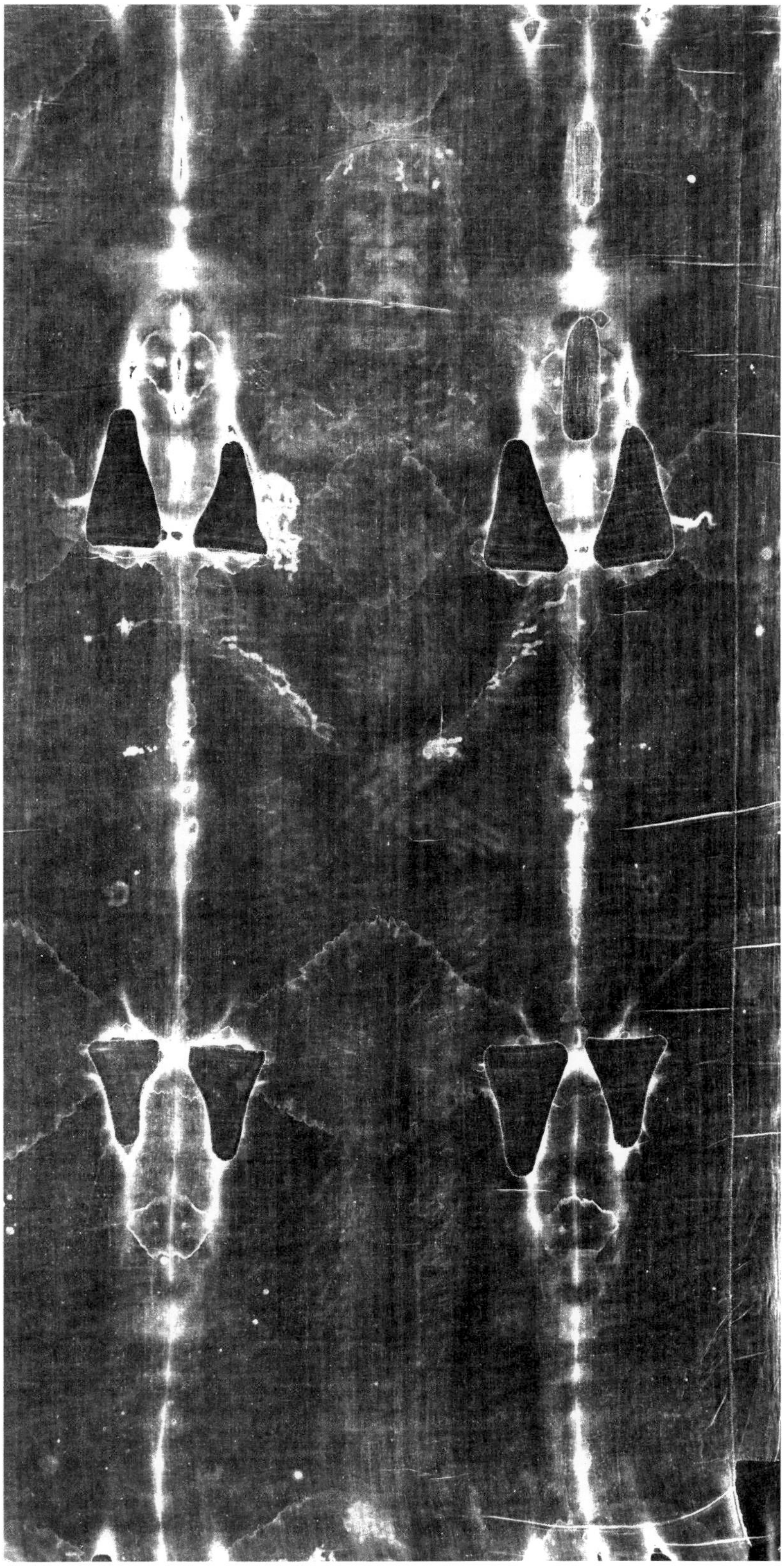

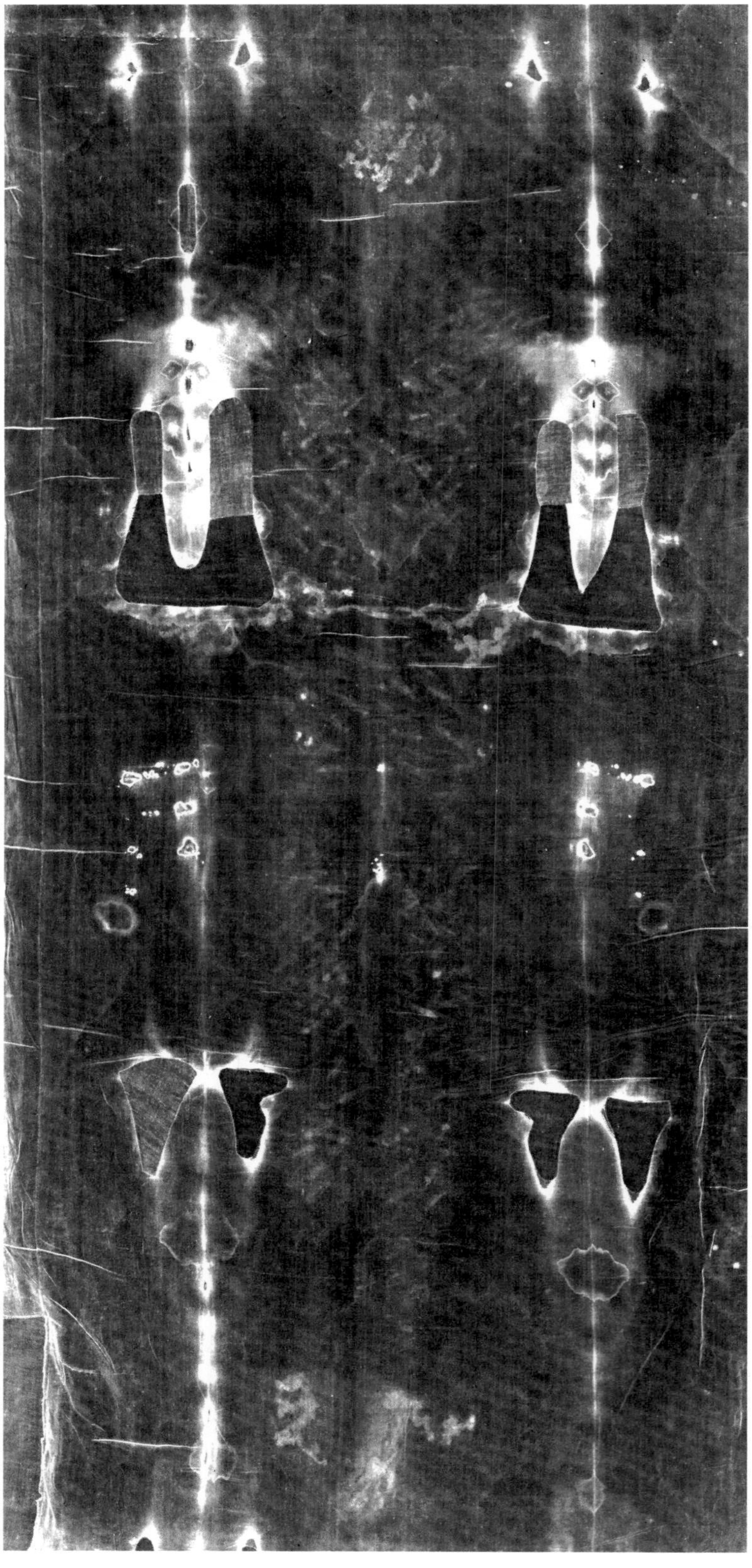

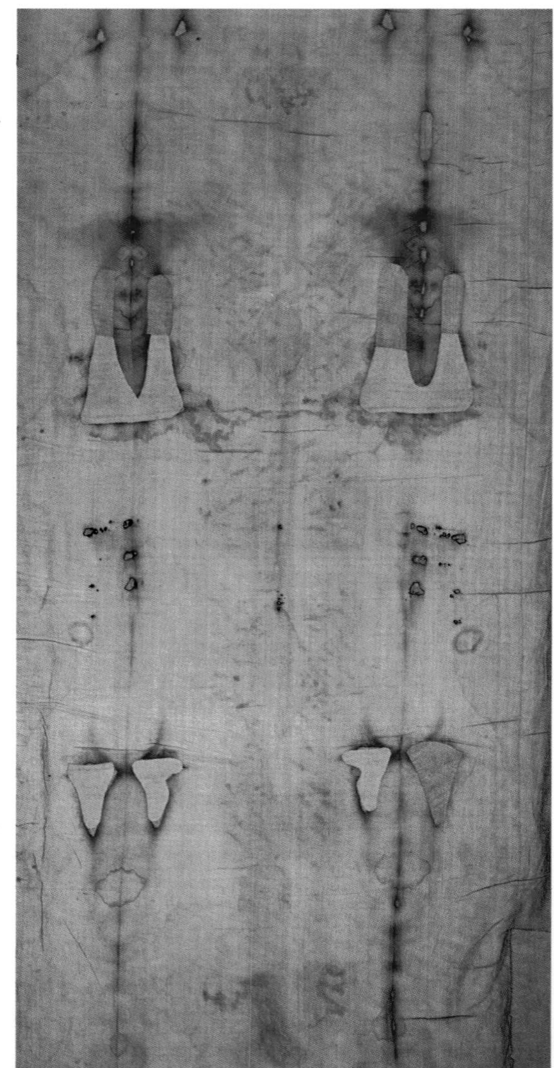

LEFT: *London fashion photographer Leo Vala, who pioneered research into the Shroud's three-dimensional properties.*

From my arrival in Turin as a neophyte and certified sceptic expecting to 'see the brushstrokes and go home', I had become far more familiar with the image on the Shroud and examined it in far greater detail than all except very few people in the world have ever done, other than my STURP colleagues. I had also become profoundly fascinated with the image on the cloth and knew that this interest might well last the rest of my life.

One characteristic of the Shroud's image demanding little deduction is that the two body imprints comprise the 'inside' side of the cloth, as this theoretically at one time enveloped a human corpse head to toe and back and front. As such they can only be mirror images of the body that the cloth theoretically wrapped. Reversing the image left to right, as on the photographic negative, therefore produces what, again theoretically, must have been the man of the Shroud's actual one-time appearance, his left hand being over his right, the chest wound being in his right side, his left foot over and partly occluded by his right, etc.

Another immediately evident characteristic is that, however the two imprints may have been created, they exhibit a body imprinting process that seems to have worked in a strictly straight-up and straight-down manner that is technically termed 'collimated'. One key indication of this is that the sides of the body are not represented image-wise on the Shroud, nor is the top of the head, so there can have been no sideways-splaying image-making process. Another key indication is that the body imprints have no light focus or visible direction of light. Conventional photographs and paintings alike almost invariably convey something about where their subject's lighting is coming from, the left side of the body, say, casting a shadow to the right. In the case of the Shroud's 'body' imprint, however, both the sides of the face, as well as the entirety of the body, are uncannily evenly 'lit', again suggesting that the image-making source was not light in its normal external form, and worked in a strictly straight-up and straight-down manner.

Also readily apparent is that there is an important distinction to be made between the Shroud's 'blood' imprints and the 'body' imprints. The 'blood' imprints can be interpreted only as direct-contact transfers from the theoretical bloodstained body, though there are a couple of instances of apparent direct spillages. The 'body' imprints, on the other hand, are quite definitely not what you would expect from a body being, say, coated with some image-producing substance, then the cloth being laid over it to create an imprint in the way that printers do by passing a sheet of paper over a bed of inked metal type. The very same subtle gradations of tone that give the Shroud's body image its unique and stunning 'photographic' appearance also preclude their causation by any such direct-contact printing process. Either such tones are the work of the very subtlest of artists, who

LEFT: *The Shroud back-of-the-body photographed in colour, with the same section of the cloth as this appears in black-and-white negative (far left). Theoretically the part of the cloth on which the body would have directly laid, the photographic effect is none the less striking.*

somehow managed to create perfect negativity without the slightest means of himself or anyone of his time being able to view the effect that he had created, or something has acted at a distance to *project* them onto the cloth.

Such observations have aroused enormous interest among professional photographers and others involved in the technology of images, as they try to understand what the Shroud's projection process might have been, and how anything of this kind could have come into being, by any conceivable means. One pioneer back in the 1960s was the professional London photographer Leo Vala who, using two slide projectors to beam negatives of the Shroud face onto a malleable Plasticine, moulded a most striking 3-D likeness of the face. This provoked him to comment: 'I have been involved in the invention of many complicated visual processes and I can tell you that no one could have faked that image. No one could do it today with all the technology we have. It's a perfect negative. It has a photographic quality that is extremely precise.' [2]

Then during the decades that followed the 1960s, photographic technology improved in ways that even Vala could not have anticipated. When in the mid-1970s the American physicist Dr John Jackson of Colorado Springs was conducting the researches into the Shroud's image that would lead to his invitation to Turin as co-leader of the 1978 STURP team, he was almost by chance introduced to a piece of equipment that had only recently been developed for the NASA space project. This was the Interpretation Systems VP-8 Image Analyzer, a device designed to enable shades of black and white to be translated into levels of vertical relief that could be viewed and adjusted via a television screen. A normal photograph records only variations in light and does not contain information about the camera's distance from the object being photographed. So when viewed via the VP-8 the result is almost invariably very collapsed and distorted, the VP-8 not having been designed or intended to produce any 'true' 3-D display, only a semblance of it.

However, when the Shroud's image was placed beneath the machine, the result was nothing short of astonishing. A consistent 'true' 3-D effect was produced whereby it was possible via the device's TV monitor to move around, viewing the contours of the body just as if viewing a range of mountains from a moving helicopter. The Shroud image's varying tones or 'intensity levels' could thereby be seen not so much as true photographic light and shade but rather as encodings of the (still theoretical) body's relief in relation to its distance from the cloth at each related image point.

Even today it is difficult for ordinary laymen to appreciate just how mind-blowing this discovery was to those physicists and other technicians who first came across it. As Dr Jackson remarked: 'When I first saw this . . . I think I knew how Secondo Pia must have felt when in 1898 he saw his photographic image.' [3] Electronics engineer Peter Schumacher, inventor and developer of the VP-8 Image Analyzer for NASA during the 1970s,

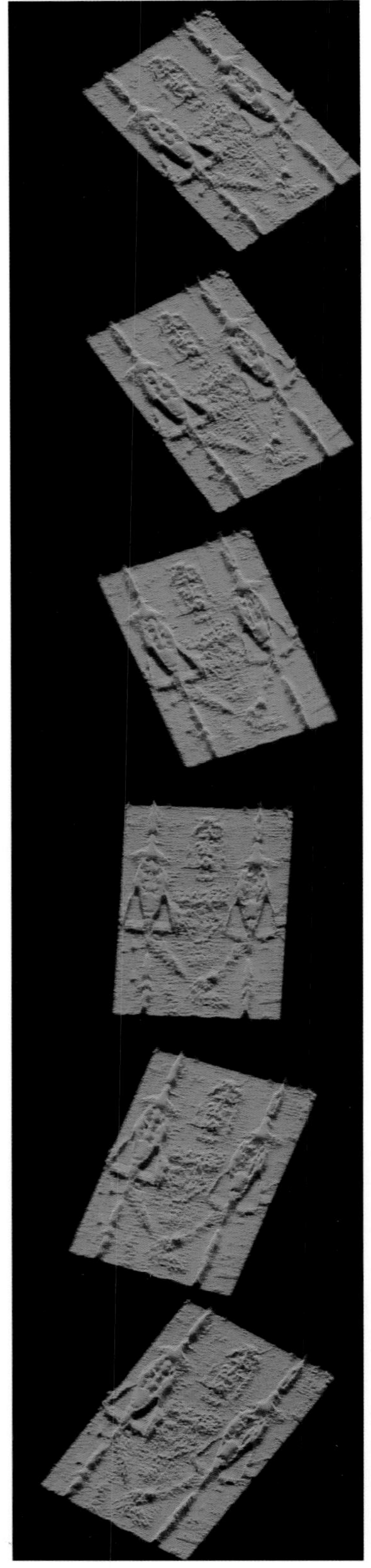

LEFT AND BELOW: *The Shroud body image seen from a variety of angles under the VP-8 Image Analyzer, showing its true three-dimensionalty. Peter Schumacher (seen above), who pioneered its development, regards this as unique and compelling evidence of the cloth's authenticity.*

BELOW: *'X-ray' properties in the hands of the man of the Shroud. The hands' markedly bony appearance as seen under the VP-8 at left, and in photographic negative at right of this.*

who personally delivered one of the machines to the home of Dr Jackson's colleague Dr Eric Jumper, recalls his astonishment as he saw for the first time the Shroud's full body image as viewed via the system he had invented:

> A 'true three-dimensional image' appeared on the monitor . . . The nose ramped in relief. The facial features were contoured properly. Body shapes of the arms, legs and chest and the basic human form. . . . I had never heard of the Shroud of Turin before that moment. I had no idea what I was looking at. However the results are unlike anything I have processed through the VP-8 Image Analyzer, before or since. Only the Shroud of Turin has [ever] produced these results from a VP-8 Image Analyzer.[4]

With regard to the idea that some medieval artist might have produced such an image, Schumacher is emphatically dismissive:

> One must consider how and why an artist would embed three-dimensional information in the 'grey' shading of an image [when] no means of viewing this property of the image would be available for at least 650 years after it was done? One would have to ask why is this result not obtained in the analysis of other works? . . . Why would the artist make only one such work requiring such special skills and talent, and not pass the technique along to others? How could the artist control the quality of the work when he or she could not 'see' grey scale as elevation? . . . Would an artist produce this work before the device to show the results was invented? [5]

Nor is even this 3-D effect all. When in the early 1980s the Eastern Michigan University chemist Dr Giles Carter was studying some of the life-sized photographs taken by the STURP team he noticed that the man of the Shroud's fingers looked unnaturally long and bony. As he pondered this it suddenly struck him that the bones of the hand seemed to be showing up as if under an X-ray. In the area of the mouth on the Shroud, he further

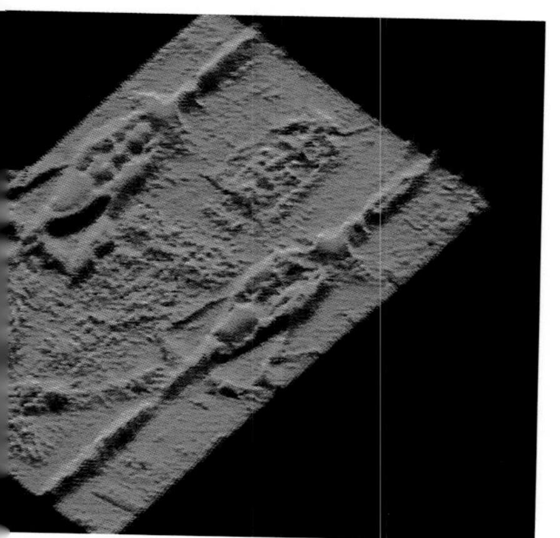

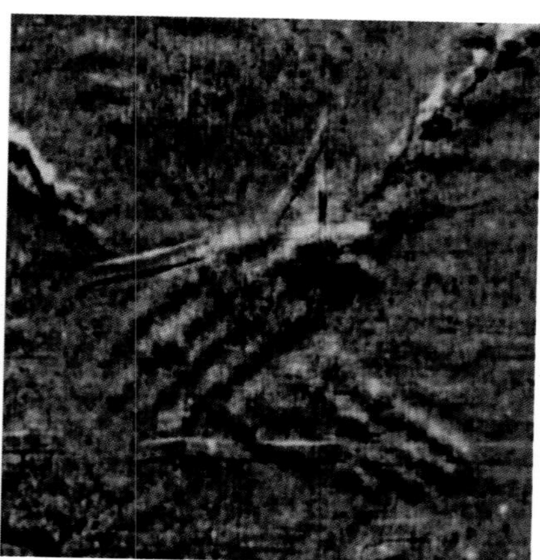

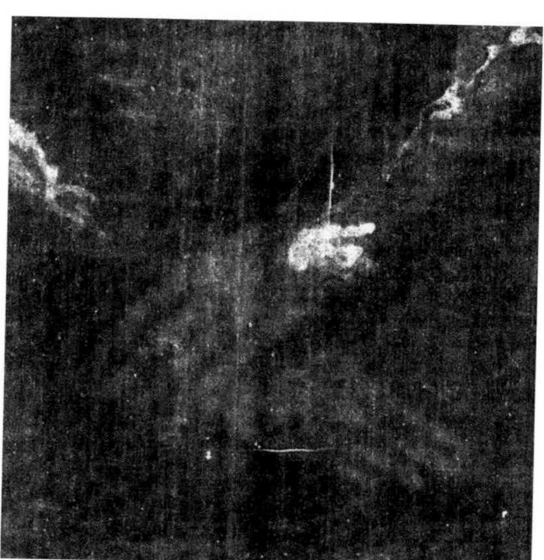

noticed what appeared to be the image of two rows of teeth. The high, pronounced cheekbones to the face also gave the impression of his seeing through to the skull. So was it possible that whatever produced the Shroud's image had not only photographic and 3-D characteristics but even a glimmering of properties akin to long-wavelength X-rays?[6]

This possibility has recently gained further credence from a special technique developed by Dr Alan Whanger[7] of Duke University, North Carolina, a retired psychiatry professor whose medical background includes extensive surgical experience and X-ray interpretation. When in 1995 Whanger tried superimposing the Shroud's positive and negative images and shifting them vertically out of alignment[8] he found that the bony structures of the hands, the wrists, the skull and teeth, as observed by Carter, all showed up yet more clearly. As Whanger comments: 'These findings have been reviewed by a number of physicians, including three professors of radiology, who all immediately agreed that this shows an autoradiograph.'

So could some forger back in the fourteenth century truly have anticipated the future sciences of photography, 3-D images and, if the observations of Carter and Whanger are to be accepted, even X-radiography in order to create the Shroud's body image? By way of qualification it is important to point out that although enthusiasts sometimes claim that medieval artists could never have had any concept of negativity, this is not strictly true. Coin engravers as far back as the days of the ancient Greeks had to produce images that were 'negatives' in the sense that they had to reproduce relief in reverse, as did the makers of seals, examples of which date easily as far back as the second millennium BC. This said, however, coin and seal dies, of whatever era, make no pretence of being anything other than the handiwork of artists and engravers, and are a very, very far cry from the true photograph-resembling subtleties of the Shroud's image.

It has also sometimes been said that, since the Shroud's body image is readily distinguishable only on stepping back from it, an artist would not have been able to see properly what he or she was doing. This again is not strictly true. Isabel Piczek is a Los Angeles-based professional artist who has created vast murals for churches and cathedrals throughout the United States. And as she points out, when she paints a seven-storey-high figure, she repeatedly has to descend from her scaffolding, view the next area that she intends to work on, hold in her mind what elements this needs, then ascend the scaffolding and paint these without being able properly to see this work in anything like the way that she intends it to be seen from below. But, as an artist long convinced of the Shroud's authenticity, Piczek is also careful to point out that this sort of 'painting blind' can be done only with the aid of outline 'cartoons' that have been pre-drawn in the studio to act as guides to where one block of colour should end and another begin.

Yet another key characteristic to be noted of the Shroud's image is that it has no outlines, suggesting that, if it was the work of a medieval painter,

BELOW: *Multi-talented artist Isabel Piczek, doyenne of the argument that the Shroud cannot be the product of any medieval painter.*

RIGHT: *The Shroud's facial image, showing striking X-ray characteristics when a photographic edge enhancement is used.*

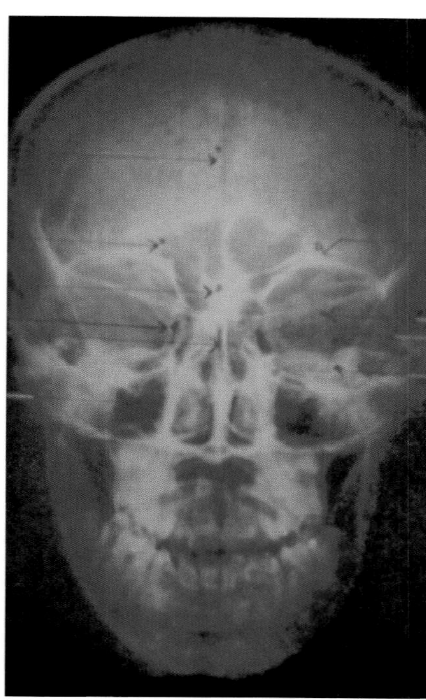

he or she anticipated the most impressionist of Impressionists by some five hundred years. Yet even the most extreme, so-called pointillist, branch of Impressionism used outlines to indicate where they should place the dots of colour with which they made up their paintings. So it is Isabel Piczek's opinion, and one echoed by photographers and image analysts, that for any medieval artist to have created an image as lacking in outline as that on the Shroud is 'technically impossible'.

Peter Schumacher has summed up the situation:

> No method, no style and no artistic skills are known to exist that can produce images that will induce the same photographic and photogrammetric results as the Shroud image induces . . . The Shroud image exhibits some properties of photographic negatives, some properties of body frame (skeletal, internal) imaging, and some properties of three-dimensional grey-scale encoding. It is 'none of these' and represents portions of 'all of these', and more.

Overall, in agreement with artist Piczek, he concludes: 'It is most unlikely that the Shroud is a work of fabrication, or trickery, or forgery of any type.' Such remarks, of course, directly contradict the fourteenth-century French bishop's claim, endorsed by the carbon dating, that the Shroud is all those things.

But what evidence might there be that the Shroud ever was a genuine first-century gravecloth? Or that it genuinely once wrapped a human body?

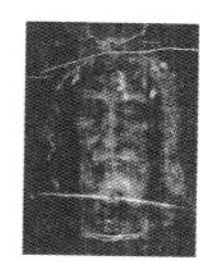

CHAPTER 3

'There's no doubt: it's a grave-cloth.'

(Physicist Dr Eric Jumper)

DESPITE the Shroud's 'photographic' qualities, even to begin to counter the argument that some cunning medieval painter simply 'faked it up' we need to show convincingly that it has size, shape and other characteristics at least compatible with ancient Jewish funerary cloths. In which regard, although the Shroud is hardly what anyone, either now or in the Middle Ages, might expect from the gospel description of how Jesus was buried 'following the Jewish custom' (John 19: 40), it actually stands scrutiny in this respect surprisingly well.

As previously noted, the Shroud's dimensions have only recently been gauged with any real accuracy, thanks to the removal of the nineteenth-century blue satin surround. However, even more important is the revelation from this same removal of how it was originally 'finished'. As is well known to textile historians, looms such as those used in ancient Egypt could span up to 350 cm, enabling the production of cloths of this width, of near unlimited length, and sometimes exceptionally fine quality. According to Dr Mechthild Flury-Lemberg, the Shroud may well have been made originally to this kind of width, but it was then cut very precisely lengthwise, followed by being joined up again with a seam 8.1 cm from one edge. This reduced it widthwise while retaining its two original selvedges, or length-side borders. Dr Flury-Lemberg insists that whoever made this seam then also hemmed the Shroud at its two ends, tell-tale characteristics of this same hand being evident in each instance.

Another of Dr Flury-Lemberg's findings, discovered only shortly before the commencement of the March 2000 Symposium, is what she calls 'a very special, almost invisible stitching with which the edges were finished', done so cleverly that it is visible only on the Shroud's reverse, or under-side.[1] This closely resembles similar almost invisible stitching on first-century AD textile fragments found in tombs in the environs of the ancient Jewish palace-fortress Masada.[2] Although for Dr Flury-Lemberg the sheer professionalism of how the Shroud was made suggests that it was manufactured in a Roman-period Egyptian (or possibly Syrian) textile 'factory' and imported into Judaea, this is the closest that anyone of real authority has come to pin-pointing the Shroud textile characteristics-wise as deriving from a period so close to Jesus' lifetime.

And further significance pertains to the 437 cm x 111 cm dimensions to which the Shroud would appear to have been deliberately cut down, such

LEFT: *Poor Clare nuns, together with the Turin microanalyst Professor Giovanni Riggi and assistant, unstitching part of the Shroud from its backing cloth to enable the underside to be viewed. Clearly visible is the nineteenth-century blue silk surround that framed the Shroud up to 1998, also the traditional red silk covering cloth.*

dimensions, allowing a little for stretch or shrinkage over the centuries, arguably suggesting the historical period when the Shroud was made.

For, indicating that such dimensions may very possibly relate to some historically known unit of measurement is that the Shroud's ratio of length to width is almost, though not exactly, 4:1. The slight inexactness reinforces the view that there may well have been some stretching or shrinking. Furthermore, if we are looking to some particularly meaningful unit of measurement, then there is really only one candidate, the ancient Near Eastern cubit, which was broadly based on an arm's length from the elbow to the tip of the middle finger, but which had acquired a bewildering variety of differing localised 'standards' back in the first century AD.

Given that over the centuries the Shroud is known to have been displayed almost universally landscape-style (except for the occasion when I viewed it in 1973!), it is arguable that any possible stretch is more likely to have been widthwise rather than lengthwise, the latter dimension of 437 cm therefore arguably the more meaningful. In which case, if the so-called Philaeterian cubit of 52.5 cm, which is known to have been used for Jerusalem's Herod Temple, is applied to it, then we find that the Shroud measures just over eight of these cubits long, and only a little more than two of them wide. If the slightly larger Assyrian cubit measure is substituted, then the correlation is even closer. So it has to be considered possible, albeit very far from proven, that the Shroud was 'finished' to conform to the ancient Near Eastern cubit measure, also to similarly Near Eastern-style 'invisible stitching', neither of these common knowledge in medieval Europe.

Such findings aside, the Shroud's particularly unexpected feature, the significance of which again remains very far from adequately explored, has to be its long, narrow shape. As already noted, the theory behind this is that the deceased was laid on one half, and the other half was then drawn over his or her head and down to the toes. But the immediate question is who, in any period, might have chosen to bury their dead in this way? Although the occasional burial shroud has survived from medieval Europe, as for example two found wrapping an English knight buried at St Bees, Cumbria[3] (today superbly conserved and displayed in Whitehaven Museum), in these, as in numerous examples depicted in European manuscripts and funeral effigies, the cloth is invariably squarish, rather than anything like the Shroud's long and narrow shape. The principal St Bees shroud, for instance, measures 252 cm square, and the body was laid on one side and the cloth's other side brought over it sideways. Its loose ends were bunched up and tied at the top of the head, reminiscent of a Christmas cracker. And, with minor variations, arrangements of this kind seem to have been fairly universal during the Middle Ages.

Likewise in Graeco-Roman ancient Egypt, in which shroud burials are commonly found, the cloths that were used tended to be only a little longer

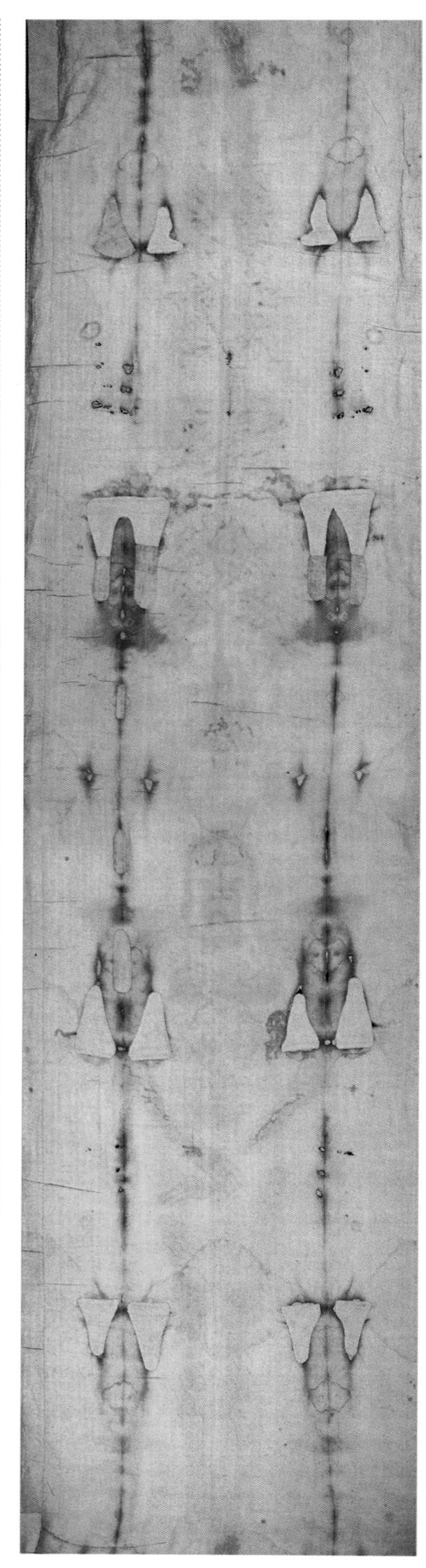

ABOVE: *(Top left) A typical shroud of the Graeco-Roman period, painted with the deceased's likeness, from Saqqara, Egypt, dating* c. *AD 180 and measuring 180 cm x 135 cm. (Top centre) The shroud of an Egyptian female, Taathyr, of similar dimensions and period. (Top right) A lead-encased burial shroud of the thirteenth century AD, found at St Bees, Cumbria. (Below) An English shroud of the Civil War period, depicted on a tomb sculpture in St John's Church, Bristol, typically showing cloth ends bunched at the head. In all cases the shrouds' dimensions and arrangement are quite different from that of Turin (left).*

than the body's height, mostly around 179 cm, with slightly shorter widths. Again there was the same sideways rather than over-the-head mode of wrapping the body, as in the case of one dating from *c.* AD 180, which, like the Shroud, was made of linen, and was found at Saqqara, Egypt. Like several other examples from this period and place, this particular specimen was strikingly painted with a full-length portrait of the deceased in which he lay in death facing his own painted face, with the images of the gods Osiris and Anubis tucked down either side of him, a rather uncanny parallel to what theoretically happened spontaneously in the case of our Turin Shroud. Also worth noting is that the Saqqara deceased's mantle features a simple decorative border along its lower edge very similar to that formed by the Shroud's lengthwise seam. Yet notably absent among such Egyptian burials (and this is true however far we look back into ancient Egyptian burial practices) is anything like the over-the-head arrangement that we see on the Shroud.

Furthermore, although no one can claim to know exactly how burials 'following the Jewish custom' were carried out in Jesus' time, it is certain-

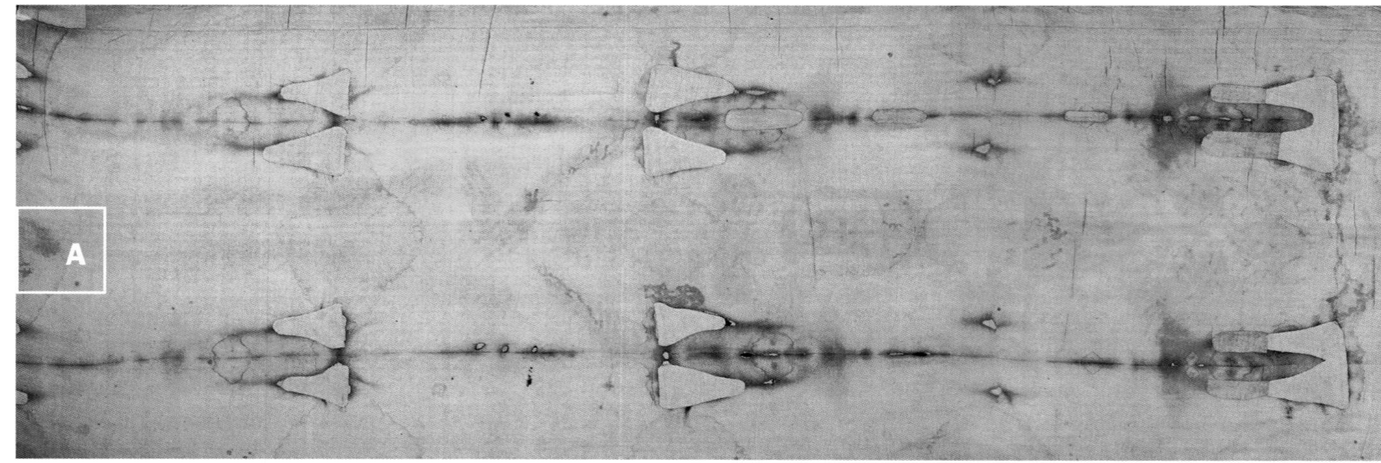

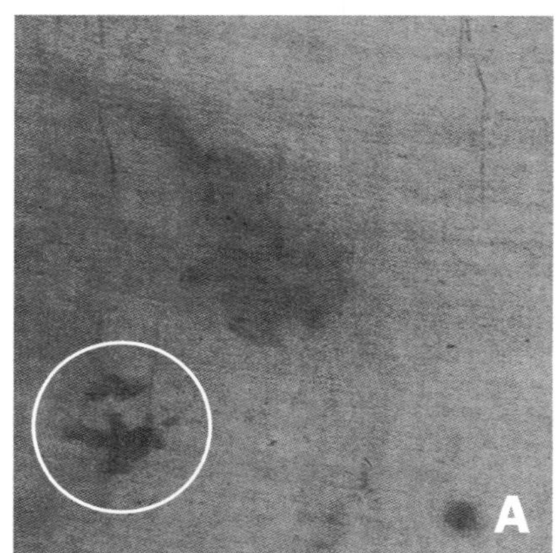

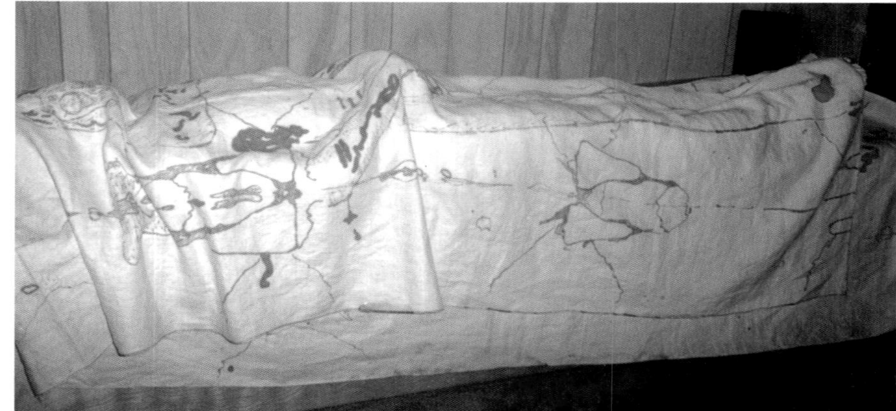

ly well enough established that these were normally not in 'shrouds', as we understand the term, at all. While modern-day Bibles often translate the original Greek word *sindon* as 'shroud' when it appears in the gospel accounts of Jesus' burial, in actuality it had a much more general meaning as a linen garment (as is self-evident in Mark 14: 51-2), rather than anything specifically funerary. And the true ancient Jewish funerary norm was for the deceased to be washed, dressed in his or her Sabbath-best clothes, if wealthy laid out on the ledge of a rock-cut tomb, and then left to rot. After about a year the de-fleshed bones would be gathered up into a stone ossuary or bone-box. It is in receptacles such as these that most Jewish human remains dating from Jesus' time have been found in and around Jerusalem. In general the idea of any 'over-the-head' cloth simply does not occur.

However there was one important exception to this otherwise all-prevailing custom – if someone had died a bloody death, as on a battlefield or by crucifixion. In these circumstances, because it was deemed important to keep all the life-blood with the body, the Code of Jewish Law[4] prescribed

TOP: *How blood marks at the far ends of the Shroud (see ringed details) match each other, providing an uncanny 'register' of how the theoretical body lay in the cloth. The half of the cloth drawn over the body did not stretch the full length of the feet. Conversely, there were several inches to spare on the half on which the body lay.*

CENTRE ABOVE: *Dr John Jackson's manikin of the Shroud body, with a mock-up of the Shroud laid over it, demonstrating how the cloth would have been laid over the body and how the far-end blood marks can be shown to match.*

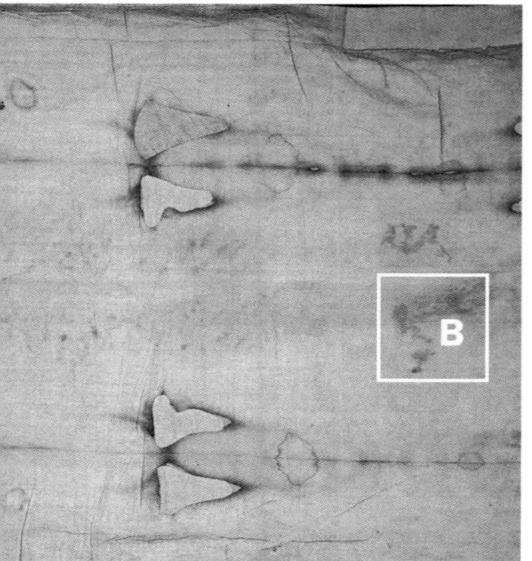

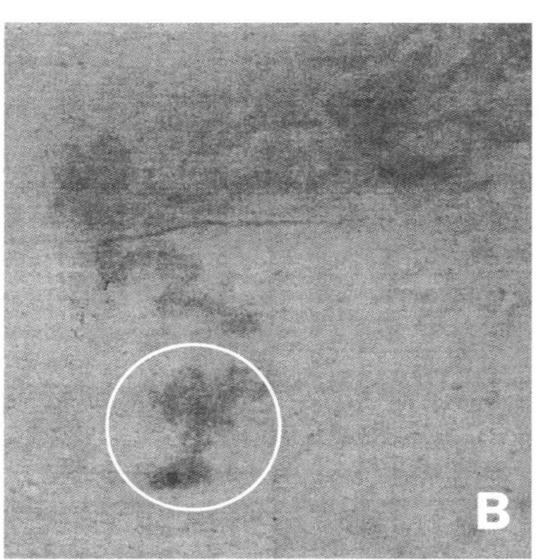

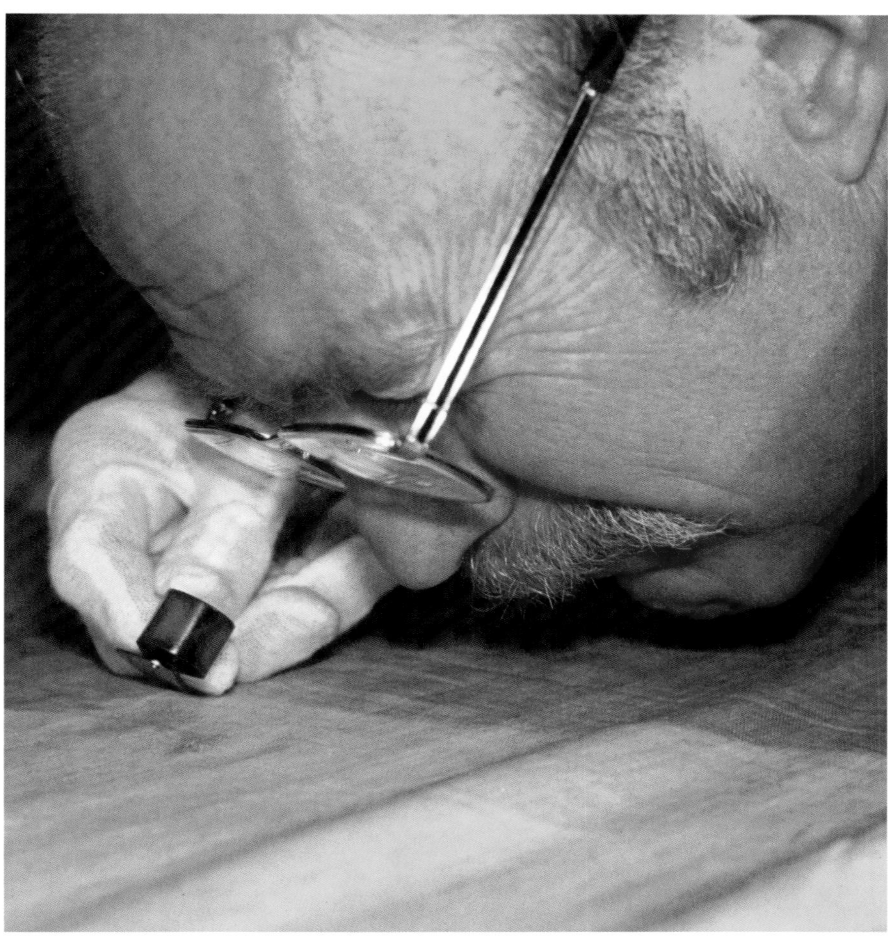

ABOVE RIGHT: *STURP's Dr Ray Rogers viewing one of the blood marks in close-up.*

that the blood should not be washed off [5], but left on the body and 'a sheet which is called *sovev* used 'to go right around' it. This text, therefore, seems to describe a specifically ancient Jewish arrangement, virtually unique in the typology of the world's known funerary practices, whereby a long, narrow cloth went over the deceased's head in precisely the very unusual manner that we see indicated in the case of the Shroud. It also throws valuable light on the otherwise enigmatic reference in the John gospel to the cloth found in Jesus' empty tomb that had specifically been 'over his [Jesus'] head . . . rolled up in a place by itself' (John 20: 7). All of which raises the question, was this cloth the same Shroud preserved in Turin today? Or, if not, how could any medieval 'relic' forger, in addition to all his 'photographic' wizardry, have known of anything historically so obscure?

No less convincing a pointer to the Shroud being genuinely an ancient Jewish grave cloth, rather than a faked semblance, is the fact that its imprints are not just a straightforward 'front-half' and 'back-half' of the 'sandwich-board' variety, as any artist-forger would have concocted it, and as artists indeed sometimes unthinkingly copied it during the sixteenth and seventeenth centuries. Instead the front half, rather than, as might be expected, extending all the way down to and beyond where the man of the Shroud's toes would have been, stops at least 2.5cm short, with the recently discovered hem showing that it never had any more length in its 'finished' form. Yet in the case of the back half a region of blank cloth carries on for as much as 8 or 10cm beyond where the toes can be seen. Because of this overlap, the Shroud would therefore have been turned back over the short front half in order to make a neat funerary 'parcel'. Although this is just the sort of mistake that someone enshrouding a genuine body might easily have made, since after all, they would hardly have been expecting any image to form, an artist-forger would almost certainly have made sure he 'imprinted' at least the body's front half in full, leaving any 'skimping' to the less important back half.

In this instance there is also the most remarkable evidence that a body was wrapped in the Shroud in precisely this 'too short front half' way. As first noted by the German researcher Dr Werner Bulst[6], at the far left-hand end of the Shroud there is a small but distinctively shaped 'blood' stain where the front of the deceased's feet would have been. At the far right-hand end, where a rill of blood can be seen to have spilled directly onto the cloth, one part of this stain can be shown to be a precise match to the one at the far left-hand end. The STURP project leader, Dr John Jackson, who has made a life-sized mock-up of the Shroud, and combined this with a styroform manikin in the shape of the Shroud 'body', takes a particular delight in demonstrating this tiny but strikingly evidential feature to those who visit his Shroud Center at Colorado Springs. And with good reason, since it shows, in a particularly homely 'who would have thought of this?' manner, that there genuinely was a three-dimensional human body once laid in this extraordinary cloth.

This neatly leads to the important issue of just how accurately the Shroud's imprints check out with an actual human body's anatomy, point by point, back and front. In 1994, as part of their attempt to 'prove' that Leonardo da Vinci forged the Shroud, the British writers Lynn Picknett and Clive Prince claimed from their measurements of Shroud photographs that the man of the Shroud's height was an absurd 6 ft 8 in (203 cm) at the front and 6 ft 10 in (208 cm) at the back.[7]

The truth is that Picknett and Prince made their calculations based on the man of the Shroud's body having been as flat as if run over by a steamroller. To determine his true height, the only reliable method is to do as Dr John Jackson did for his Shroud Center, that is, to cut a length of cloth to the same dimensions as the Shroud, mark it up with the salient body features, then invite volunteers to 'fit' this Cinderella-slipper-style. In fact Dr Jackson's first attempt at this was back in the 1970s when he and his colleague Dr Eric Jumper were working at Colorado Springs Air Force

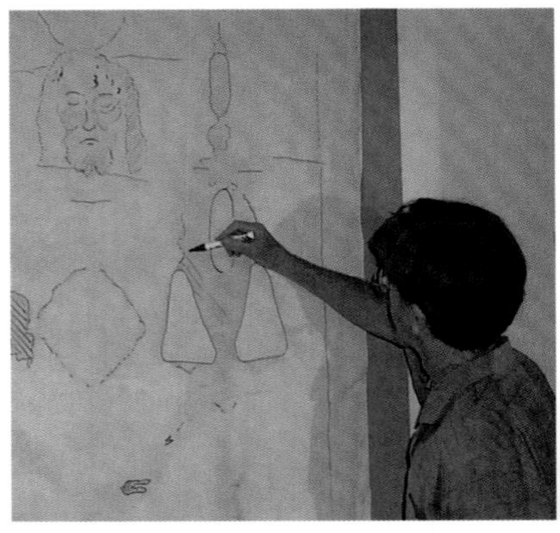

ABOVE: *Author Ian Wilson making a life-sized mock-up of the Shroud, using a projected slide and measurements conforming to known fixed points on the Shroud. When this is worn as below salient points fit closely.*

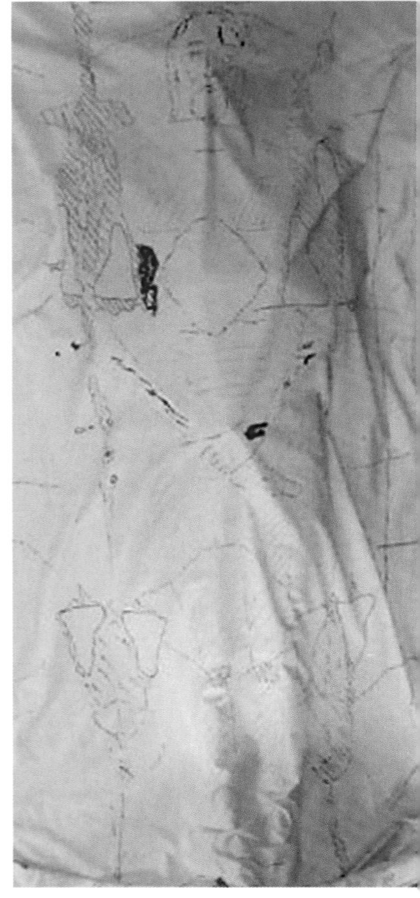

RIGHT: *Sculpture teacher and human anatomy expert Professor Lorenzo Ferri making a life-sized statue of the man of the Shroud, according to his assessment of how the body lay in death.*

BELOW: *Dr John Jackson and colleagues with a life-sized mock-up or working replica of the Shroud, and volunteers recruited to 'fit' the cloth Cinderella-slipper-style. Those found to fit were around 180–183 cm (5 ft 11 in to 6 ft) in height, demonstrating that this was the man of the Shroud's approximate height.*

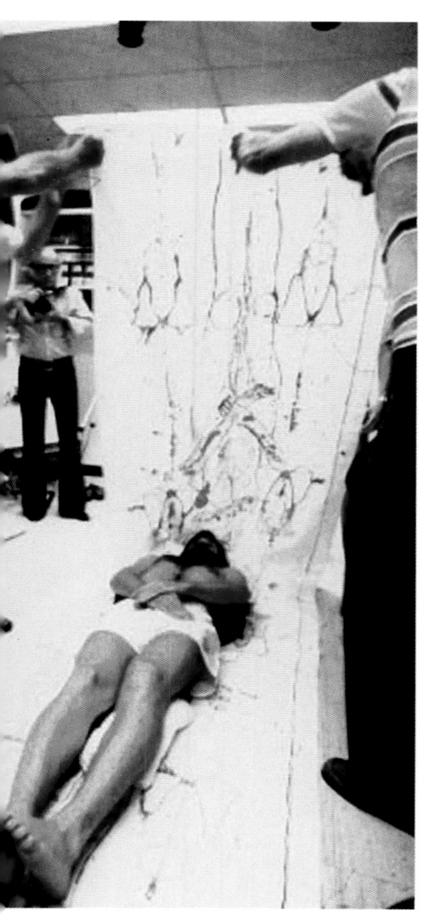

Academy, a facility where they had access to any number of cadet volunteers for this purpose, but he has repeated and refined the method several times since. Had Picknett and Prince used anything like Jackson's careful methodology they would have found the closest 'fit' to the Shroud to have been, not 6 ft 10 in, but, rather more credibly, 5 ft 11 in (180 cm).[8]

That is a height that, as it happens, very closely approximates to my own. To prove the falsity of the Picknett–Prince claims, I therefore made

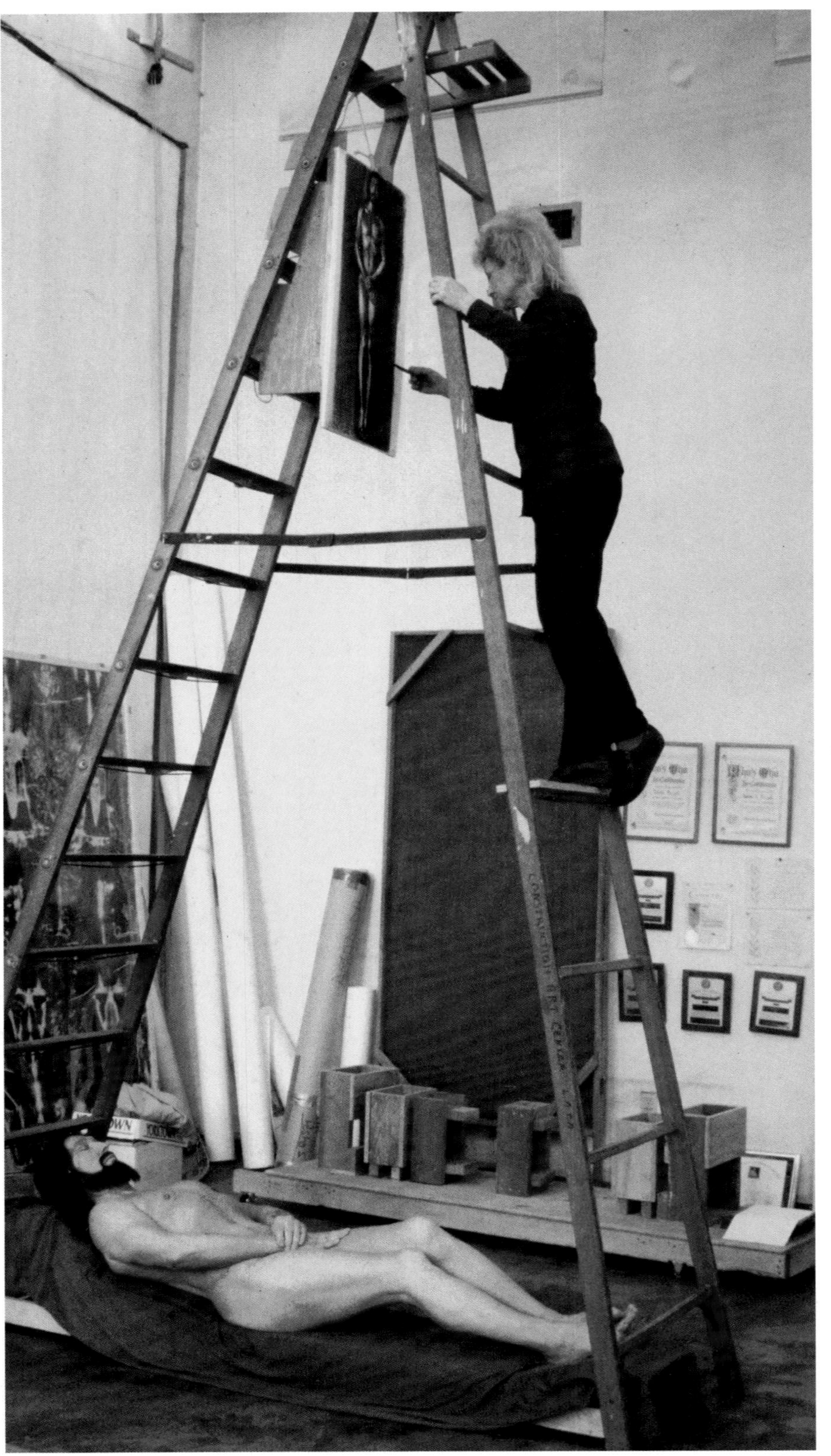

LEFT: *Liturgical artist Isabel Piczek with a life model in 'Shroud pose' in the studio, demonstrating the impossibility of any artist having made an anatomically accurate image from the viewpoint that the Shroud's image demands.*

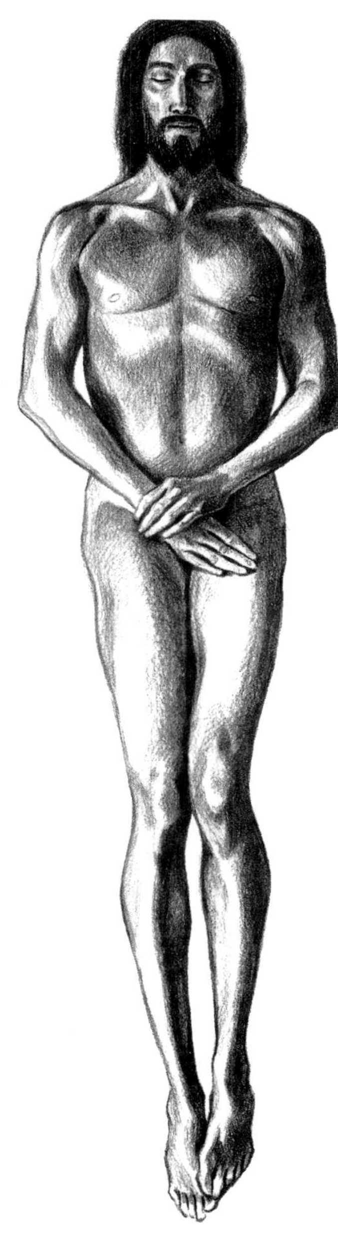

Drawing by Isabel Piczek of one of her life models reconstructing the Shroud pose.

a cloth model of the Shroud to the original's exact dimensions, helped by my wife Judith. Then with the aid of a slide projector I marked this up with the Shroud imprint's 'body' features, just as Dr John Jackson had done before me. As Judith's photographs confirm, my 5 ft 11 in frame very readily matches this imprint point for point, back and front, as anyone approximating this same build can check for themselves. Furthermore, anyone who regards this as too tall for anyone living in antiquity should be aware that despite the widespread supposition that people in past ages were significantly shorter than ourselves, there is in fact no serious shortage of six-footers among the skeletons found in ancient graves. Overall then, even from this simplest of demonstrations, the Shroud's imprints make perfect anatomical sense.

But, if by this virtually mechanical means we can calculate the man of the Shroud's height, can we go further? Can we reconstruct how the whole (still theoretical) body would have looked as laid out in the Shroud, thereby corroborating as far as possible that it was once a genuine human body's grave-cloth? An important point here is that, remarkable as the Shroud's imprint is in its three-dimensionality, although the way that the imprint has registered gives us a great deal of visual information about the body's front and back contours, it does not necessarily do so for its full depth. Indeed, as Jackson's and Jumper's own calculations indicated, the image registration on each side seems to have a depth of no more than 4 cm. So the Shroud's image, even as so remarkably viewed via the VP-8 Image Analyzer, presents but a topmost slice of the body's front and back, leaving unseen the greater part of the remainder. But can we reconstruct it?

Onto the scene at this point steps the professional artist, with eyes ideally trained by long hours working with the nude model in traditional life classes, and therefore able to see a human body in its proper depth thanks to an understanding of the principles of foreshortening – that is, those parts which will look too short, or not appear at all, because of the effects of perspective. As the Italian sculpture teacher Lorenzo Ferri noted in the 1960s, while pioneeringly reconstructing how the man of the Shroud's full body would have looked, the Shroud's imprint exhibits a marked foreshortening to the legs. The head and upper torso also seem to be raised at a significant angle to the horizontal plane, as if resting on some kind of head-rest, or fixed in this attitude due to the effects of rigor mortis.

Accordingly, following Ferri's death, in the early 1990s the Los Angeles artist Isabel Piczek took up much the same line of research, and because she routinely hires life models to pose for the preliminary studies for her vast murals and mosaics, she used some of these to help her. She soon found that there is indeed a lot more to this 'correct seeing' of the Shroud image than at first meets the eye.

One of Piczek's first discoveries was that the only way to obtain the right view of any present-day body posed in the Shroud manner, for the purpose of checking it against a life-sized photograph of the Shroud image, is to use a very tall ladder and ask the model to lie directly underneath it. Because of the frequent vast scale of her commissions, for which she has to make actual-sized working drawings, Piczek always keeps a five-metre ladder in the high, airy studio that she shares with her sister Edith, and the top of this provided just the right vantage-point. It also showed the absurdity of any artist even handling a 437 cm long cloth while balancing in this awkward position, let alone trying to paint onto it.

The next problem was that Piczek's hired models found it quite impossible to hold the required pose unaided, demanding as it does that while lying flat they keep their head and upper torso several inches from the horizontal. This necessitated having a specially angled posing platform constructed to provide support. Once this was done, and she began directing her models to hold their bodies in exactly the mode that she 'saw' on the Shroud, a very distinctive 'burial pose' for the man of the Shroud soon emerged. Corroborating Ferri, the head and upper back were raised and the knees bent. But an immediate difficulty was that these and other details differed markedly from the altogether flatter mode that John Jackson and Eric Jumper had reconstructed using their Air Force cadet models. So who was right – Piczek, with her professional artist's instinctive recognition of foreshortening, and her vast experience working with professional, nude life models; or Jackson and Jumper, with their high-tech scientific equipment and briefs-clad Air Force cadets?

My interest in the Shroud is based on a life-long enthusiasm for the history and practice of figurative art (while a history undergraduate I also attended life classes at Oxford's Ruskin Art School), and I could see the same foreshortening that Isabel Piczek saw. My inclination was, therefore, to favour her interpretation. And given that, as already remarked, my height approximates to that of the man of the Shroud, a logical way of exploring the issue further seemed to be to become a Piczek model for a day and under her direction experience the 'feel' of her version of the burial pose for myself.[9] To this Isabel Piczek readily agreed, and accordingly

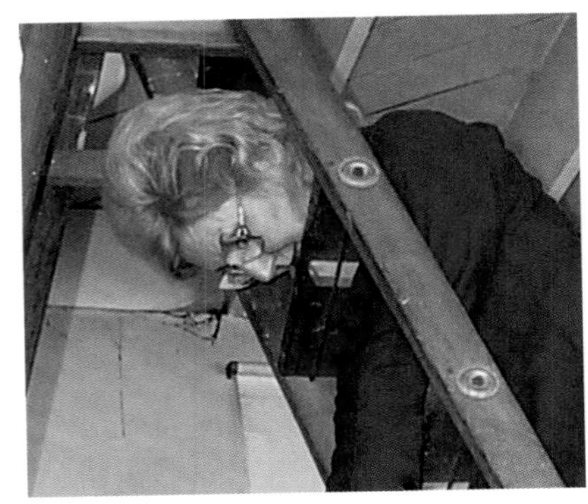

ABOVE: *Isabel Piczek, at the top of her ladder, directs author Ian Wilson into the Shroud pose, while referring to a life-sized photograph alongside him (below). Note how the platform is specially constructed so that the model's back is tilted upwards in a position which is otherwise impossible to hold. On the facing page (left) can be seen the same pose as photographed from almost the top of the ladder, showing how the flexion of the knees is scarcely apparent from this viewpoint, also how the pose is hardly the 'pious modesty' one that sceptics often claim.*

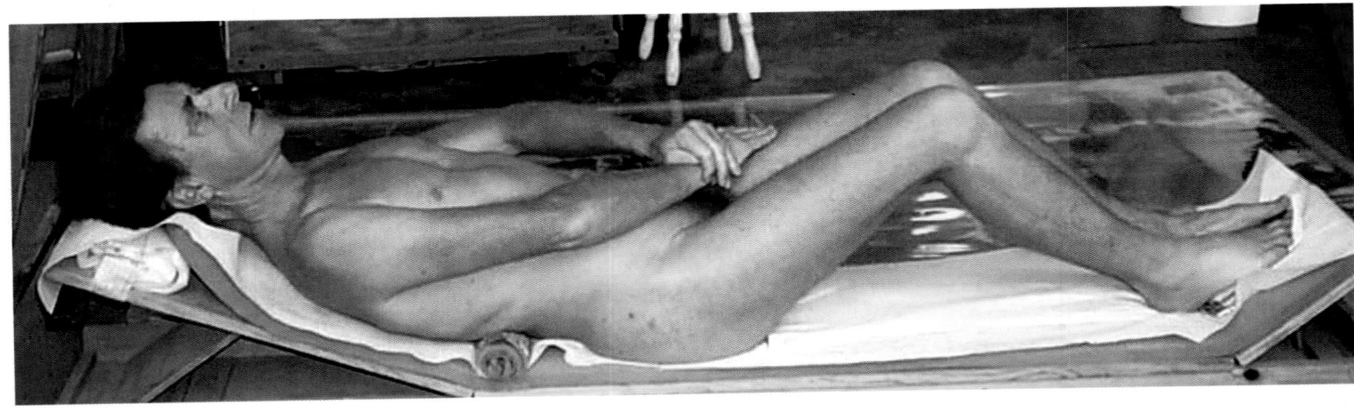

on the morning of Wednesday 5 July 1999, Isabel Piczek's assistant Alfonso fetched the posing platform from its storage and laid it below the tall ladder, with a life-sized photograph of the Shroud negative alongside. I took my clothes off, settled onto the platform and assumed an approximation of the pose. Isabel Piczek then climbed to the top of her ladder and began to call for inch-by-inch adjustments, aided by my wife Judith giving the occasional manual shove.

Sceptics often label the Shroud's distinctive pose, with the hands crossed over the genitals, as a 'modesty' one typical of a pious artist. However, when you actually assume it, as I did fully naked, you quickly find that any such 'modesty' is but a semblance. My right hand rested only on my left upper thigh, and the left on it, with neither even touching my genitals. These were occluded only when viewed from Isabel's directly overhead position, and then only just. But in any case burials both in antiquity and in the Middle Ages were quite commonly done with the hands crossed over the genitals, as observable both on ancient Egyptian sarcophagi and in medieval manuscript illuminations. So the 'modesty' argument should not be used either for or against the Shroud's antiquity.

The second finding from the experience was the extent to which my upper back and head were indeed raised. Although this is far from obvious

BELOW: *The sarcophagus of an Egyptian priest,* c. *340* BC *(right), showing the same burial pose as that indicated on the Shroud (centre) and as posed by author Ian Wilson (left).*

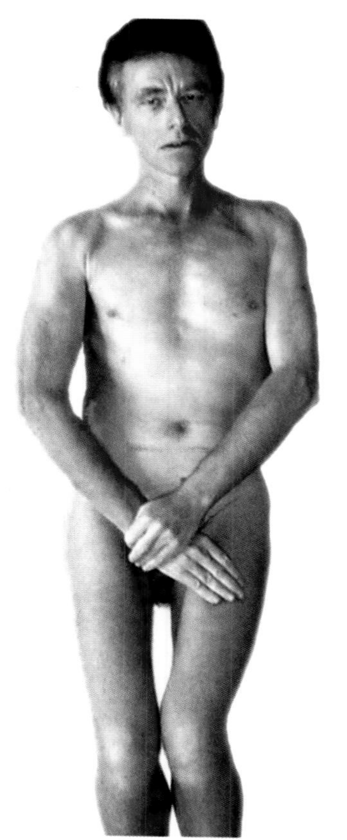

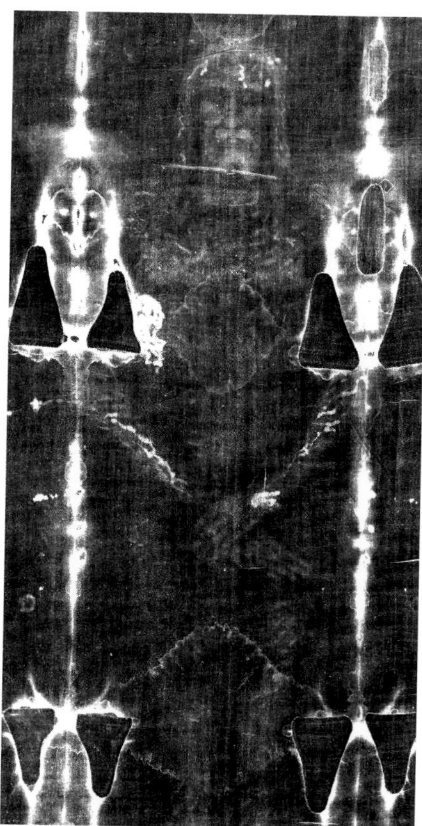

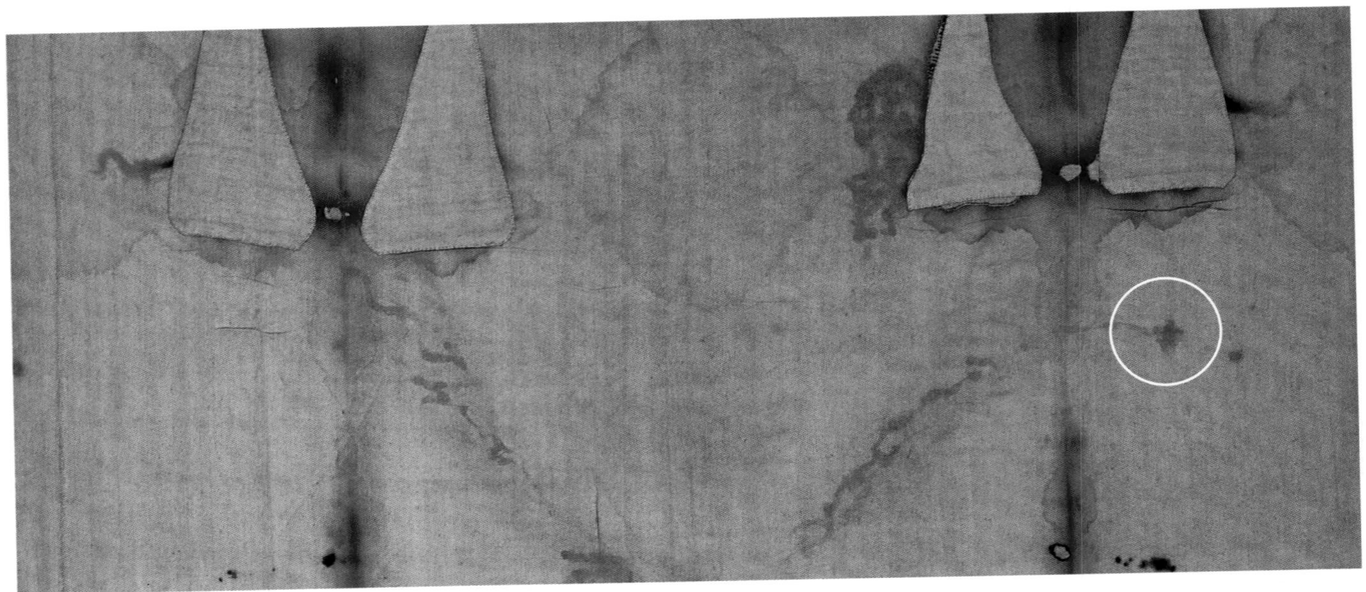

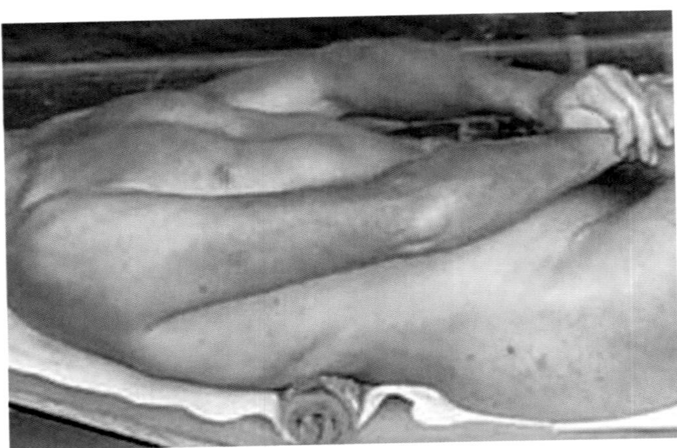

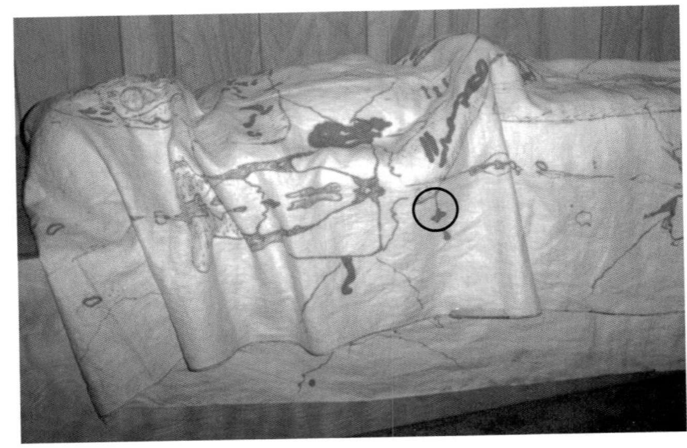

when viewing the Shroud's straight-on frontal and dorsal images, it is very evident when you are laid on the platform and the Piczek visual methodology is applied. So could the original burial have included a headrest? In fact there is historical support for this, since several First Temple Jewish tombs in Jerusalem and its environs still feature these,[10] although as we shall see in the next chapter, it is also possible that the theoretical body may have become fixed in this position, with its upper torso pushed forward, from the way that it had hung on the cross.

Another discovery was just how markedly bent I needed to keep my knees, enforced by an angled footrest at the foot of the posing platform, which was designed again to hold the model's body in the correct position. Here in earnest was the deep foreshortening that Piczek had repeatedly insisted that the Shroud, despite its rigidly frontal aspect, conveys to anyone with the requisite anatomical knowledge. Instead of my legs resting

TOP: *A drop of 'blood' from the man of the Shroud's right elbow (ringed). This appears to have trickled from the body as it lay in the cloth, and from the length of its fall before being checked at the horizontal plane, the height of the elbows above the horizontal can be accurately calculated. The author's right elbow (above left) may be a little too high, but that of the Jackson model (above right) is definitely too low. Research on these points is far from concluded.*

Italian sculptor Luigi Mattei's reconstruction of the man of the Shroud's burial pose, as made for a Year 2000 exhibition in Bologna. There remain many differences between one interpretation and another that are yet to be resolved.

almost completely flat, as in the Jackson and Jumper reconstructions, they rose at quite a marked angle from the horizontal, the entire body surface from heels to buttocks not touching the platform. To me all this indicated a body that, for all that it might look like one laid to rest, had in fact been locked in the greatest tension. So was what I was experiencing, with the exception that the arms were no longer outstretched but forced over the genitals, something at least of the very last position that the man of the Shroud had assumed as he hung on the cross?

One unexpected finding concerns the positioning of the arms. While the Shroud's direct frontal aspect might lead to the supposition that the elbows rested nearly on the floor on either side of the body, it was learnt from actually assuming the pose that the elbows have to have been raised several inches from the floor. Although the attitude felt very awkward, rather as if my arms had been forcibly brought together in this mode from some completely different position, the fact that it was the correct one, as even Isabel Piczek had not previously realized, is corroborated by a drip of blood that is to be seen on the Shroud between the third set of poker holes and the triangular patches next to the chest wound. This can only have spilled from the elbow and trickled down the side-draping of the Shroud to be checked, where we see it pool by the part of the cloth that rested in the horizontal plane.

My impression of the pose's awkwardness and discomfort was confirmed when Isabel Piczek directed to me to lower my right shoulder relative to the left. I had anticipated her asking me to do this, since Shroud-interested physicians had long noted that the man of the Shroud's right shoulder appeared to have been dislocated. But actually doing so brought powerfully to mind that what to me was merely a pose had arguably once meant human pain. For if my arm was uncomfortable, how much more so must it have been for those that once hung from nails hammered through living flesh and bone?

To what extent Isabel Piczek's version of the Shroud pose is more accurate than the Jackson and Jumper one will no doubt be debated among Shroud aficionados for decades to come. There remain difficulties and issues that can be resolved only by further experiments of the kind that Isabel and I conducted.

But overall there can be absolutely no doubt that the Shroud makes perfect sense as having been used as a burial cloth, and having had a real dead body laid in it. In this light it also, of course, gives rise to new questions. For what do qualified physicians and pathologists, in the wake of the radiocarbon dating, continue to make of the various bloodstains and other pathological features that are to be seen on the cloth? Do they still find these medically convincing? Does the Shroud still make anatomical and medical sense as having belonged to someone who genuinely underwent, not only a Jewish burial but all the rigours of a Roman crucifixion?

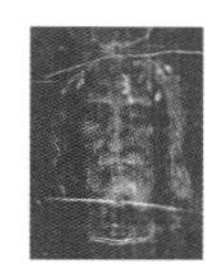

FACING PAGE: *Crucifixion scene from the Holkham Bible picture book, a fourteenth-century manuscript thought to have been created in northern France, the region where the Shroud was said to have been 'cunningly painted'.*

CHAPTER 4

'The most pitiable of deaths'

(Historian Josephus)

GARY VIKAN, a Baltimore art professor who believes the Shroud to be the work of a medieval artist, has recently expressed the opinion that people living in the Middle Ages might well have had quite a lively understanding of crucifixion and what it would have meant, so that any knowledge of this kind that the Shroud exhibits is nothing to be surprised about.[1]

In fairness to this argument, the fourteenth century was undeniably a time of the most intense interest in, and graphic portrayal of, the more lurid physical details of Jesus' crucifixion. The previous century had witnessed medieval Europe's greatest saint, Francis of Assisi, manifest on his own body wounds which apparently replicated those in Jesus' hands, feet and side, and whatever their causation they created a vogue for mystics and charlatans alike to imitate such 'stigmata'. Performers in miracle plays vied with each other to create the most realistic re-enactments of Jesus' passion and crucifixion. Bands of flagellants went from town to town stripped to the waist, frenziedly whipping themselves until the blood streamed down their backs. Artists of the time reflected and furthered this trend, as in the British Museum's Anglo-French Holkham Bible picture-book. Created during the lifetime of Geoffrey de Charny, the first known owner of the Shroud, this includes more than forty scenes of Jesus' passion, death and burial illustrated with a luridness akin to modern-day children's horror comics.[2]

BELOW: *St Francis of Assisi* (c.*1182–1226*)*. The 'stigmata' wounds that appeared on his body, seemingly replicating those of Jesus, created many imitators, also a vogue of interest in the more lurid physical details of Jesus' crucifixion.*

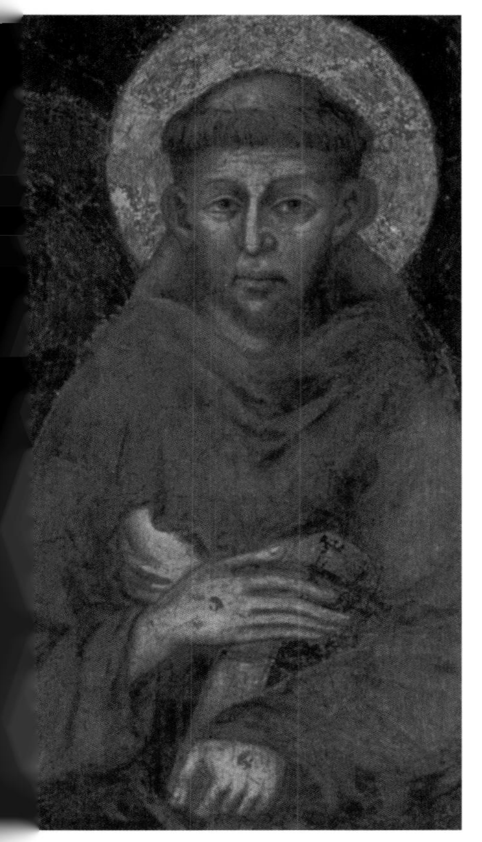

Yet, if from all this the Shroud might be interpreted merely as a product of this time, a consensus of the medical appraisal of its imprints tells a very different story. More than sixty years ago the Paris surgeon Dr Pierre Barbet viewed the Shroud at 'less than a yard' distance when it was briefly brought out onto the Turin Cathedral steps in September 1933. The experience fired him to undertake the most intensive study of the Shroud man's apparent injuries, which it had only recently become possible to study in real detail thanks to the superb Enrie black-and-white photographs taken two years earlier. And Barbet's conclusion was emphatic: 'To describe these imprints as the work of a forger is an attitude which is absurd and . . . impossible to hold.'[3]

As might be expected, during the subsequent decades there have been some medical experts who have disagreed with Barbet on matters of specialist interpretation. None the less, even in the teeth of the radiocarbon dating announcement of 1988, the current international consensus among

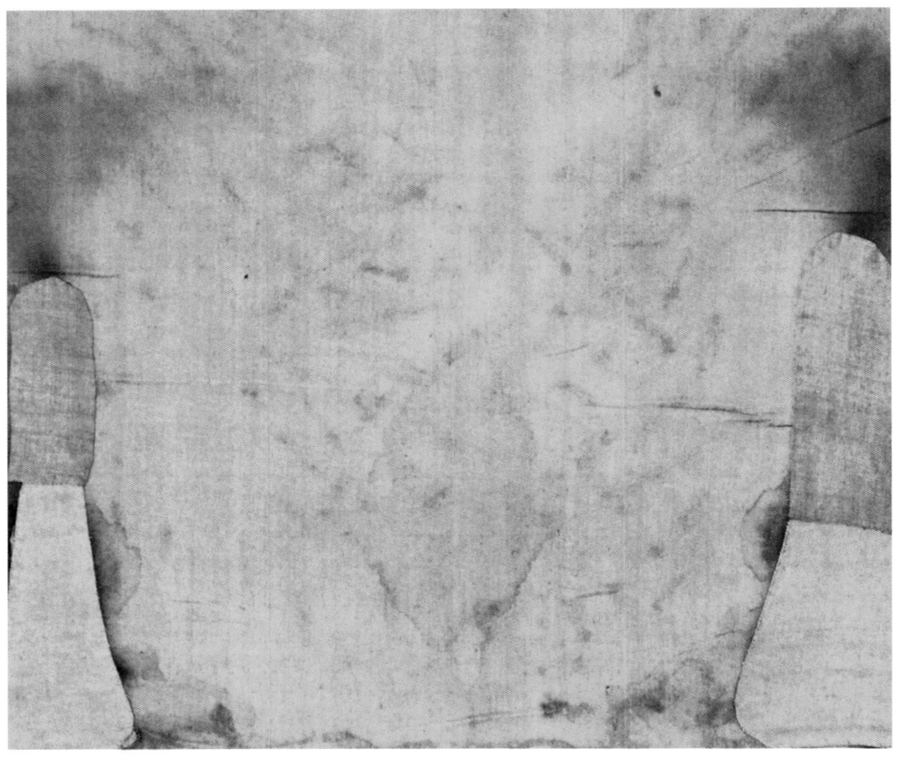

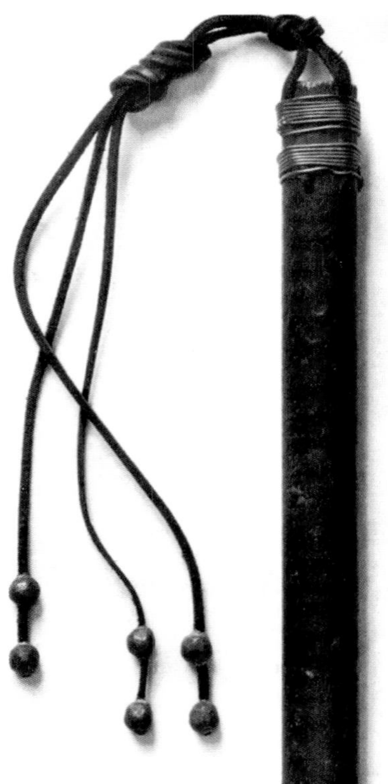

ABOVE LEFT: *The upper back region of the Shroud's back-of-the-body imprint, showing it to be peppered with faint dumb-bell-shaped marks corresponding to the double pellets of lead or bone that tipped the Roman scourge weapon the* flagrum *(above right).*

physicians, anatomists and pathologists who have seriously studied the Shroud remains that the injuries it represents make perfect medical sense as deriving from a real-life individual who genuinely underwent crucifixion and its preliminaries.

Thus all over the Shroud man's body there can faintly but persistently be distinguished some hundred dumb-bell-shaped marks, which from their distribution, falling as they do on the front and back of the trunk and legs, can meaningfully be interpreted only as injuries from a scourging or flagellation. In their subtleties of shape and definition, their angles of fall and their areas of fall, these markings are quite different from, and considerably more convincing than, any of those on the innumerable medieval depictions of this punishment. As is apparent from close medical inspection, each individual mark indicates, theoretically at least, a contusion or raised welt that would have been caused by the source of the dumb-bell shape impacting on the body's flesh. In 1973 I completely failed to notice any blood associated with these but, prompted by Barrie, who had seen small bloodstains during his close-up work in 1978, I too observed these during my March 2000 viewing, particularly on the shoulders, the thighs, the backs of the knees and the calves.[4] Clearly, the impact of the dumb-bell shape not only broke the skin but actually tore the flesh.

In which regard dictionaries of classical antiquities make it easy enough to identify the source of that dumb-bell shape as from a Roman

ABOVE: *A reconstruction of how a Roman scourging was carried out. It can be seen on the Shroud how the lash fell, convincingly corresponding to how such a whip would have been wielded.*

BELOW RIGHT: *Close-up of the blood flows on the Shroud's back-of-the-head imprint. These appear to have derived from a cap of spikes, as reconstructed (below), rather than the neat circlet often imagined by artists.*

flagrum, examples of which are depicted on Roman coins and in Roman catacomb paintings. This was a fearsome solid-handled two or three-thonged whip tipped with twinned *plumbatae* or pellets of metal or bone, the dumb-bell shape of which match the Shroud very well.

Historically, Roman scourging with the *flagrum* is known to have involved the victim being stripped naked, chained to a column and then given what might be a near unlimited number of lashes, dependent on the gravity of the crime and whether he or she was a Roman citizen. Medically the effects of this set of injuries alone would have been debilitating in the extreme. The New York forensic examiner Dr Fred Zugibe, long convinced by the injuries visible on the Shroud, was one of those specially invited to the Turin Symposium of March 2000, and together we studied the 'scourge marks' during our very privileged examination of the Shroud in the Cathedral sacristy. As he comments of these, they would have caused intense 'trauma to the nerves, muscles and skin reducing the victim to an exhausted, wretched condition with shivering, severe sweating, frequent displays of seizure, and a craving for water.'[5]

As mentioned back in Chapter 1, all around the Shroud man's forehead and again around the back of his head, we noted a series of reddish-coloured, irregularly spaced trickles, as if something spiked had caused his scalp to bleed in several places. Even for a layman, these fairly obviously suggest the 'crown of thorns' that all four gospels describe as having been thrust on Jesus' head to humiliate him – although the Shroud indicates that this was very much more like a crude, tangled clump of some barbed plant, than the neat circlet imagined by most artists. However, it is again the medical specialist who notes not only the medically convincing character

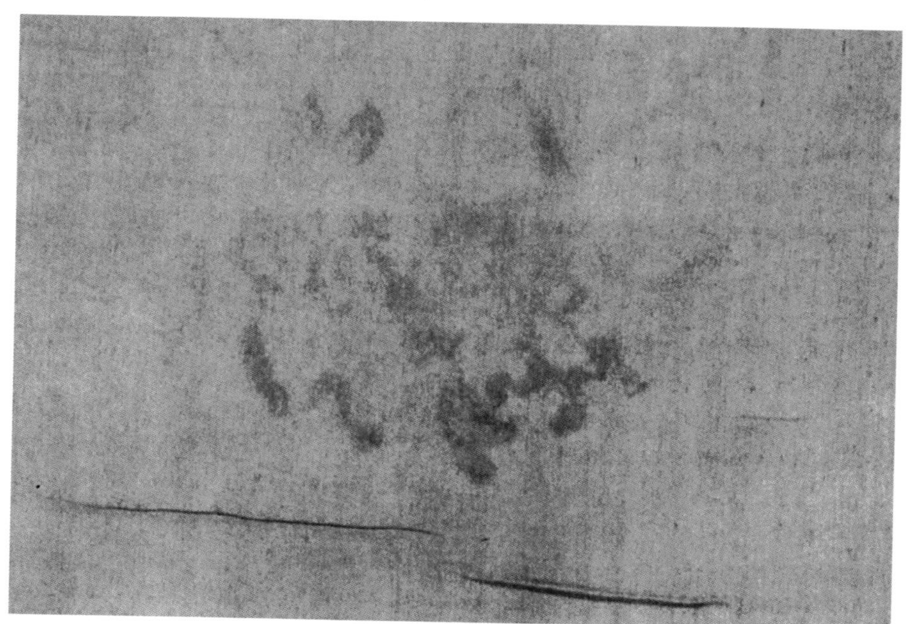

of each blood trickle – with even venous and arterial flows being distinguishable from each other relative to the location – but also what would have been the accompanying trauma. As Dr Zugibe remarked, the densely distributed blood vessels to be found all around the human head are intertwined with an equally complex distribution of nerves, as a result of which the pain would have been of the kind when nerves are touched by a dentist's drill.

However, the Shroud features that must inevitably command the greatest medical interest are the streams of apparent blood which can be seen to have trickled down the forearms, with further stains also at the feet. Although it is automatic even for the layman instinctively to identify these bloodstains as being from crucifixion injuries, the issue that immediately comes to the fore, for both layman and medical specialist alike, is just how much is historically known about this particular execution method.

Despite the innumerable sculptures and paintings of the crucifixion that are to be seen in churches ancient and modern, the Christian gospels provide surprisingly little factual information concerning how Jesus was crucified. We cannot be sure whether he was hung facing towards or away from the cross, though very recent Shroud evidence now suggests the latter, in view of tiny fragments of wood found in the back of the head region, mixed with the 'crown of thorns' bloodstains[6] (see Chapter 5). Even the universal idea that Jesus was nailed, as distinct from hung via ropes, is based only on the John gospel's description of the resurrected Jesus inviting 'Doubting Thomas' to inspect his hands (John 20: 27). Although the Romans are recorded as having crucified thousands in their more savage moments,[7] and the stripping and scourging mentioned as its preliminaries are also referred to by classical writers, those same writers are squeamishly frugal in explaining the practical details of how the procedure was actually carried out. For instance, were nails used for both hands and feet? Was the victim nailed onto the crossbeam of his cross on the ground, then hauled upwards by ropes? Or was he made to stand in position on a platform, the nails hammered in and then the platform kicked away?

Whatever the answer, what the Shroud quite unmistakably shows is that the 'hand' nail, certainly in the case of the only arm which is fully visible to us (the left), has to have gone through the wrist, not the palm, as previously imagined by virtually every artist in history. It was Dr Pierre Barbet who conducted the first serious researches on this, demonstrating from cadavers and amputated limbs how there is a convenient space in the wrist called Destot's Space that a nail can easily pass through – though in the case of a live person at the price of excruciating pain from the nerve touched at this point. As Barbet further found, when he drove a nail through this the weight of a body was readily supported on a cross, unlike in the case of the palms, in which the flesh would tear and the body fall.

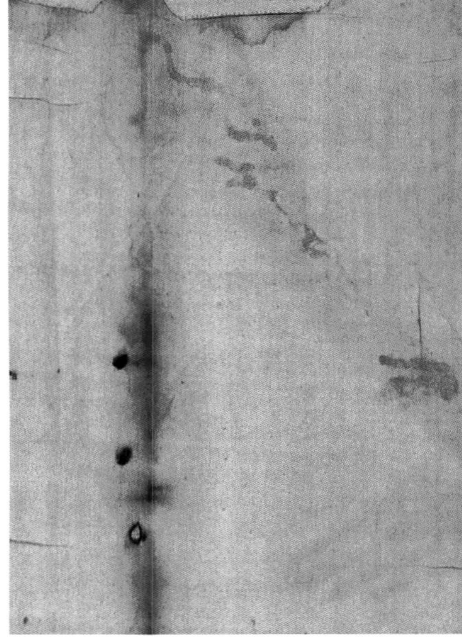

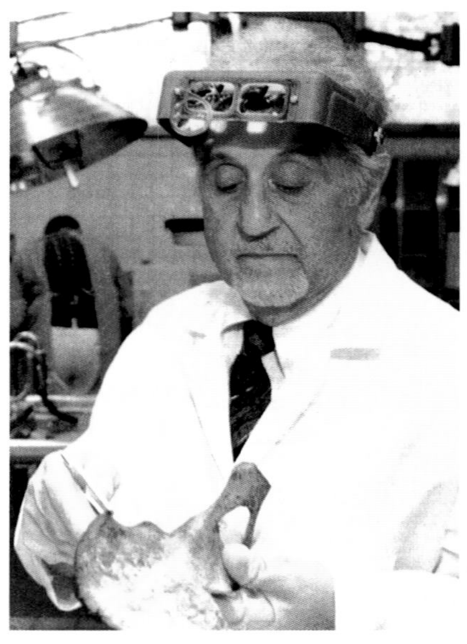

TOP LEFT AND RIGHT: *The area of the crossed hands imprint visible on the Shroud, as seen in natural colour and photographic negative respectively. Anatomists have deduced that the exit point of the nail has to have been through the wrist, but disagree about the exact spot.*

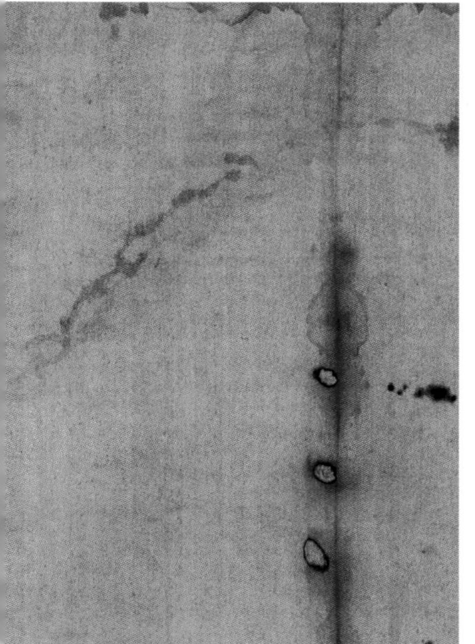

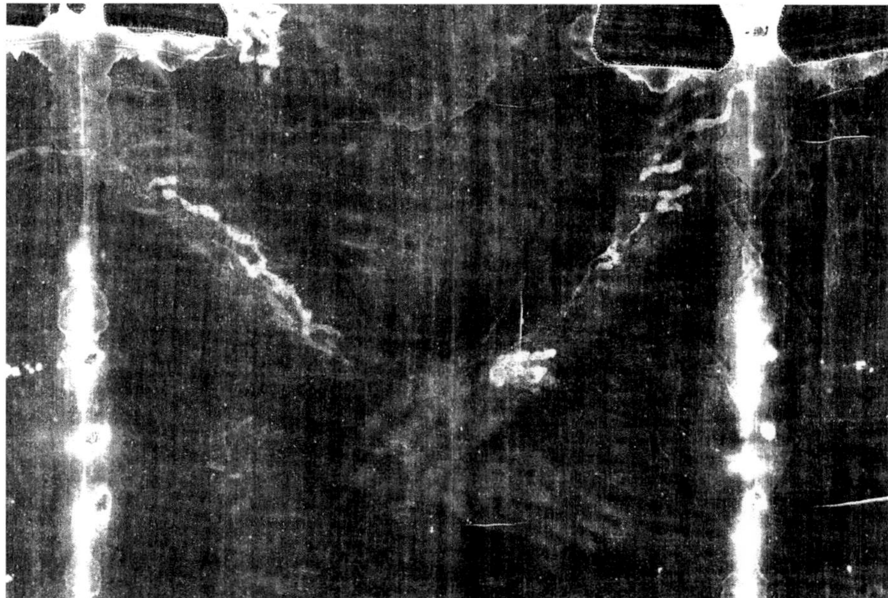

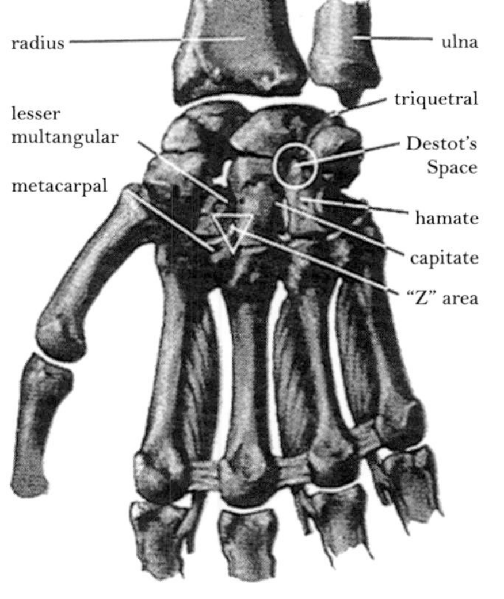

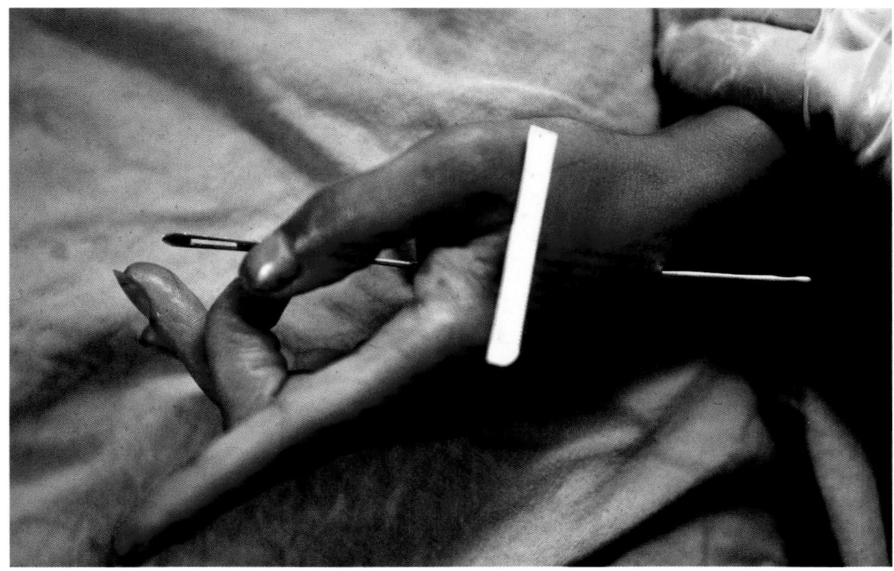

New York medical examiner Dr Fred Zugibe (left) argues for the nail having passed through the thenar furrow, the 'Z' area on the anatomical drawing (above). The fact of a suitable path for a nail here was proven to Dr Zugibe from his examination of a murder victim who had received an injury at this point, as shown right.

Although many medical specialists have continued to this day to accept Barbet's finding, Dr Fred Zugibe is one important exception. Instead of Destot's Space, Zugibe favours each crucifixion nail having been driven through the unseen palm side of the hand at the point of the so-called thenar furrow (he calls this opening the 'Z' space), thereupon travelling obliquely to exit among the bones of the wrist on the other, non-palm side of the arm, just as the Shroud indicates. In remarkable corroboration of this, Zugibe has been able to cite an example of precisely such an injury that he came across in 1994, in the course of his day-to-day forensic work:

> A young lady had been brutally stabbed over her whole body. I found a defence wound on her hand where she had raised her hand in an attempt to protect her face from the vicious assault. Examination of this wound in her hand revealed that she was stabbed in the thenar furrow in the palm of the hand; the knife had passed through the 'Z' area and the point exited at the back of the wrist exactly where it is displayed on the Shroud. X-rays of the area showed no signs of broken bones.[8]

As was physically demonstrated by Zugibe, had the woman been a crucifixion victim, being nailed to the cross through the 'Z' area would actually have offered better support than in the case of Destot's Space, it being capable of supporting hundreds of pounds without tearing. However, driving a nail through this area would damage the sensory branches of the median nerve, 'resulting in one of the most exquisite pains ever experienced by people and known medically as causalgia.'

But, while this feature of the Shroud injuries might be medically very convincing, does there exist any independent evidence of how crucifixion was actually carried out? Only one ancient skeleton bearing definite signs of crucifixion has so far been excavated – that of a young first-century Jewish man called Jehohanan, whose remains were found in 1968 in an ossuary in an ancient cemetery just outside Jerusalem.[9] Because Jerusalem's ultra-Jewish lobby insists on the quick re-interment of any excavated bones, the examination carried out by the late anatomist Dr Nicu Haas was necessarily rushed, and, although superficially exhaustive, it has subsequently come in for substantial criticism and modification.

For instance, Haas identified an indentation on the radius or forearm bone very close to the point where it joins the wrist bones. This, he suggested, had been caused by the chafing of a crucifixion nail, hammered into the wrist slightly higher up than indicated on the Shroud, but none the less supporting the view that the wrist was the right location for nails in ancient crucifixions. Following Haas's death, however, Israeli archaeologist Joseph Zias and medical specialist Eliezer Sekeles noted on other bones similar indentations which were patently unconnected with any nailing. They, therefore, judged Haas's interpretation to be 'not convincing'.[10]

Whatever the validity of this judgement, Zias and Sekeles were on even stronger ground with regard to Haas's interpretations of the nailing of Jehohanan's feet, on which Haas himself had been far from firm in his own conclusions. Haas's concept was that a large nail had transfixed both Jehohanan's ankle bones, his assumption being that this nail had been driven through the two ankles positioned side by side as the body hung in some kind of side-saddle position. However Zias' and Sekeles' fresh study established that the bones came from only one ankle, not two; the 11.5 cm nail was not in any event long enough to go through both ankles and then

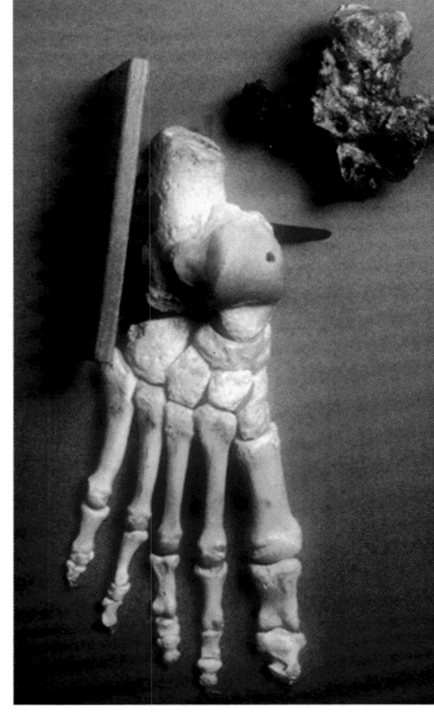

ABOVE: *The ankle bone of crucifixion victim Jehohanan pierced with an 11.5 cm long nail, alongside the bones of a modern-day foot, nailed in like manner. The plaque of wood, replicating an actual specimen found attached to Jehohanan's ankle, is thought to have been a device to prevent the crucified from pulling his foot over the nail-head in an attempt to relieve the agony.*

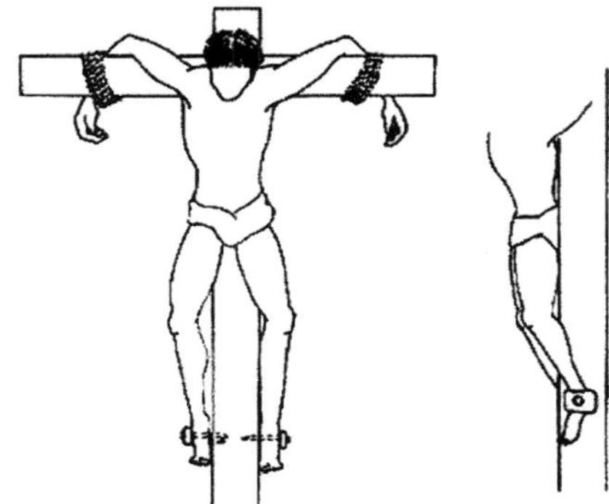

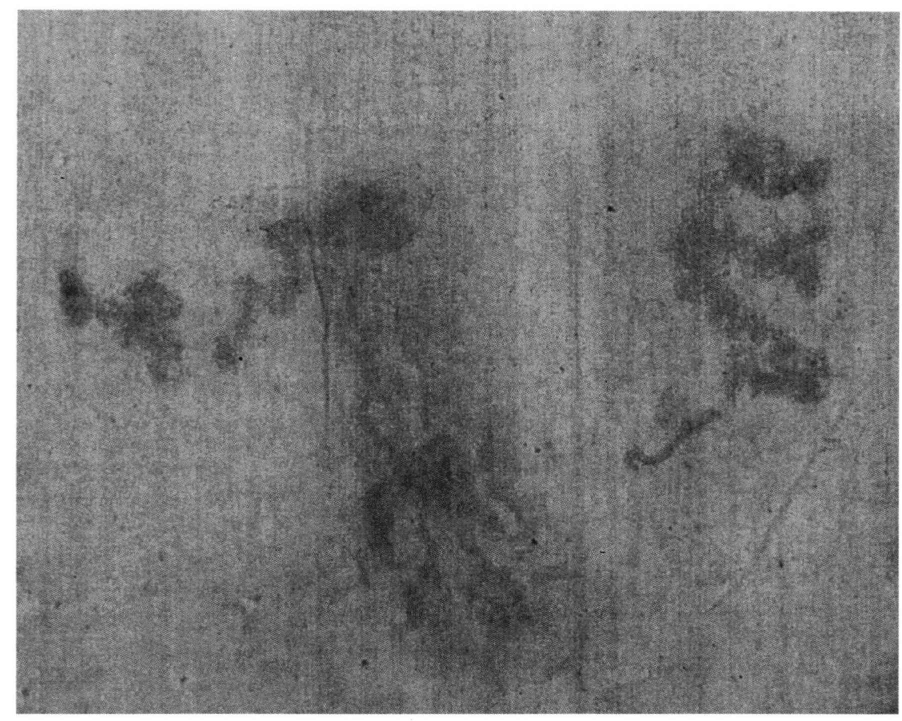

RIGHT: *The apparent bloodstains to the feet on the Shroud's back-of-the-body imprint. Note at left the rill of blood which seems to have spilled directly onto the cloth from either the heel or the ankle, suggesting that the man of the Shroud's ankles may have been fastened in the same manner as Jehohanan's.*

anchor them securely to a cross upright. According to Zias' and Sekeles' revised interpretation, Jehohanan's feet most likely first dangled on either side of the upright, and were then fastened to it by nails hammered through each ankle sideways on, forcing him to straddle it.

How this squares with the Shroud is not very clear, since most pro-authenticity medical specialists see a slightly darker 'blood' stain between the middle metatarsal bone area in the 'bloody sole' on the Shroud's back-of-the-body half and assume this to have been the point where the nail was driven through, with the left foot having been laid over the right, and a single nail going through both insteps. What they have mostly ignored, however, is the very distinctive rill of blood that can be seen to have spilled directly onto the foot region of the Shroud's back-of-the-body half, presumably at the time the body was laid in it, which from its position looks to have come from the soft area just above the heel and behind the ankle. If this deduction is correct, then the revised Jehohanan findings in respect of ankle nailing may be rather more supportive of the Shroud's authenticity than its many detractors (including Zias and Sekeles), realize.

But what did all this mean medically for the poor unfortunate who had to go through this horrifying ordeal? Although we have remarked on the fact that classical writers skimped on crucifixion's practical details, they did not try to play down its terrors. In the first century BC Cicero called crucifixion 'the most cruel and atrocious of punishments'.[11] A century later the Jewish historian Josephus, chronicling the Jewish revolt of AD 66–70, described how the people of a besieged town opted for surrender rather than let the Romans execute a young captive before their eyes using this 'most pitiable of deaths'.[12] Josephus' contemporary Quintilian likewise remarked that the Romans specifically chose well-frequented thoroughfares to carry out their crucifixions so that the greatest number of people could 'watch and experience the horror of it',[13] and thereby be suitably deterred.

Accordingly, in order to gain at least some greater insight into what crucifixion actually meant medically, during the early 1980s Dr Fred Zugibe had a cross specially made and set this up in his office. He then invited volunteers to let themselves be fastened to it, using cuffs at the wrists and straps at the feet, so that he could monitor the effects that mere suspension in the crucifixion mode would have on them. Zugibe's finding was that, even without his volunteers being required to undergo anything of the agonies of nails through their wrists and ankles, their ordeal was quite traumatic enough. As he observed:

> The chest appeared fixed, and abdominal (diaphragmatic) breathing became very obvious . . . Between six and eight minutes after the beginning of suspension, a marked sweating became manifest in most individuals, which encompassed the entire body and in some instances actually drenched the volunteers, running off the toes to form a puddle on the floor.

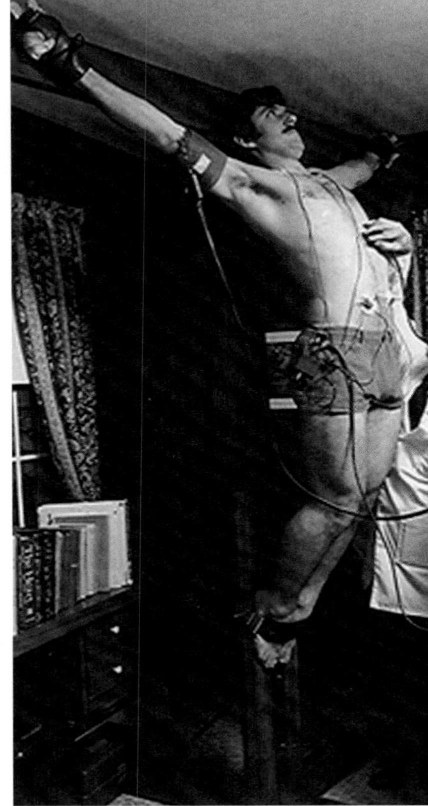

Despite the scientific rigour of Zugibe's methodology, some doubt lingers concerning whether his method of fastening the volunteers' feet – both flat against the cross – was historically correct. It is obvious to anyone that there is a difference in the strength of the impression left by the lower part of the Shroud man's right leg compared to the left, and likewise with the feet themselves. This suggests that, however the feet may have been arranged on the cross, it may not have been the neat side-by-side mode that Zugibe had his volunteers adopt; and Zugibe himself accepts that there are alternative possibilities.

Such difficulties aside, one important observation from the Zugibe experiments was that, despite the volunteers' discomfort, their bodies tended hardly to touch the cross, but instead arched outwards so that only the soles of the feet and the back of the head had any kind of contact with the cross upright.

The Los Angeles artist Isabel Piczek has similarly explored the physiological effects of crucifixion, due to the not uncommon need for crucifixion scenes in her huge church murals. When these are required she routinely asks the figure model to allow himself to be roped to a cross that she sets up in her studio. On such occasions the model may need to hang suspended for hours on end, with just the occasional rest-break – though

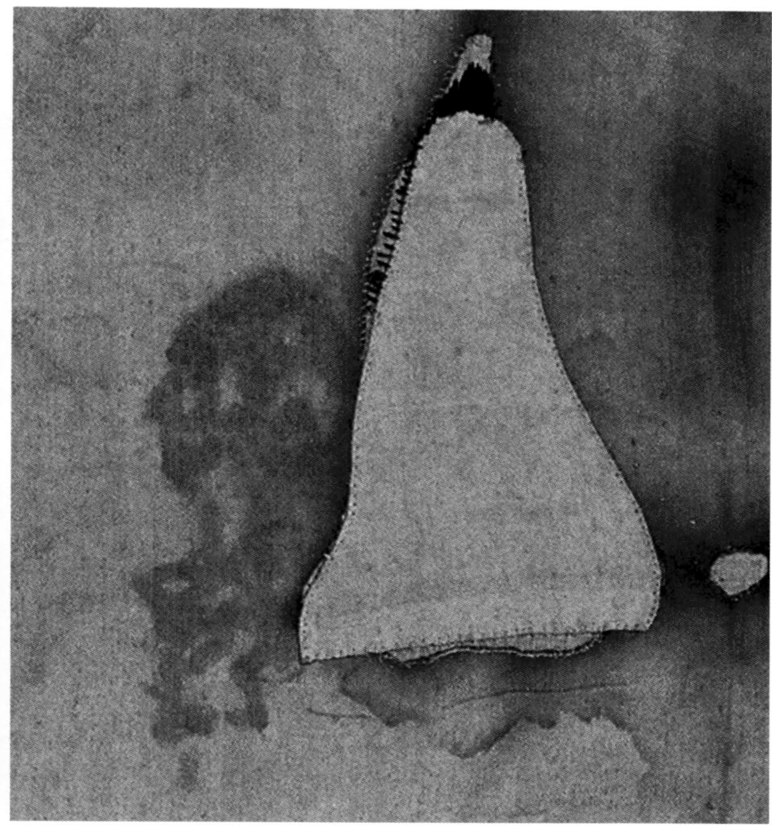

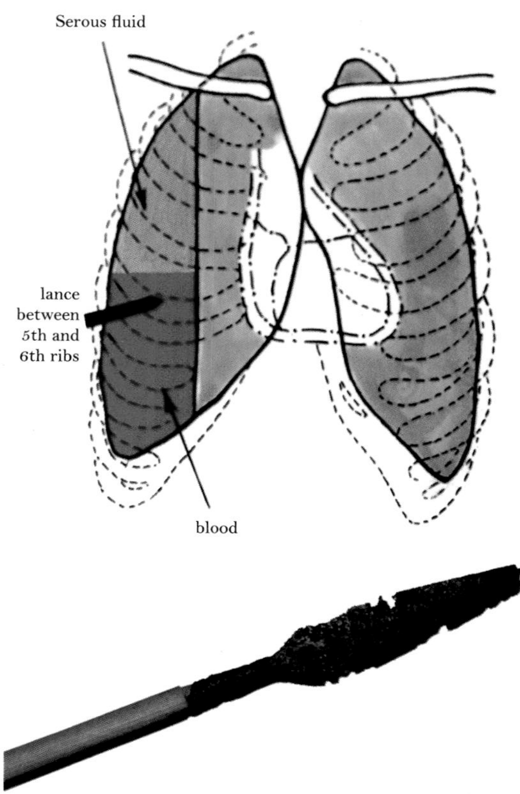

FAR LEFT ABOVE: *Dr Fred Zugibe with a volunteer 'crucifixion' victim fastened to a cross, enabling Zugibe to make a detailed study of the physiological effects of being suspended in such a manner. If the Zias interpretation of the foot nailing is correct, then the actual mode of crucifixion may have been as in the drawing (left).*
ABOVE LEFT: *Detail of the chest wound on the Shroud, its elliptical shape corresponding to that of the Roman* lancea *(right), the very weapon reported in the gospel of John as having been plunged into Jesus' side to check that he was dead.*
ABOVE RIGHT: *How fluid build-up in the chest cavity may well have been responsible for the 'blood and water' that reportedly spilled from this injury.*

to make things easier Piczek mostly ropes the arms only, allowing the feet to be free but standing on tip-toe. Even so she invariably finds that the model's chest expands alarmingly, and that he suffers breathing difficulties, which increase as breathing out becomes more difficult and as the blood pressure falls dangerously. The ends of the fingers and the toes turn white, then blue, and become increasingly painful. Despite air-conditioning the model sweats with astonishing copiousness, just as Zugibe observed of his volunteers. Also the abdomen becomes strangely distended, while the genitals correspondingly shrink in size. Among the many reasons for Piczek's unswerving belief in the Shroud's authenticity is that she quite instinctively sees on it the expanded chest, the distended abdomen, and the 'invisible' genitals, just as she has become used to seeing these features manifest on the models whom she 'crucifies' in her studio.

Besides the 'crown of thorns' and 'crucifixion nail' 'blood' stains on the Shroud, there is of course one other 'bloody' injury, the wound in the Shroud man's chest. The exit point of the blood is elliptical at its top edge, as if from a bladed weapon with this shape, and this corresponds readily enough with surviving specimens of the Roman *lancea* or lance. This was a general-purpose weapon that was standard issue for Roman auxiliaries, and the very type, in Greek *lonche*, described as having been used for the

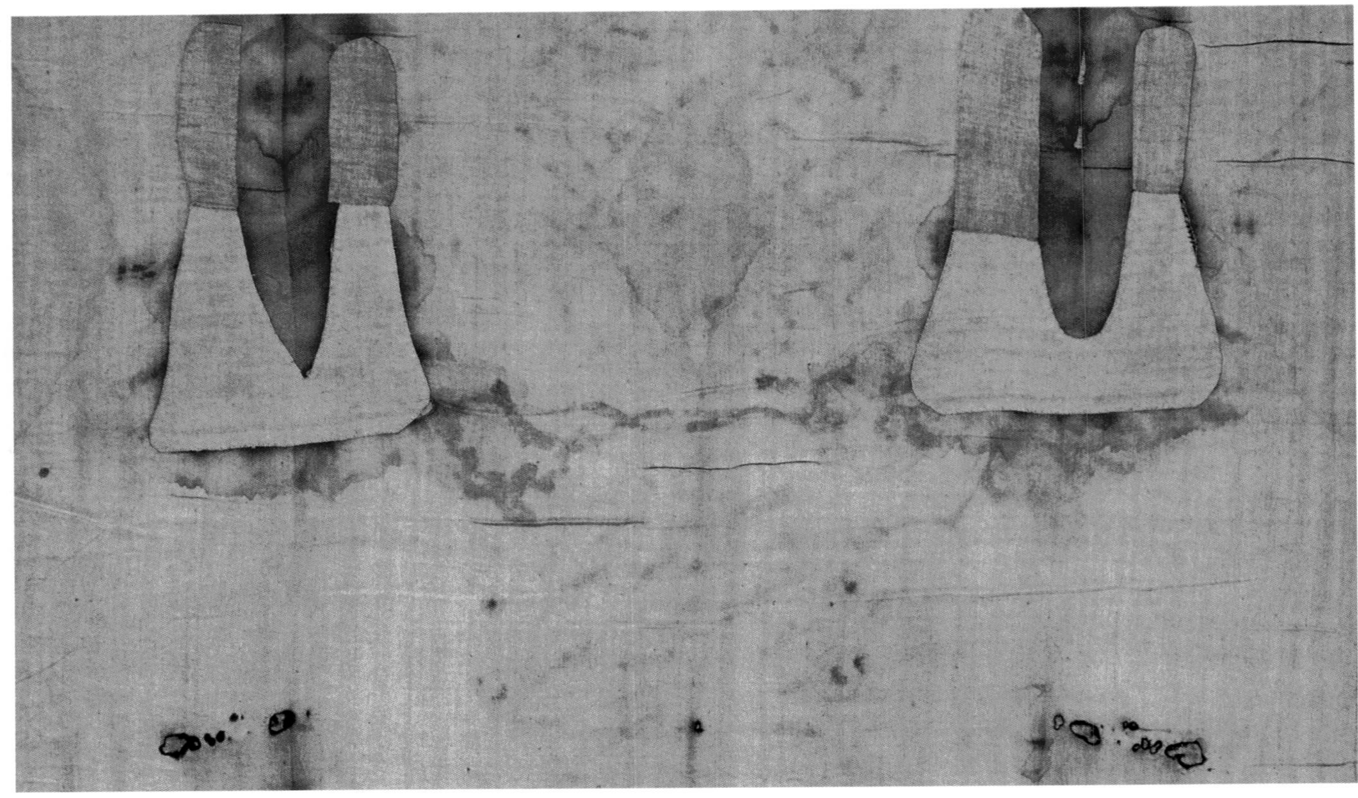

ABOVE: *Spillage of apparent blood across the small of the back, seemingly caused when the Shroud man's body was laid on the cloth. Even to the layman this looks convincingly like a real-life blood spillage, quite different from the crucifixion wounds depicted by artists.*

coup de grâce inflicted on Jesus: 'One of the soldiers pierced his side with a *lance* and immediately there came out blood and water.' (John 19: 39).

In this gospel this particular injury's purpose is evident enough: to check that Jesus was genuinely dead. And, although we are not told which side was pierced (i.e. the right or the left), that the wound should be in the Shroud man's right side is important, since that is the only side which could have had spillable blood, from the heart emptying on that side, together with 'water' or pericardial fluid, which medical specialists agree would have accumulated copiously from the percussive injuries that the man had sustained. The complex trickle of 'blood' which meanders across the small of the back on the back-of-the-body imprint is readily interpretable as being spilt from the same wound directly onto the Shroud at the time that the body was laid on it after having been carried, most likely on a stretcher-type bier as is commonly used to this day in the Near East, to the tomb.

Ironically, despite the confidence of medical practitioners, from cues such as these, that the Shroud man really was dead (assuming that he was a real person rather than a painting), the subject continues to be beset with non-medical sensationalists who every once in a while argue that because dead bodies cannot bleed, the heart must still have been pumping.[14] Dr Zugibe, for one, is roundly dismissive of such arguments. Perhaps surprisingly for the layman, from the bloodstains he sees on the Shroud he insists

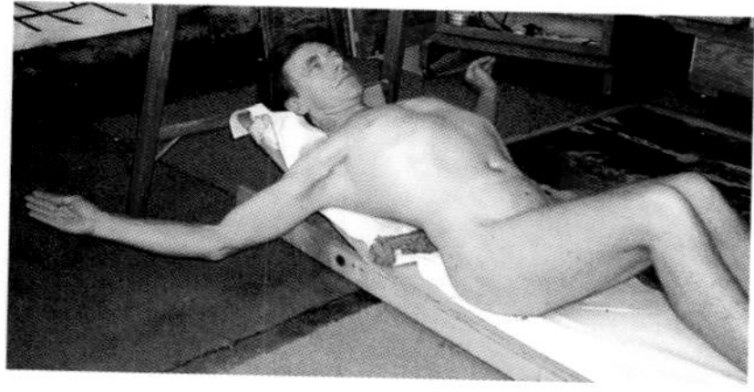

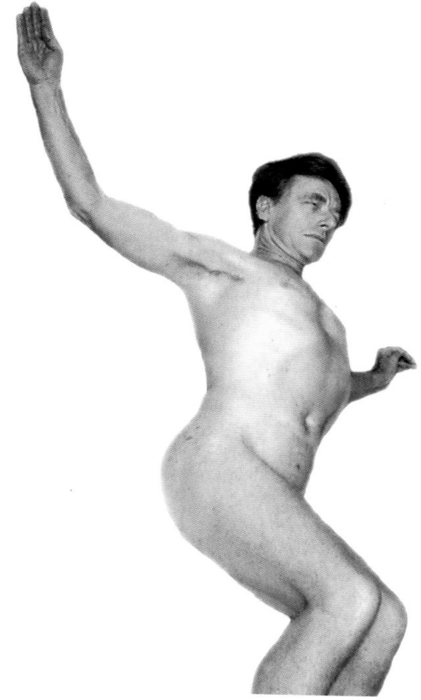

ABOVE: *How the Shroud man's body seems to have been 'frozen' in a crucifixion position. Author Ian Wilson demonstrating how the burial pose reconstructed by Isabel Piczek translates the way the body once hung on the cross, merely by outstretching the arms while still recumbent. The lower photograph has been tilted through 90°. This suggests that the man of the Shroud's body was locked in rigor mortis which for burial purposes had to be broken in respect of the arms.*

that the body was sluiced before burial, and stresses that the blood of victims of a violent death can often stay surprisingly fluid, 'bleeding or oozing from lacerations, bullet wounds, stab wounds, traumatic injuries and the like'[15] being commonly observed when moving bodies around in the autopsy room. To him it is mostly post-mortem blood of this kind that we see on the Shroud. Had the man of the Shroud been still alive, he points out, the Shroud would have been literally saturated with blood from the numerous lacerations and wounds because 'we in forensic pathology know that even tiny wounds bleed profusely when the heart is beating.'[16]

Additionally, pathologist after pathologist, including the London Hospital's Professor James Cameron, expresses confidence that the man of the Shroud really was dead for a completely separate reason: that just as Isabel Piczek sees clear evidence of foreshortening, they see unmistakable signs of rigor mortis. From my very subjective experience of assuming the Shroud burial pose under Isabel Piczek's direction, as described in the last chapter, one very powerful impression was that this was a body which was very stiff and still under tension, as if still locked in much the same attitude as when it had hung on the cross. By way of verification of this, Isabel directed me, while still on my back on the posing platform, to extend my arms out sideways into the 'crucifixion' mode without moving any other part of my body. If the photograph of this is tilted through 90° it indeed looks most eerily as if I am hanging on a cross. As Isabel Piczek comments, the Shroud body is self-evidently 'frozen in a crucified position'.[17]

The pathologists, of course, go further, Zugibe speaking of 'the incontrovertible evidence of rigor mortis', and Cameron noting how the hands exhibit evidence of what he calls 'de-gloving', arguably the same skeletal effect as was remarked on by Drs Giles Carter and Alan Whanger (see page 38). Perhaps the most compelling elucidation of all, however, has come from a mortician or funeral director who attended a Shroud lecture given by the late Chicago theology professor Fr Francis Filas at which a slide of the back-of-the-body negative image was shown. At the end of this lecture the mortician came up to Filas and said that although he had known nothing about the Shroud beforehand, he was now quite sure it was genuine. Asked why, he said it was the sharpness of the Shroud man's buttocks. To him the gluteal muscles showed nothing of the sagging from the weight of the body that would be expected of any living person laid in the cloth. Rigor mortis can set in very quickly, almost instantly in cases of violent deaths, and to the mortician it was quite obvious that this had locked the Shroud man's buttock muscles in the tension that these were under during his very last moments alive on the cross. To him this represented, even by itself, the most convincing evidence that the Shroud once contained a very real, and atrociously traumatized, dead body. And so it should for us.

But what we have seen so far rests purely on visual clues. So what about the evidence of actual hands-on, *physical* analysis?

GONDRAND
STRP

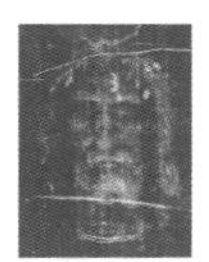

CHAPTER 5

'It's blood!'

(Chemist Dr Alan Adler)

IN 1898, when the Shroud was directly owned by Italy's King Umberto I, the holiness attributed to it meant that a lot of persuasion was needed even to gain permission for it to be photographed. The very idea of any direct, hands-on scientific examination would have been unthinkable.

In 1946, however, when Umberto's grandson, Umberto II, was exiled from Italy, effective control of the Shroud passed to Turin's archbishop. And, with the whole tenor of twentieth-century society becoming increasingly science-based, sooner or later something so intriguing as the Shroud simply *had* to be subjected to direct scientific scrutiny.

Accordingly, between 16 and 18 June 1969, Turin's then archbishop, Cardinal Michele Pellegrino authorized a small group of Italian scientists, together with one photographer, to make a preliminary, observation-only survey, principally to check on its condition. This was followed on 24 November 1973, immediately after the television exposition of that year, by a one-day examination by a secretly convened 'commission of experts'. This commission's composition was again almost exclusively Italian, although a Belgian textile specialist, Professor Gilbert Raes, was permitted to remove a snippet of the linen for textile examination purposes, and a Swiss criminologist, Dr Max Frei, was allowed to apply twelve strips of sticky tape to different parts of the Shroud's surface, and to take these away for analysis.

However, by far the most exhaustive scientific examination to date was to occur five years later, by which time Cardinal Pellegrino had been succeeded by Anastasio Ballestrero. Early in 1978 Fr Peter Rinaldi, the Italian-born, New York-based pastor who had facilitated my viewing in 1973 informed America's Dr John Jackson and his fellow researchers that Ballestrero had given the green light for them to conduct such an examination some time around the six-week period of the Shroud's public expositions (the first in forty years), which were being held between 27 August and 8 October of that same year. Under the dynamic leadership of nuclear systems specialist Tom D'Muhala, an impressive team of some two dozen American specialists calling themselves the Shroud of Turin Research Project (STURP) had for two years been quietly developing a scientific test plan to examine the Shroud, with Barrie Schwortz as one of the two official photographers. Equally impressive was this team's accompanying assemblage of equipment, comprising some of the most state-of-the-art

FACING PAGE ABOVE: *Members of the STURP team unloading the eight tons of equipment they brought with them from the USA for the scientific examination of the Shroud in 1978. Italian customs in Milan held it for five days before allowing it to be forwarded to Turin.*

FACING PAGE BELOW: *At the end of six weeks of public expositions, the Shroud is carried on a silk-covered board into the special suite of Turin's Royal Palace allotted for the five days of scientific examination.*

image analysis technology to be found anywhere in the world, even the transport of which demanded eighty crates weighing a total of 8 tons.

Although this equipment arrived in Italy on 28 September, in principle giving an adequate setting-up time prior to the allotted examination period of 8–13 October, it was not enough for the customs officials at the receiving airport, Milan. Alarmed by 'radioactive' notices, they immediately impounded the whole consignment, demanding a minimum sixty-day 'quarantine' before the equipment could be released for its intended task.

Thankfully frantic diplomatic activity resolved the log-jam after five days, and the crates duly arrived in Turin, enabling the team to set themselves up in the magnificently frescoed suite of Turin's Royal Palace which they found to have been allotted to them. Despite the suite's magnificence, it was less than practical for the task in hand, the power supply, for one, being hopelessly inadequate. This was but one of many difficulties but eventually all was ready to receive the subject of the exercise. Around 10.45 pm on the night of Sunday 8 October twelve young men arrived at the suite carrying a 5 m long sheet of 2 cm plywood draped with an expensive-looking sheet of red silk. When the silk was pulled back, the Shroud was revealed beneath, fastened to the plywood by somewhat rusty-looking thumb-tacks at 60 cm intervals. When the tacks were dextrously removed by Cardinal Ballestrero's deputed 'keeper of the Shroud', Monsignor Cottino, and several Poor Clare nuns, the Shroud was laid on the gleaming stainless-steel test-frame which the STURP team had brought with them from the States, enabling the task of determining just what was or was not responsible for the Shroud's enigmatic 'body' and 'blood' images to commence.

The Shroud's overall dimensions were measured, then its thickness was gauged with a micrometer and determined at 0.343 mm, or just a little heavier than shirt cloth. Dr Max Frei then took a new set of sticky-tape samples, which will be described in detail in the next chapter. Then, with the aid of Poor Clare nuns, one of the Shroud's sides was unstitched from the backing cloth sewn on to it in 1534, allowing parts of the normally inaccessible underside to be viewed for the first time in four hundred years. This was done to enable Prof Giovanni Riggi and his Italian scientific team to perform their experiments.

Given only two weeks' notice that he would be examining the Shroud, Riggi had developed several impressive experiments. The first was to use an endoscopic camera system, normally reserved for peering inside the body as a medical diagnostic tool, in order to photograph the Shroud's underside. When he placed the device between the two cloths, the camera's focusing light provided a small circular area of light through the cloth. This was initially positioned under the image area of the Shroud but revealed little or nothing of interest. However, as soon as the light was placed beneath the 'No. 3' bloodstain in the forehead area, it revealed the density of that particular stain, leading STURP team co-director Eric

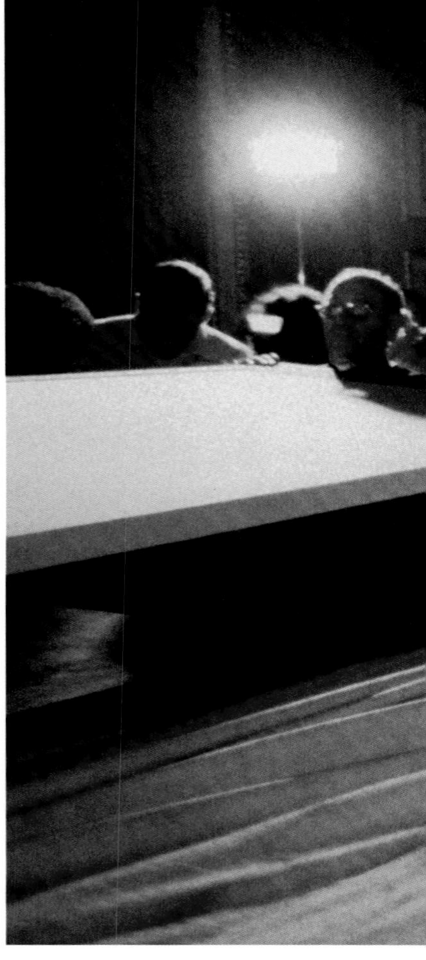

ABOVE: *The Shroud is transferred from the simple wooden board on which it had been fastened for display onto the stainless steel test-frame the STURP team had constructed specially for their work.*

RIGHT: *STURP scientists Ray Rogers (left) and John Jackson (centre) are the first to look at the underside of the Shroud in over four hundred years, following the unstitching of the cloth at one side from the backing sheet onto which it was sewn in 1534.*

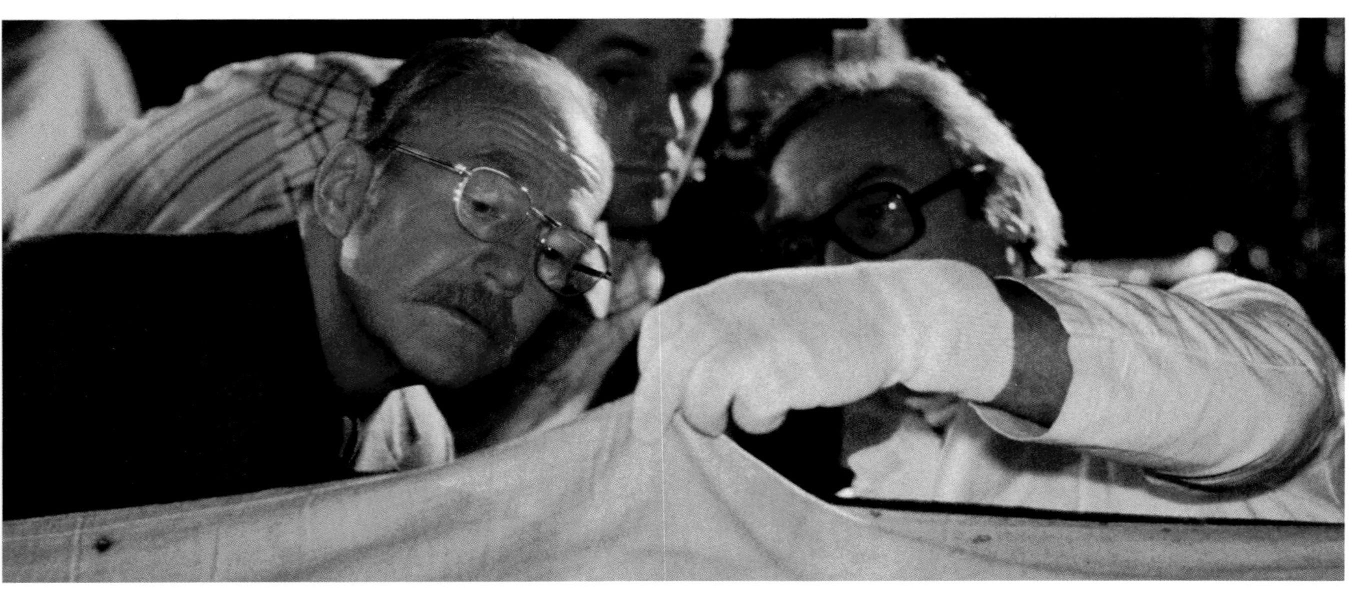

Jumper to insist that Barrie photograph the entire Shroud in a similar fashion, which he did shortly after. This quickly established that, while the images of the 'blood' stains penetrate right through the cloth, those of the so-called 'body' variety (i.e. the face, the hands, etc.) do not. In essence, this was one of the first things that STURP 'learned' about the Shroud.

Riggi's next experiment was to use a special vacuum with sterilized filters to remove any debris or loose materials from the underside of the cloth but little of importance was found in the results. Then STURP began their main pre-planned programme of tests.

Various scientific photographic methods were tried, in addition to conventional colour and black-and-white photography.[1] Taking advantage of a small breathing space between scheduled experiments Barrie was able to place photographic lighting behind the Shroud, rather like viewing a photographic slide on a light-box, and this clearly showed beneath the patches the exact extent of the damage caused by the 1532 fire. This further revealed that, while the 'blood' stains showed up dark against the light, indicative of some solid, analysable substance being present and absorbed into the cloth, the 'body' stains simply disappeared, as if they lacked any substance that might block the light, strongly indicating that they were a surface phenomenon only.

The American team included radiography technicians, and these methodically X-rayed the cloth in plate-size sections, their most notable finding being that both 'blood' and 'body' imprints alike failed to show up on their plates. This indicated that neither variety had sufficient atomic weight to interfere with X-rays. For anyone familiar with X-rays of old master paintings, in which the artists' solid, lead-based pigments commonly show up very strongly, the inference is that any theoretical 'cunning painter' of the Shroud would have to have been very clever indeed to avoid anything like this which might have disclosed his handiwork.

Another technique commonly used for old masters is ultraviolet (UV) photography, which can often show up otherwise invisible brush-strokes. In the case of the Shroud, however, instead of anything of this kind its chief revelation was hitherto unseen halos around the major bloodflows, medically yet another highly convincing finding, since rims of serum are commonly left around wounds as the solids in the blood contract as part of the scab-making process, and these fluoresce just as on the Shroud. Although ultraviolet light undoubtedly accentuates such serum halos, during our March 2000 examination Dr Zugibe and I noted the one surrounding the bloodstains to the foot on the back of the body image to be clearly visible to the unaided eye.

A portable photomicroscope was also part of the STURP team's equipment, and with this they were able to view and photograph specially selected areas of the Shroud under high magnification, though repeatedly their focus was impaired by vibrations from large passing vehicles being

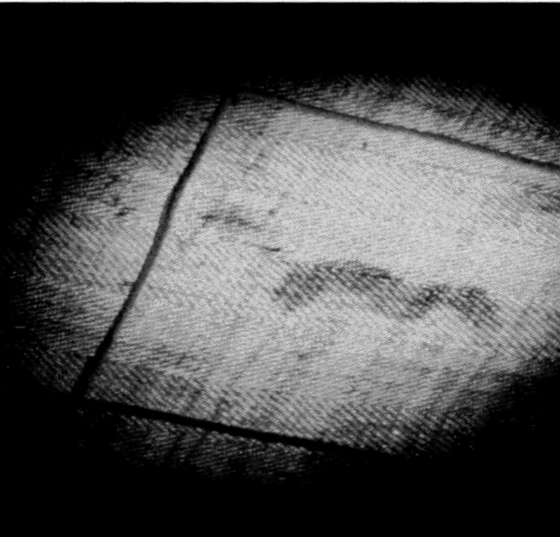

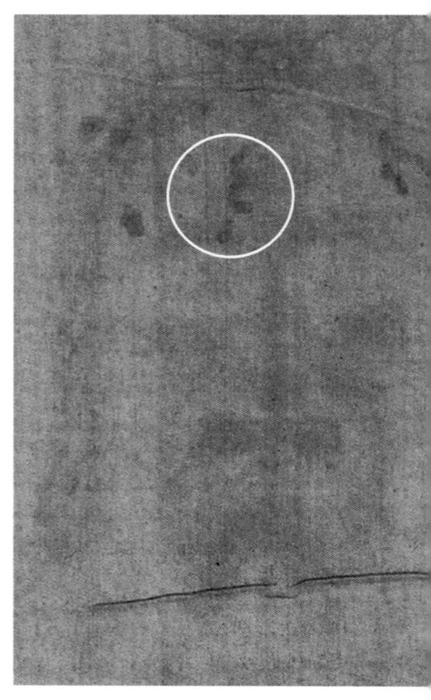

FACING PAGE: *The apparent bloodstain on the forehead of the man of the Shroud, seen in natural light (top), and illuminated from underneath (centre). The location of this bloodstain can be seen ringed (below).*

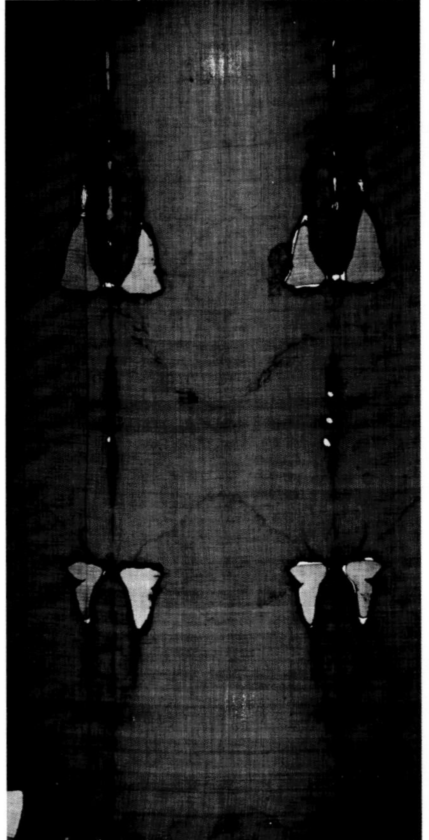

RIGHT AND FAR RIGHT: *The frontal and back-of-the-body halves of the Shroud back-illuminated, clearly showing the damage from the 1532 fire, also how the blood shows up solid against the light.*

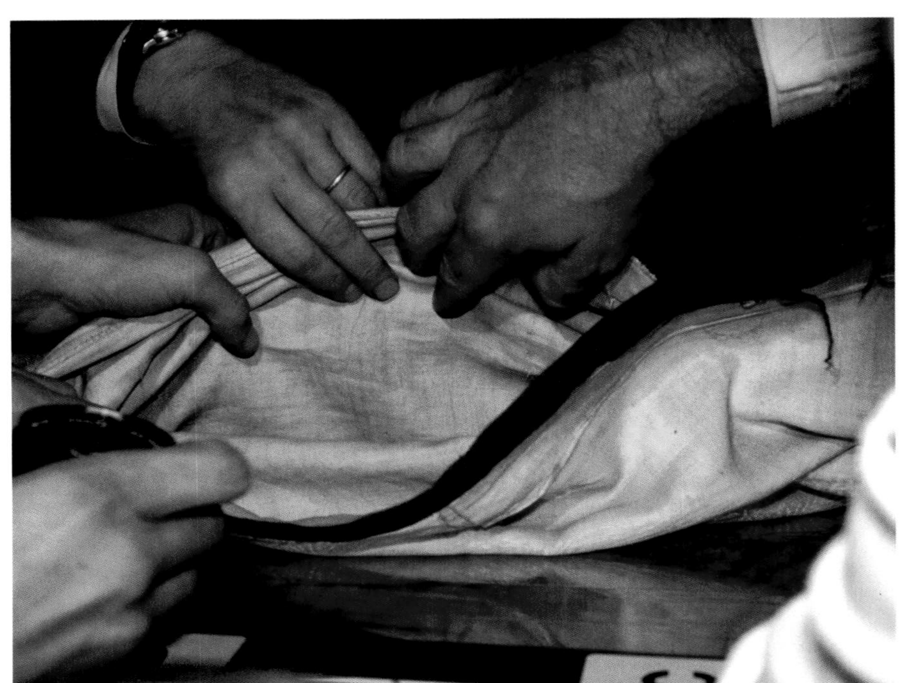

BELOW RIGHT: *View of the underside of the Shroud, as revealed from the unstitching of the end edge.*

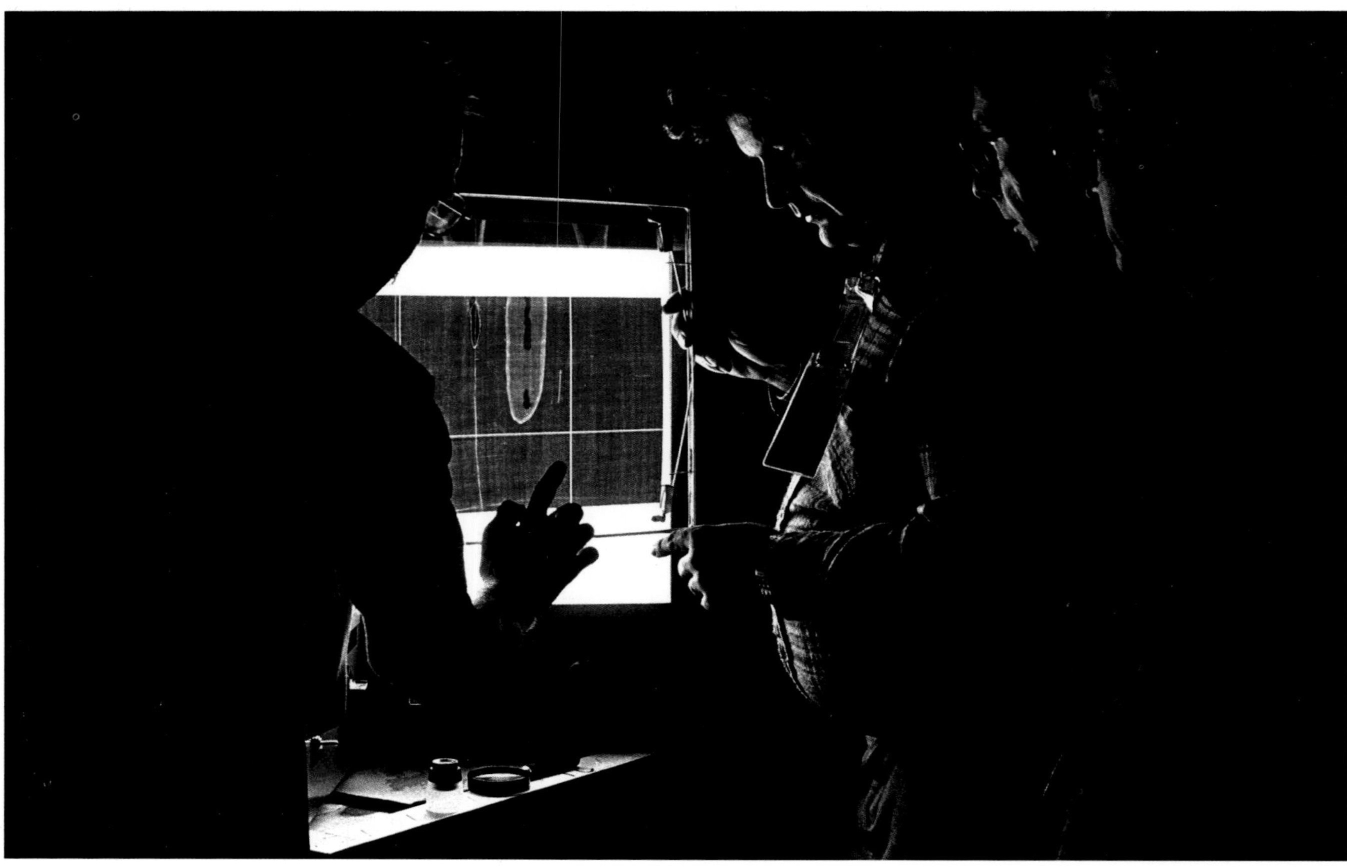

ABOVE: *STURP scientists examining the results of their X-ray work. This revealed that, whatever comprises the Shroud's imprint, the heavy lead-based pigments commonly seen when old master paintings are X-rayed are absent.*

FACING PAGE ABOVE: *A photomicroscope being used to examine the Shroud on site, with (right) a close-up of the 'body' image area.*

FACING PAGE BELOW: *A special applicator being used to obtain sticky-tape samples from the Shroud's surface. These samples were intended for study under greater magnification back in the USA.*

transmitted through the centuries-old wooden flooring, and by draughts coursing through the palace rooms that wafted the suspended cloth as if it were a sail. In the course of this work, they clearly saw that the 'blood' areas comprised reddish-brown particulate matter which had some definite semblance to old, dried blood. The 'body' areas, by contrast, seemed to be some inexplicably substanceless discoloration of the fibres.

Inevitably the best way of discovering what constitutes the 'body' and 'blood' images had to be direct sampling. To this end, using a specially designed, pressure-controlled tape applicator, also a sticky tape specially formulated by the 3M Corporation so that no glue residue would be left on the cloth, STURP members applied thirty-two tapes to a carefully selected cross-section of regions of the Shroud. The regions targeted comprised 'blood' image, 'body' image and (as 'control') non-image and water-stain areas, the aim being for the detritus collected on the tapes to be analysed by specialists back in the United States.

The first port of call for these tapes was Chicago, where the initial findings of the noted microscopist Dr Walter McCrone proved far from encouraging. McCrone had received considerable public attention because of his then recent discovery of the fraudulence of the so-called Vinland

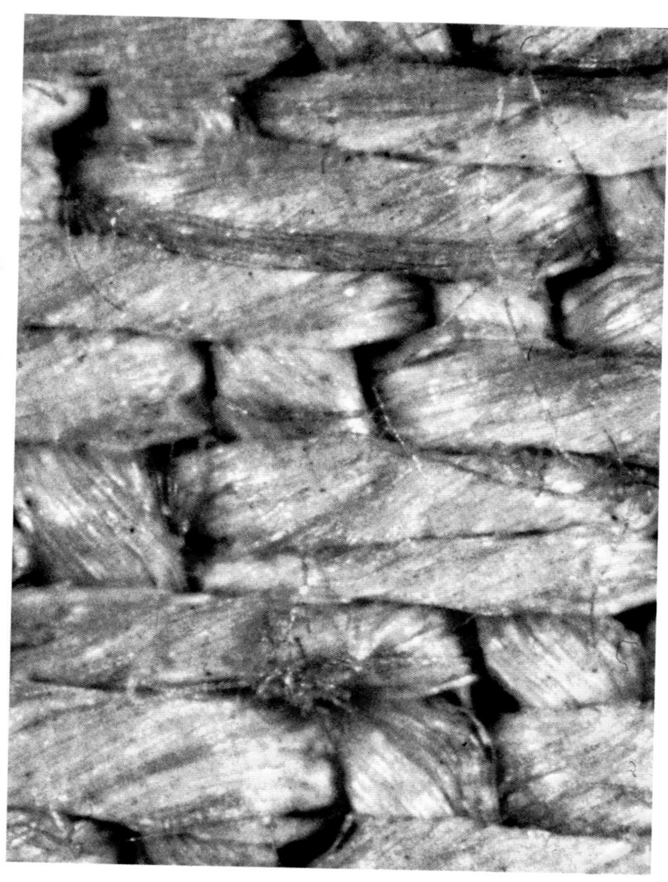

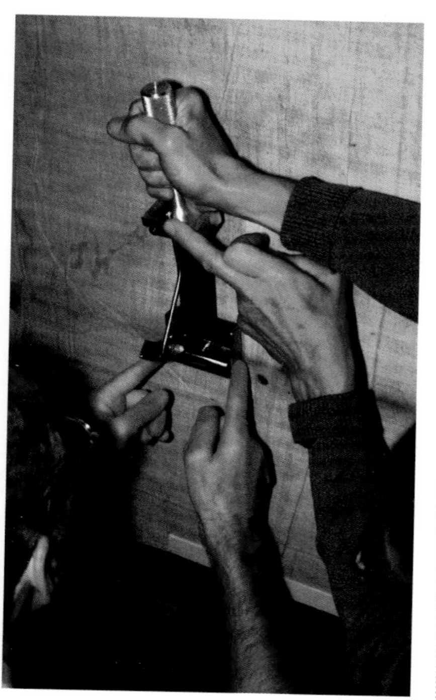

Map (thought to support Viking discovery of America before Columbus), and he quickly dismayed those scientists who had worked directly on the Shroud in Turin by declaring the cloth's image to be nothing more than a conventionally created painting. According to him, its 'body' imprint had been painted with a fine iron-oxide pigment in a gelatin protein binding medium. The 'blood' stains had been created in much the same way, simply with the addition of some cinnabar, the 'vermilion' of medieval and Renaissance artists' pigments.[2]

To the team who had been to Turin McCrone's findings simply did not make sense, so they were very relieved when a second opinion, from the Yale University chemist Dr John Heller and the Jewish-born blood expert Dr Alan Adler, produced completely different interpretations.

As Heller and Adler showed, McCrone was correct that the Shroud indeed has iron oxide particles scattered across its surface. And, like him, they too found particles of vermilion and other artists' pigments. But they were emphatic that neither of these materials was responsible for the Shroud's 'body' and 'blood' images. The artists' pigments, for instance, are random, and quantitatively distributed no more strongly in the image than the non-image areas. Their presence is easily explained as mere strays left on the Shroud's surface from the sixteenth- and seventeenth-century practice of pressing freshly painted artists' copies against it to give them special holiness. Several painted copies of the Shroud bear inscriptions attesting to their having been deployed in this way, as in the case of one in Toledo worded: 'This picture was made as closely as possible to the precious relic . . . at Chambéry [i.e. the Turin Shroud] and was laid upon it in June 1568.'[3] According to Heller's and Adler's analysis,[4] and consistent with the 'on-site' observations, the Shroud's fibres which represent the 'body' image have no identifiable substance added to them that might be responsible for this image. It is as if they have simply been degraded, or 'aged', at those places where the imprint appears, in much the same manner that newspaper turns yellow when exposed to strong sunlight, except that the 'yellowing' has occurred selectively, at strengths relative to the (theoretical) body's distance from the cloth at any one point.

As Dr Adler continues to argue,[5] in the wake of Heller's death and having been granted a relatively recent direct viewing of the cloth to facilitate conservation recommendations, 'the body' image areas are superficial in the extreme, lying only on the very top of the Shroud threads. They do not penetrate the cloth, nor do they exhibit any capillarity or absorptive properties. They are more brittle than their non-image counterparts, as if whatever formed them corroded them. They are uniform in coloration, they are not cemented together, neither are they 'diffused' as they would be if they derived from some dye or stain. They do not 'fluoresce' or reflect back any light. Most emphatically, they are not made by pigment contact. As further noted by former Kodak technician Kevin Moran of Belmont, North Carolina, who has recently been able to make direct studies of body image on the sticky tapes taken by Dr Max Frei: 'Since the linen fibres are some 10 to 30 microns in diameter and appear as smooth fibre optics, the section where the darkened [i.e. image] fibre meets the clear [i.e. non-image] fibre looks like a precision line formed on a modern semiconductor.'[6] This is something completely outside any conceivable technology, medieval or modern.

ABOVE: *The Italian forensic medicine specialist Professor Baima-Bollone extracting 'bloodstain' thread from the Shroud during the 1978 examination.*

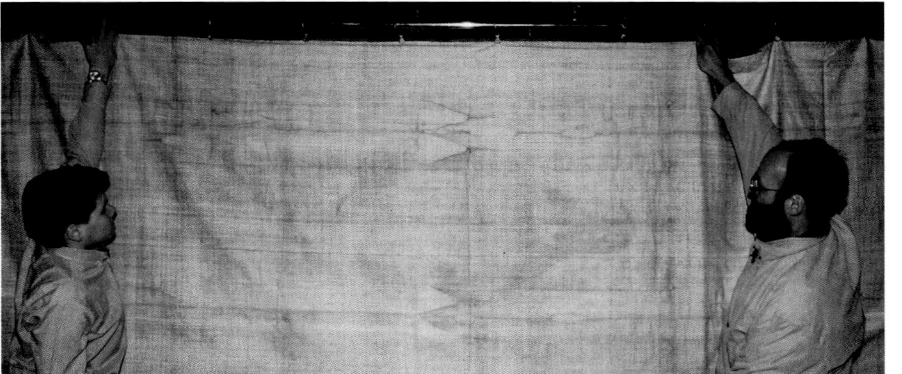

LEFT: *A seventeenth-century artist's copy of the Shroud from Broumov, Czech Republic, of the kind that were traditionally pressed against the Shroud's surface to give them extra holiness. Stray paint particles found on the Shroud's surface almost certainly derive from this custom.*

RIGHT: *Close-up of a blood area on the Shroud, as photographed using the portable photomicroscope.*

As for the 'blood' stains, according to Heller's and Adler's studies these derived from genuine clotted wounds, and they pass eleven different diagnostic tests, enabling them to be pronounced to be true blood in any court of law. Blood constituents such as proteins, albumen, haem products, and the bile pigment bilirubin (on which Adler is an acknowledged expert) can all be determined to be present. One remarkable feature noted by Adler is that where blood occurs in the same region as body image, the cloth fibres lack body image characteristics below the bloodstain, suggesting that the blood was on the cloth before the body image-making process began.[7] That is hardly the way any artist might be expected to work.

Characteristically, throughout the last two decades McCrone has firmly stuck to his original verdict, even to the extent of self-publishing a book on his findings.[8] Yet, despite this, not even those otherwise most convinced of the Shroud's fraudulence have come forward in his support. For instance, although he accurately predicted, years in advance, the date that the radiocarbon dating would find for the Shroud, the radiocarbon-dating scientists declined to beat a congratulatory path to his door. He has also seen his greatest glory, his highly publicized debunking of the Vinland Map, overwhelmingly overturned by higher-tech methods than his own[9] – resulting in the Map's owners, Yale University, formally reinstating it as genuine after all.[10] Not least, when the professional artist Isabel Piczek tried applying to clean, untreated linen small squares of canvas that she had recently painted using typical Renaissance-period pigments, she found that sub-micron-sized iron-oxide particles easily became transferred and were just like those that McCrone claimed to be the

Shroud's image.[11] All in all, McCrone's interpretations now have little going for them.

Even so, while the origin of the Shroud's 'body' image remains far from clear (and we will be returning to a fresh consideration of this towards the end of the book), it is important to have the strongest possible confirmation of the Heller-Adler claim that the Shroud 'blood' really is blood. Thus although Alan Adler has carried out immunological tests which in his view establish beyond reasonable doubt that it is from a primate – and as Adler notes, the photographic evidence hardly favours the subject being a shaved orang-utan – critics have argued that its colour is too red.

However, as Dr Adler has explained, when someone is severely beaten, or otherwise suffers severe traumatic shock, the haemoglobin from the broken blood cells goes through the liver, which then converts it into bile pigments such as bilirubin. Since bilirubin is yellow-orange, and when it is mixed with other blood products that have oxidized brown, the result is very credibly the red colour still visible on the Shroud.

In fact, quite independently of Drs Heller and Adler, other findings have served to confirm that what appears to be blood genuinely is blood. For instance the Italian pathologist Dr Pier Luigi Baima-Bollone, who has carried out thousands of autopsies, and who has had more Shroud 'blood' sample than was accorded to Dr Adler, has not only confirmed it to be blood, but confidently identified it as of the AB group.[12] Although this group is comparatively rare among Europeans and is found in only 3.2 per cent of the world's population as a whole, its incidence is 18 per cent among Jewish populations of the present-day Near East.[13] Caution is needed, however, since some researchers have noted a tendency among blood samples more than several centuries old always to test AB.

Ancillary to the blood itself, during the 1980s the Utah-based archaeologist Dr Eugenia Nitowski, studying sticky tape number 3DB, taken from the small-of-the-back area of the Shroud 'blood' stains, found what she has confidently identified as a microscopic muscle fragment that had arguably been dislodged by one of the scourge strokes. Also, as earlier mentioned, among the same blood from the back of the head have been found tubules of wood. Arguably these were transferred from the wood of the cross as the man of the Shroud desperately pressed his head against it in an attempt to relieve at least something of the horrifying pains in his hands and feet.

But arguably of the greatest importance, even though they are as yet far from fully secure, are studies, both in Italy and the United States, which, completely independently of each other, have identified DNA in the Shroud 'blood'. On the afternoon of 21 April 1988, just a few hours after having cut off the snippets of the Shroud used for radiocarbon dating, the Italian microscopist Dr Giovanni Riggi took a 1.5 mm 'blood' sample from the back-of-the-head region. In June 1993 he provided some of this sample

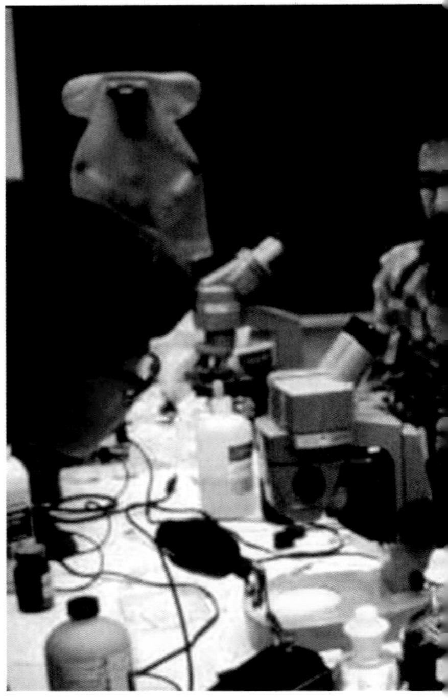

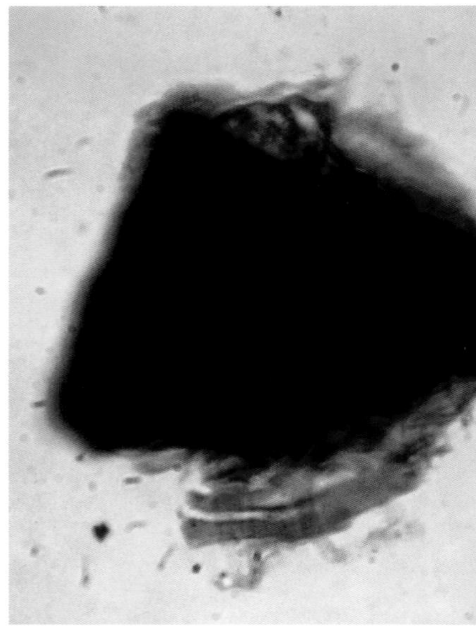

ABOVE: *Found on a sticky-tape taken from the region of the small-of-the-back bloodstains, what some suggest to be a muscle fragment, possibly removed during the scourging.*

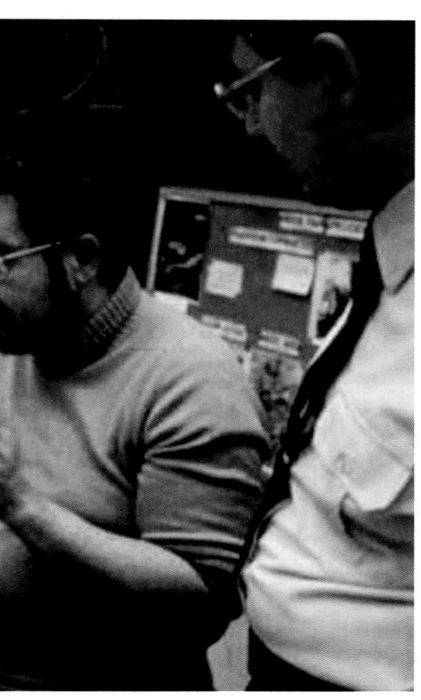

ABOVE: *Seen at centre, Jewish-born Dr Alan Adler, a world authority on blood chemistry, at work on Shroud 'blood' samples. From eleven independent scientific tests, he is in no doubt that the samples are human blood.*

to a visiting American microbiology professor, Dr Leoncio Garza-Valdes, who took it back for analysis at the University of Texas' Center for Advanced DNA Technologies at San Antonio, Texas. There the laboratory director, Dr Victor Tryon, and his technician wife, Nancy Mitchell Tryon, quickly established that the sample was human blood of the AB group, just as Baima-Bollone had before them. They also determined that it had both X and Y chromosomes, indicating that the individual from whom it came was male. Three unmistakable gene segments were identified, beta globin from chromosome 11, amelogenin X from chromosome X and amelogenin Y from chromosome Y, a finding quite impossible if the Shroud 'blood' were merely iron oxide as contended by Walter McCrone.

Regrettably, because Riggi and Garza-Valdes did not at the time observe the right protocols with Turin's then archbishop, Cardinal Giovanni Saldarini, this San Antonio DNA testing carries no official recognition. Furthermore, the Shroud's detractors can and do argue that contamination is such a serious problem in any DNA analysis that it could have come from anyone who merely coughed over the Shroud or had a cut finger at any time during the Shroud's history. (As Barrie has pointed out, members of the STURP team will undoubtedly have left some of their DNA on the Shroud.) The best material for the analysis of ancient cases is also said to be not nuclear DNA, as was used in this instance, but mitochondrial, that is, the kind found in parts of the cells used for generating energy. Unlike nuclear DNA, which carries genes from both mothers and fathers, mitochondrial DNA is inherited unchanged down the maternal line, and is also said to be rather more sensitive in the case of minute samples, though fewer laboratories are prepared to handle it, and much less data is potentially obtainable from it.

But while the debate over the Shroud's DNA therefore necessarily remains far from resolved, a major new development, also with its own bearing on the Shroud 'blood', concerns a relic with its own authenticity controversies, the so-called sudarium of Oviedo. Although this bears bloodstains, like those on the Shroud, with every semblance of authenticity, because these are not accompanied by any similarly meaningful body image I have long shied from taking any interest in them – until a recent development.

This was the emergence of a new, serious researcher on the subject, Mark Guscin, a British-born classicist resident in Spain, with an excellent book *The Oviedo Cloth*[14], the first on the subject in the English language, published in 1998. In this he shows that historically the Oviedo cloth's origins can with reasonable plausibility be traced back to early first-millennium Jerusalem, having been moved from there to Spain in the seventh century apparently to keep it safe from the Persian invasions of that period. By early in the ninth century, due to Arab incursions into southern Spain, it had quite definitely moved north to Oviedo, since the cathedral's still extant *camera santa* or holy room was specially built for it at that time. And in 1075 it was similarly reliably recorded as being taken out of its still extant *arca* or chest in the presence of King Alfonso VI. Its certain history, therefore, significantly antedates that of the Shroud. It is also free of the early accusations of forgery that so dog the Shroud.

But exactly like the Shroud, far more revelatory than the Oviedo cloth's history is its self-documentation. Although it bears no photograph-like 'body' image in the manner of the Shroud, Mark Guscin and his Spanish colleagues have very convincingly demonstrated that its 'blood and body fluid' stains exhibit shapes so strikingly similar to those on the Shroud that there has to be the strongest likelihood that both were in contact with the same corpse.

Two groups of stains particularly indicate this. The first are what I would call the nasal stains, which appear to derive from a nose and mouth soaked in bloody fluids. These are repeated mirror-image-style, apparently because of the cloth having been partly doubled on itself. Forensic analysis indicates that they consist of one part blood and six parts pulmonary oedema fluid. This finding is therefore strikingly consistent with the strong body of medical opinion that the man of the Shroud's lungs would have filled with fluid caused by the scourging. They are also very compatible with gospel writer John's observation that at the conclusion of Jesus' crucifixion 'immediately there came out blood and water' (John 19: 34), as from the same oedematous fluid, when a lance was plunged into Jesus' chest.

In the case of the Oviedo cloth's back-of-the-head group of bloodstains, if these are photographed to the same scale as their equivalent on the Shroud, and then matched up to each other, there are again enough similarities to indicate, in Dr Alan Adler's words, 'that these two cloths were in contact with the same wounded body'.[15]

If the Oviedo cloth really is genuine, what might its function have been? As envisaged by Guscin and his colleagues, whoever 'wore' it seems to have had it, partly folded back on itself, wrapped around the left side of his face, then pinned to the hair at the back of his head, arguably while hanging upright as if on the cross. This actually accords very readily with known Jewish scruples concerning leaving the face of any dead person exposed, scruples which, however strange they might seem, are hardly any different from the continuing practice even in our own time of covering the face of anyone who has just died in hospital or is lying at the roadside dead from a road accident. That this is how the cloth was deployed is in fact very clear from the holes that it still bears from the pins that would have been used to hold it in position.

According to Guscin and his colleagues, experiments involving the time it takes for blood and pulmonary fluid stains to differentiate have determined that the individual who had this cloth affixed to his head must

FACING PAGE ABOVE: *The Oviedo cloth that is reputed to have screened Jesus' face when he was brought down from the cross, in the manner demonstrated by Mark Guscin (seen above). Even the original pin marks consistent with this arrangement can still be seen. The most prominent stains, which mirror each other, are thought to derive from fluids from the nose, as in the reconstruction seen at right. The area boxed on the cloth corresponds to the back of the head, and features 'crown of thorns'-type puncture wounds, some uncannily matching those on the Turin Shroud.*

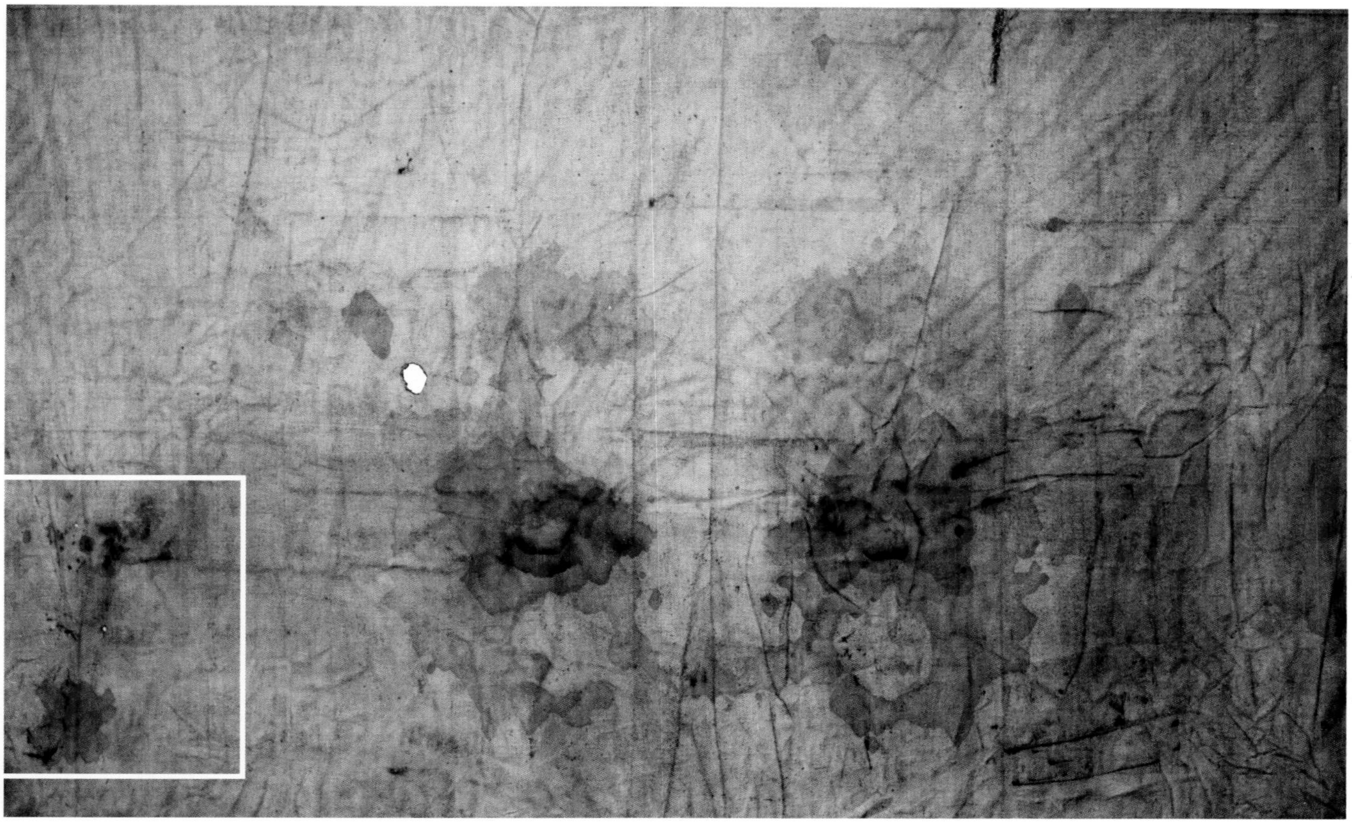

have lain on the ground for some forty-five minutes, arguably after having been taken down from the cross. However, the cloth would have had to be removed by the time he was laid in the Shroud.

Exactly as with the Shroud, blood samples suitable for DNA analysis have been taken from the Oviedo cloth. In 1994 the American Shroud researcher Dr Alan Whanger visited Oviedo and, with full ecclesiastical approval, took three sets of samples, each consisting of one thread from a bloodstained area and one from an adjoining blood-free area as control. After sealing and labelling, these were taken to a freezer at the Spanish Ministry of Justice in Madrid where, at the time of writing, they still await official approval for the testing to take place.

Obviously, if the DNA from the Shroud and the Oviedo sudarium happened to match, even though the segments are fragmentary, this would be the most powerful possible evidence that the two cloths once wrapped one and the same person. But other matches are already known. Exactly as in the case of the Shroud, whoever bled onto the Oviedo cloth was of the same comparatively rare AB blood group. Furthermore, as we are about to discover, there are similar uncanny parallels with the Shroud in respect of the microscopic detritus in the Oviedo cloth's otherwise unstained areas.

CHAPTER 6

'Those are the flowers of Jerusalem!'

(Botanist Professor Avinoam Danin)

When I left Turin on 24 November 1973 after my first-ever viewing of the Shroud, it was in complete ignorance that on that very same day the cloth was being examined in great secrecy by the members of Cardinal Pellegrino's special 'commission of experts'. Equally unbeknown to me, one of those experts was the Swiss criminal investigator Dr Max Frei, whose specialty was to press sticky tape onto a fabric's surface in order to sample its dust, then to identify the territory within which the fabric had been moved by identifying the species of plants represented by the pollen grains found among that dust. It was a technique Frei had pioneered for obtaining evidence from suspects' clothing in the course of his forensic investigations.

Accordingly it was an extraordinary surprise and delight for me when three years later came news that Frei had discovered on the Shroud pollens of plants peculiar to Israel and Turkey, very strongly indicating that the Shroud had at one time been kept in these locations.[1] This potentially corroborated my own ten-year-long historical researches, at that time largely unpublished and unknown, showing that the key to the Shroud's pre-1350s history seemed to be in what is today Turkey. It also raised the question of what further light Frei's botanical science might be able to shed on the mystery of the Shroud's early history.

In great excitement I contacted Dr Frei and that same summer travelled to meet him at his home in Thalwil, near Zurich, Switzerland. There he told me that he needed to make field trips to Turkey and Israel in order to pursue his researches further, as a result of which he and I one year later visited these locations in the company of film-maker David Rolfe.[2] In the course of these travels I personally observed Frei collecting a variety of botanical specimens. Then in October 1978, as part of the STURP scientific examination, he took a further twenty-six sticky-tape samples from the Shroud's surface, with Barrie Schwortz photographically documenting each removal. Yet, although he worked most methodically, beginning with the back-of-the body end and working round the cloth, his ostensibly amateur-looking procedures, particularly his use of 'dime store' sticky tape, and the fact that he massaged this deep into the Shroud's surface, raised more than a few eyebrows among the more high-tech-minded STURP Americans working alongside him – despite his method of obtaining pollen ultimately proving hundreds of times more successful

LEFT: *Dr Max Frei taking sticky-tape samples from the Shroud at the start of the STURP scientific examination in 1978. Looking on is STURP scientist Ray Rogers who strongly disapproved of Frei's use of a 'dime store' roll of tape, instead of the carefully formulated tape and applicator that the STURP team had brought with them.*

than STURP's. As Barrie recalls, when at one point Frei was about to apply the tape to the Shroud's facial image, John Jackson reached out and physically stopped him from doing so, requiring some fast diplomatic intervention by Prof Luigi Gonella, the then scientific advisor to the Archbishop of Turin.

Unruffled, Frei kept up a friendly correspondence with me, making clear that his work with the tiny pollen grains demanded much time and patience, and that, when his researches were complete, he had every intention of publishing them in the form of a fully definitive scientific report. Sadly, however, he was never able to achieve this; in January 1983 he died of a sudden heart attack.[3] Five and a half years later, almost unnoticed amid the attention given to the carbon dating, his entire collection of Shroud sticky tapes, along with his unpublished manuscript, passed to the United States, ceded by his widow, Gertrud, who hoped that her husband's work might thereby be carried on. On 23 July 1988 examples from this tape collection were formally viewed on video-linked microscopes at a meeting at the Academy of Natural Science, Philadelphia. At this meeting Dr Walter McCrone, who was specially invited to attend, acknowledged that quantities of pollen grains, whatever their age and geographical derivation, were undeniably present on these tapes. The Shroud researcher Paul Maloney, then acting as the collection's custodian, later reported on the preliminary statistical analysis that he had personally conducted: 'Eighty-eight pollen grains were counted in approximately 2 square centimetres on a dorsal "sidestrip" tape . . . A hundred and sixty-three grains were counted on the same size area on a tape from the left arm, but an astounding *circa* 300 grains were counted on a tape taken from near the face in a comparative size area.'[4]

Yet only three months after the Philadelphia meeting the bombshell struck: the Shroud had been radiocarbon dated to the Middle Ages. This quickly dissipated all the impetus that had accumulated behind the Frei tapes' acquisition; health problems on the part of Paul Maloney served only to exacerbate the inertia. Taking advantage of the hiatus and of Max Frei's inability to defend himself, detractors of the Shroud began trying to destroy Frei's entire professional reputation. It was put about that any Near Eastern pollen on the Shroud, if it existed at all, simply came from the cotton gloves that the STURP team had insisted be worn by all who handled the Shroud during the 1978 examination, Frei included.[5] Frei was all but accused of outright fraud, and, although his expertise was in botany, a minor and undeniably ill-advised role that he played in the bogus Hitler diaries case[6] was exaggerated out of proportion.

As a further complication, and partly as a result of Paul Maloney's indisposition, the care of Frei's sticky tape collection fell to Shroud researcher Dr Alan Whanger. In 1985 Whanger had noted a faint image in the background of the Shroud that he perceived as that of a chrysan-

FACING PAGE ABOVE: *STURP's Dr John Jackson (right) lodges an official complaint against Frei necessitating intervention by Turin's Prof Luigi Gonella (centre).*

BELOW LEFT: *A specimen of* Linum mucronatum, *one of the pollens which Frei found on the Shroud.*

BELOW RIGHT: *The pattern (arrowed) in the Shroud's background that Dr Alan Whanger identified as a chrysanthemum. This is just behind the top of the man of the Shroud's head, which can be seen in the lower right corner of the picture.*

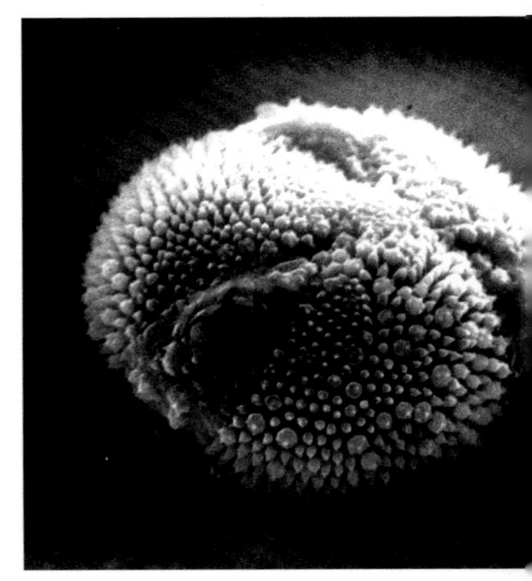

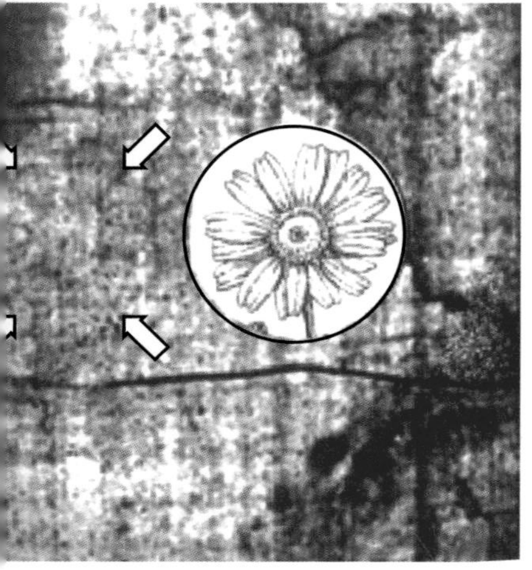

themum. From this he proceeded to see elsewhere in the Shroud's background a quite bewildering variety of other flowers, many of which he identified as of Middle Eastern origin. He further reported seeing numerous other objects both on the man of the Shroud's body, and in the cloth's ostensibly plain background. These included 'two lepton coins of Pontius Pilate, one over each eye; two desecrated Jewish phylacteries [prayer boxes], one on the forehead and the other on the left arm, an amulet of Tiberius Caesar, a crucifixion nail, a Roman spear, a crown of thorns, a sponge tied to a reed [John 19: 29], a large hammer, a pair of pliers, two Roman scourges . . . two sandals, a scoop . . . two brush brooms, a pair of dice, a coil of rope, several letters on the title or titulus [the 'King of the Jews' placard of John 19: 19], and possibly partial images of the cloak, the tunic and two more nails'.[7] All of these objects, as well as the 'flowers',

Whanger argued (and continues to argue), must have been placed within the Shroud at the time of the man's burial, somehow becoming imprinted onto the cloth in much the same manner as the body.[8] Yet not least of the problems is that Jewish funerary practice for at least the last two thousand years has positively shunned wreaths of flowers and grave goods being laid with the dead.[9] For such reasons Barrie Schwortz and I, along with many others who favour the Shroud's authenticity, dismissed Alan Whanger's insights as having too much of a 'faces in clouds' character to be considered in the same scientific league as the pollen evidence.

Yet, in fairness to him, in the case of the flower images in particular there are some very good reasons to be wary of too readily dismissing his insights. During the preliminary examination of the Frei sticky tapes in Philadelphia in 1988 it became evident that pollen grains were not only present in quantity on these tapes, but also that there was a surprising additional detritus of plant parts and other floral debris. For instance, on just one tape, 4bd in Frei's notation, no less than forty-five shreds of plant parts have been reliably observed, including one whole anther full of pollen. This strongly suggested that at least some of the pollen Frei found on the Shroud came to be there not by mere chance (i.e. as grains borne by the wind and by insects, as Frei for one had supposed), but that instead actual whole flowers must at some time have been laid on the cloth's surface.

Reinforcing the need for this to be considered seriously is the fact that plants and flowers can make Shroud-like images of themselves by a process that is as yet far from being fully understood. In collections of pressed plants that have been preserved in botanical collections all over the world there can be found examples of plants that have left astonishingly clear images of themselves on the sheets of paper between which they have been pressed (paper, it should be noted, is compositionally closely akin to linen in the sense that both are cellulose). More than fifty years ago the French pharmacist Dr Jean Volckringer, the man who single-handedly blocked thalidomide from being prescribed in France, assembled a fascinating collection of such plant-image specimens and pioneered a careful study of them *vis-à-vis* the Shroud.[10] In April 1982 my wife and I visited Volckringer at his home in Montrouge, Paris, and personally viewed this collection. Volckringer showed us how, just as in the case of the Shroud's images, the plant images take on a startlingly lifelike photographic realism when they are viewed in negative. He also pointed out how it can often take several decades for each image to form, during which time the condition of the plant specimen itself will usually have deteriorated substantially. Yet, fascinatingly, the image that slowly develops on the paper will be of the plant in its original, pristine state.

For a scientific explanation of the image-forming process, Dr Alan Whanger has looked to a German researcher, Oswald Scheuermann, who

RIGHT: *Professor Avinoam Danin of the Hebrew University, Jerusalem, an acknowledged world expert on the flora of Israel. He has confidently identified plants of Israel on the Shroud, represented both by pollens and in the form of imprints.*

BELOW LEFT AND RIGHT: *Positive and negative images of the imprint of a* Scrofularia alpestris *plant as picked in the High Pyrenees in 1856 and preserved between two thick sheets of paper (from the collection of Dr Jean Volckringer). Such images are not infrequently to be seen created by pressed plants in botanical collections and, as in the specimen here, they can be strikingly 'photographic' both in positive and negative.*

can reproduce something similar to the Volckringer plant image effect by an instantaneous electrostatic process called corona discharge.[11] Yet partly because this process seems too closely related to the much-criticized Kirlian photography, both Barrie Schwortz and I, along with many other Shroud researchers, continued to view the Whanger–Scheuermann arguments with considerable scepticism.

However, as early as 1984, when he was still in good health, Paul Maloney began corresponding with Dr Avinoam Danin of the A. Silberman Institute for Life Sciences at Jerusalem's Hebrew University about the Frei tapes. Danin is an acknowledged world authority on the flora of Israel, and much to Maloney's surprise and satisfaction, he responded with considerable courtesy and lack of dismissiveness, despite his academic eminence and his unswerving Jewishness.

This encouraged Alan Whanger, in company with his wife Mary, to call upon Danin (who in the meantime had become Professor) during a visit to Jerusalem in September 1995. As guests at his home they showed him some of their photographs of the portions of the Shroud on which they 'see' flowers, whereupon, after less than twenty seconds' perusal Danin exclaimed 'Those are the flowers of Jerusalem!' One 'flower' that he had no difficulty perceiving (and with regard to which even I can acknowledge a flower-like shape in the relevant sector of the Shroud), was the very first one that Alan Whanger had identified on the Shroud, the crown chrysanthemum or *Chrysanthemum coronarium*. Danin further noted, to the side of the man of the Shroud's right cheek, several flowers of rock rose or *Cistus creticus*. Despite having remained oblivious throughout his life to any flower images on the Shroud, Dr Max Frei found this rose represented among the pollens from a sticky tape, 6bd, taken from the centre of this very same area.

Two years later, upon visiting the Whangers at their North Carolina home, Danin observed on a Shroud photograph an image that he regarded as most interesting of all – that of a bouquet of bean caper plants, namely *Zygophyllum dumosum*. As he has remarked: 'During rainy winters this species sprouts leaves whose petioles look like sausages with two leaflets at their head. When summer comes, the leaflets drop and only the petiole is left. The petioles shrink slowly during the summer . . . The only species of *Zygophyllum* that exhibits this behaviour is *Zygophyllum dumosum*'.[12]

The overwhelmingly important feature of this discovery is that *Zygophyllum dumosum* grows only in Israel, Jordan and the Sinai. The northernmost extent of its distribution in the world coincides with the line between Jericho and the sea-level sign on the road leading from Jerusalem to Jericho. Westwards it does not reach as far as the Suez Canal, southwards it peters out before St Catherine's Monastery in the Sinai desert, and eastwards it extends no further than the longitude line of the Jordanian capital, Amman.

When I first met Prof. Avinoam Danin, at the Shroud international conference held in Turin in 1998, I was immediately impressed both by his impeccable credentials and by the authoritative and objective way in which he presented his findings. However, the cautiousness ingrained into me as an historian kept me wary of accepting that any flower images were there, continuing to June 1999 when a major Shroud conference took me to Richmond in Virginia. Because Richmond is a mere couple of hours' drive from their home in Durham, North Carolina, the Whangers very kindly invited my wife and me to visit them to view at first hand the highly detailed photographs on which they, in company with Danin, see the various images. So on Monday, 20 June 1999 Judith and I duly arrived, were introduced to the Whangers' colleague Philip Dayvault, and then ushered down to the basement room that is now very much the Whangers' workplace for all their Shroud researches.

First, to assure us of his awareness of the 'faces in clouds' objections, Whanger showed us slides of various examples of 'trick' images used in psychological and psychiatric testing. Then on life-sized Shroud photographs he began pointing out the various features that he and Mary interpret as instruments of the passion that have left images of themselves. Though time and again Judith and I conceded that we too could see vague artefact-like shapes in these areas, we strongly resisted interpreting them in the way that Alan and Mary did.

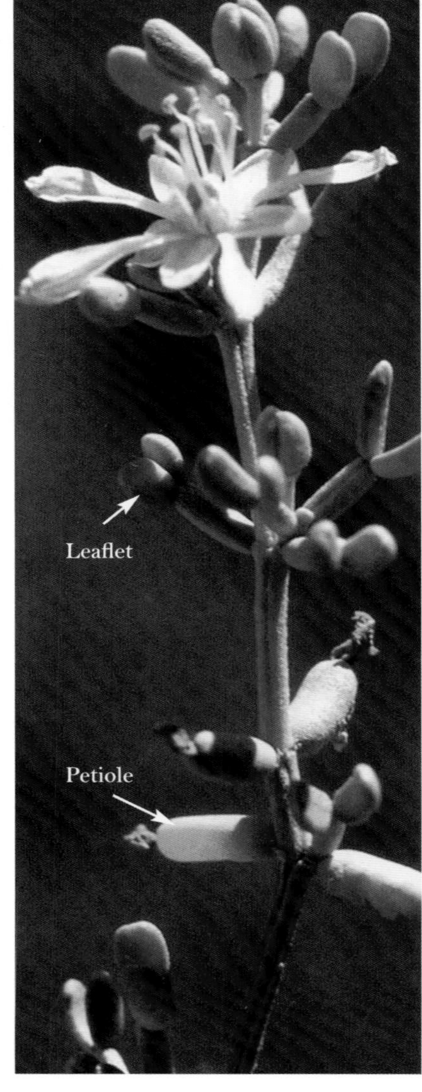

ABOVE: Zygophyllum dumosum, *or bean caper. Professor Danin sees an imprint of this very distinctive plant, with its leaflets and petioles, on the chest of the man of the Shroud. The plant is exclusive to Israel, Jordan and Sinai, as indicated on the map (facing page, below left). As striking corroboration, Dr Max Frei found this plant represented among the Shroud's pollens.*

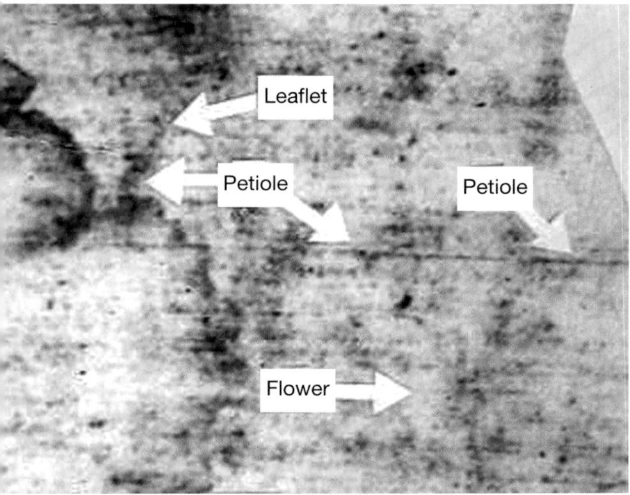

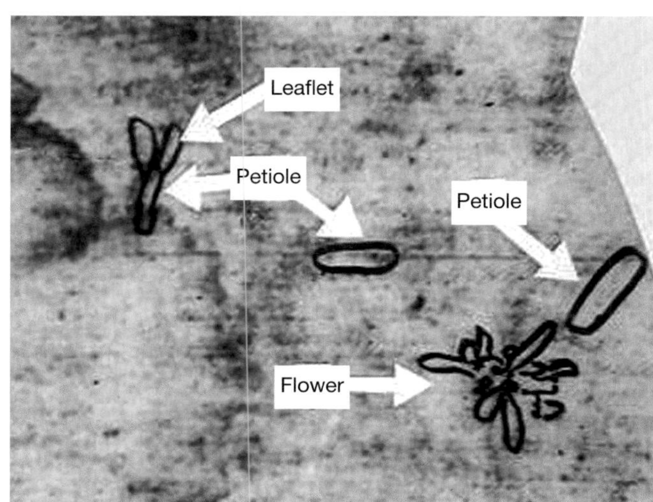

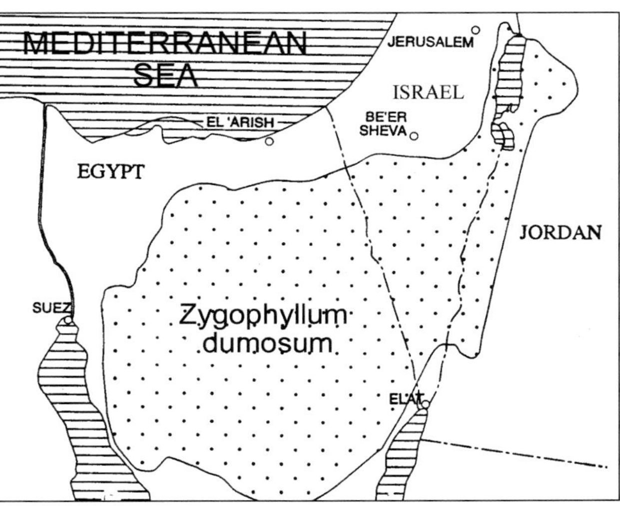

OP LEFT AND RIGHT: *Location of the alleged* Zygophyllum dumosum *mprint on the Shroud showing natural ppearance (left), and enhanced (right).*

ABOVE RIGHT: Cistus creticus, *or ock rose, a specimen of which Professor anin sees to the side of the man of the Shroud's right cheek. Dr Max Frei found a specimen of pollen from this plant on the sample he took from the very same area.*

Then Alan pointed out to us some of the different flower images. In various instances, as in the case of the chrysanthemum, a flower-like shape was undeniably there. The problem was that, when other areas of the cloth image were viewed the same way, all sorts of shapes were discernible that might be construed to be flowers, some conforming to the Whangers' interpretations, others not. Rightly or wrongly, therefore, Judith and I could only reject them.

Yet it was impossible to dissociate totally from this very marked difference of opinion whatever might be learned in tandem to it from the Frei sticky-tape collection. Normally stored in a bank vault, it had been specially brought out for us and we found it comprised albums with carefully ordered slots for each different sample, each mounted within a glass slide. At the original sampling each tape had been carefully folded back on itself to hermetically seal in its contents, and it was quite obvious which section

Frei had handled as 'lead' tape and which he had pressed directly against the Shroud, thus confounding claims that the pollen was just modern contamination. Judith and I were also introduced to the computer-linked microscope in which Alan Whanger has invested in order to study these tapes.

For demonstration purposes one of Frei's Shroud tapes was placed under the microscope, and the Whangers and Philip Dayvault encouraged me to explore its non-lead areas for the pollen grains it bore. For me the immediate surprise was to find just what a complete universe of such debris can exist on one insignificant-looking piece of sticky tape. It was possible to travel across the tape for what seemed miles, viewing it both through the microscope and on the linked computer-screen. In the course of this 'journey' the occasional little red fragment would come into view, which I recognized as from the sheet of red silk that traditionally covered the Shroud until Dr Flury-Lemberg removed it after the 1997 fire. Then at last there appeared a circular-shaped pollen grain, quite unmistakable, and large as pollen grains go.

As was immediately revealed by cross-comparison with images of pollen grains stored in the Whanger computer, this was *Gundelia tournefortii*, a plant that Max Frei had already identified on the Shroud, and which Danin had reported as present on the Shroud in abundance pollen-wise, and also in image form. Since *Gundelia*'s pollen is normally insect-borne, Dr Uri Baruch, an Israel Antiquities Authority palynologist, had seriously doubted Danin's claims, having had personal experience of collecting all too few grains of this type during field trips to various sites in the Judaean Mountains and Judaean Desert. Because of this scepticism Baruch, like ourselves, had visited Whanger's basement some eighteen months earlier. From this he satisfied himself that *Gundelia* pollen grains are numerous on the Frei tapes, and therefore that whole flowers from Jerusalem's environs must have been directly laid on the Shroud's surface. In which regard, the highly significant feature of *Gundelia tournefortii*, as both Danin and Baruch emphasise,[13] is that, exactly as in the case of *Zygophyllum dumosum*, it does not grow in Europe. Its distribution is distinctively Middle Eastern, extending from western Turkey through Israel, Syria and northern Iraq and Iran, with just some spillage into the southernmost fringes of the former Soviet Union.

Whatever might be the truth concerning the plant images, therefore, in this basement room in North Carolina I was looking at near proof positive that the Shroud must have been in the land of Israel at some time in its history. It was evidence hugely supportive of the cloth's authenticity, and thereby rendered as so much waste paper all the unworthy allegations against Dr Max Frei.

Yet, in the case of *Gundelia*, even this finding was far from all. For, as Whanger's and Danin's quantitative study of the pollen representation has

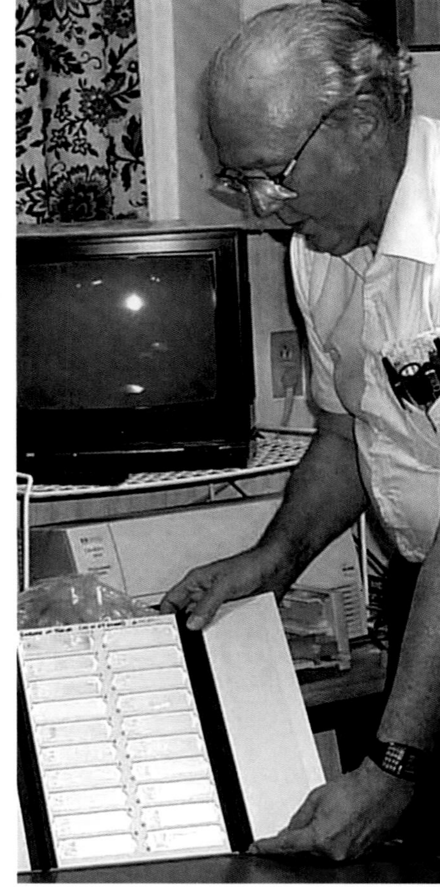

ABOVE: *Dr Alan Whanger holding one of the albums containing Dr Max Frei's collection of sticky-tape specimens taken from the Shroud. Each tape was carefully numbered, and a record was kept of the location on the Shroud from which it was taken.*

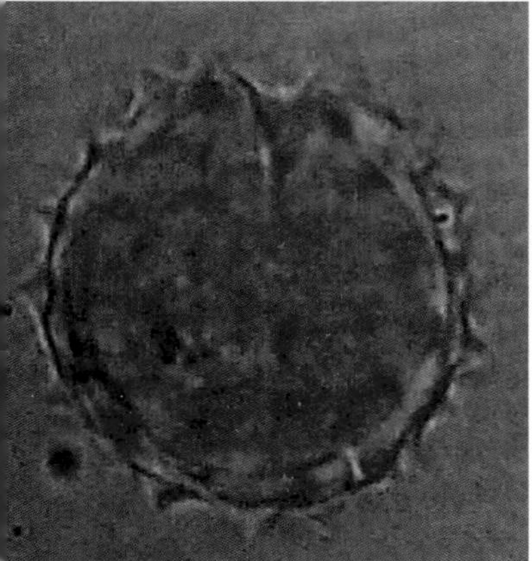

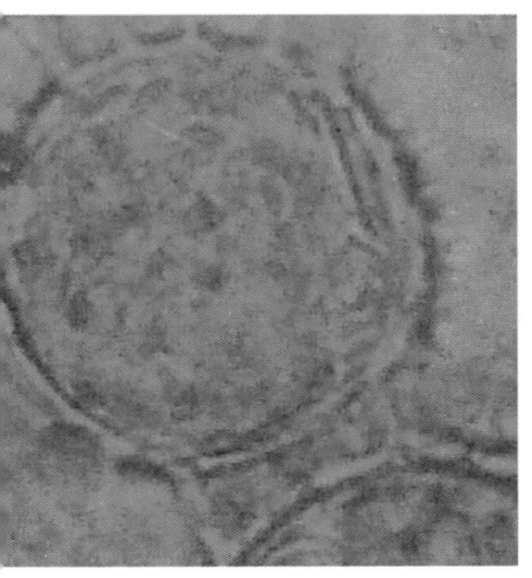

ABOVE LEFT: *Pollen specimen of* Gundelia tournefortii *(top) found by author Ian Wilson on the Shroud in the course of studying one of the Frei tapes, with (below) a control specimen for comparison purposes.*

ABOVE RIGHT: *Author Ian Wilson studying a Frei sticky tape on the Whanger microscope.*

revealed, among the by no means exhaustive 313 pollen grains that they had analysed as part of their programme, no fewer than ninety-one were identifiable as *Gundelia*; the plant comprised nearly one-third of the pollens found and 'logged' on the Frei sticky tapes, and an extraordinary 44 per cent of all those so far classified.[14]

One immediate corollary of this is that very far from Holy Land or Middle Eastern pollens being an insignificant proportion of all those present on the Shroud, they represent in fact a quite disproportionately huge amount. It is as if the six hundred years that the Shroud has definitely been in Europe have counted for very little in terms of pollen representation.

In the same context another important fact concerning *Gundelia tournefortii* is that it is insect- rather than wind-pollinated. In the case of many plants this has meant that they are not represented on the Shroud. For instance, the mainly insect-pollinated olive, though widespread both in the Near East and in western Europe, has furnished not a single specimen in the Frei collection. This is because it would have required an insect to have been on an olive tree just before landing on the Shroud during one of its open-air expositions; a very rare chance indeed.

So for *Gundelia* pollen to be so strongly represented has to mean either that a whole swarm of insects flew from *Gundelia* plants to land on the Shroud – highly unlikely – or that at some time some person or persons unknown deliberately laid flowering *Gundelia tournefortii* plants on it. Of course they may not have done so for funerary purposes. For instance, the Eastern Orthodox liturgy for Good Friday involves rose petals being scattered on altar cloths,[15] so some similar liturgical rite cannot be ruled out. But it is quite definite that whoever did this has to have done so somewhere within the Middle Eastern geographical area where the plant is known to grow, an area specifically including Jerusalem. They also have to have done so at a time of the year when *Gundelia* is known to bloom, and therefore produce pollen, a time that botanists quite independent of Danin[16] can narrow to between March and May. So is it mere coincidence that this was the very period of the year within which Jesus' Passover-linked crucifixion occurred?

All of this raises the question of just what sort of plant is *Gundelia tournefortii*? At which point the surprise is that it is an extremely fearsome-looking thorn, with prickly leaves and a thistle-like head that bears the sharpest of spines. Its greatest known usefulness appears to be as a low-grade winter fodder for goats and sheep when there is nothing better available for them. So it is certainly not obvious as the kind of plant that might have been used as a funerary bouquet, even supposing there was evidence that the Jews of Jesus' time had such a custom. Likewise, while it is possible that the plant's spikiness might have caused it to be used for the 'crown of thorns' laid on Jesus' head – a view certainly favoured by Dr Alan Whanger – Danin for one is ambivalent on this. And Dr Fred Zugibe, having carefully compared photos of *Gundelia* with the bloodstains around the back of the Shroud man's head, similarly expresses doubts.

In fact the very distribution of *Gundelia* pollen grains as these occur on the Shroud is contra-indicative of any such scenario. The greatest concentration of specimens (fourteen) has been found on tape 4/3Aa, which Frei took from the very edge of the Shroud's front-of-the-body half, at the level of the crossed hands, with the next highest incidence ten specimens on tape 12 Cd, from the spillage of blood from the ankle on the back-of-the-body half of the cloth. Conversely only a few *Gundelia* have been found in the region of the head.[17]

So what purpose might *Gundelia* have served being enclosed in the Shroud? And, besides the pollen grains, is there any visual evidence for its presence?

The answer to the first question is ephemeral. If we look to the gospel of John description of Jesus' burial, this tells us that Jesus' body was 'wrapped *with the aromatics* in linen, following the Jewish burial custom' (John 19: 40). So one of the Christian gospels very positively tells us that *some* kind of plant or vegetable matter, seemingly for air-freshening

ABOVE: *A specimen of* Gundelia tournefortii *photographed in spring by Prof. Avinoam Danin in the northern Negev region of Israel, a little to the south of Jerusalem. This single plant, of distinctively Middle Eastern provenance, accounts for one third of all the pollen specimens so far found and 'logged' on the Shroud by Prof. Danin and his colleague Uri Baruch. Note the plant's fearsome spikes, raising the as yet unresolved puzzle of why it should be so strongly represented on the Shroud.*

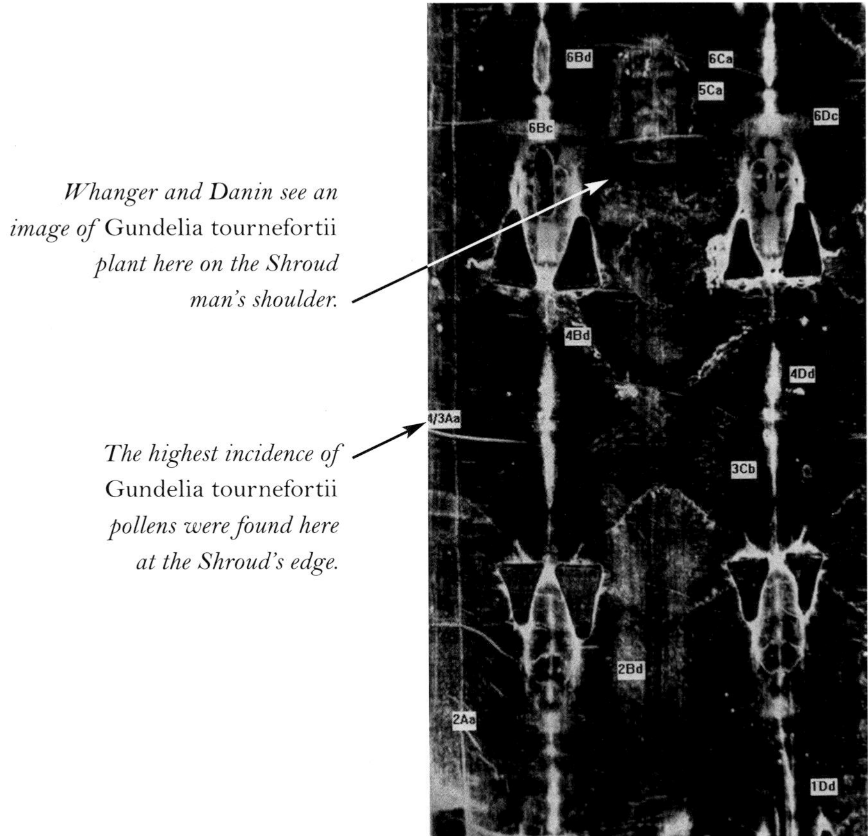

Whanger and Danin see an image of Gundelia tournefortii *plant here on the Shroud man's shoulder.*

The highest incidence of Gundelia tournefortii *pollens were found here at the Shroud's edge.*

ABOVE RIGHT: *'Map' of the locations of the sticky tapes which Dr Max Frei applied to the Shroud in order to obtain his pollen specimens. Curiously, the tape with the greatest number of specimens of* Gundelia tournefortii, *tape 4/3Aa, was taken from the Shroud's edge.*

purposes, was put next to his body. But while it might resolve matters wonderfully if we knew *Gundelia* to have some perfuming or fumigatory properties, its odour is said to be very nondescript, the closest resemblance being artichoke.

The answer to the second question is, at first sight, little less ephemeral. In unison, both Whanger and Danin identify on Whanger's life-size black-and-white Shroud photos a *Gundelia* inflorescence on the man of the Shroud's right shoulder. The STURP ultraviolet photos had first shown up a striated feature in this area that was initially supposed to be a furrowing of the shoulder from the thongs of the scourge,[18] and on the evidence of photographs alone I saw little grounds for changing this opinion.

But at the March 2000 viewing of the Shroud I was very close to Danin as we were ushered into the Cathedral sacristy. Indeed, he had brought binoculars, and kindly lent me these while we both waited for those who were standing in front of us to give way. Then, as we were able to get within touching distance of the Shroud, the spontaneity of his reaction was quite infectious. As his eyes focused on the shoulder area, in almost child-like delight he recognized, as only one of his so specialized botanical expertise could, the *Gundelia* inflorescence's presence on this. Such was his excitement that moments later Archbishop Poletto was called over to have the feature explained to him, and Danin's retracted blue plastic biro was being deployed as a pointer fractions of an inch above the Shroud's surface. Quite obvious was that for Danin, the world's leading expert on the flora of Israel, here, on this piece of cloth displayed in a northern Italian Cathedral side-room, was utterly unqualified recognition of a plant that he positively *knew* to come from the environs of his own Jerusalem. And in my observing this recognition, I could only bow to his very special 'eye' for such things – as he subsequently explained to me, a 'gift' from his childhood. The natural daylight lighting Turin Cathedral's sacristy was clear and even, and as, during the two hours allotted to us, my eyes continued to rove the Shroud's surface, quite apparent was that flower images are not just an aberration of black-and-white photographs. Faint flower-like shapes are quite definitely there on the cloth itself, and while no doubt many can deservedly be dismissed as merely of the 'faces in clouds' variety, the 'hard' evidence of the pollens, combined with my first-hand observation of Danin's very special eye at work, now persuades me to believe that some at least are 'real'.

For, whatever anyone else may make of Danin's botanical 'eye', what cannot be emphasized enough is that the location-type evidence, even from the pollens alone, is quite overwhelming. As Uri Baruch found, there are some instances in which he cannot be as specific about plant species as Frei was, but instead refers to a plant type. Possibly Frei may have been a little over-enthusiastic in his identification in these cases, or (since his death robbed us of ever knowing his full insights), it may have been because he found a way to manipulate the specimen in order to see it better. Either way, such differences are essentially minor, and the sceptics' slurs on Frei's memory are proved to be unfounded. As Danin sums up, particularly from superimposing the known distribution sites of *Gundelia tournefortii*, *Zygophyllum dumosum* and *Cistus creticus*, together with three further specific pollen types confirmed to be on the Shroud,[19] the very narrow geographical region that all these plants share in common is the mere twenty miles between Hebron and Jerusalem.[20] So the conclusion is inescapable, in the very teeth of the radiocarbon dating, that at some time in its history the Turin Shroud positively *must* have been in the same environs in which Jesus of Nazareth lived and died.

In which regard, bearing in mind the Turin Shroud's several intriguing parallels with the Oviedo cloth, as noted in the last chapter, it is of further interest that not long before his death Dr Frei took sticky-tape samples from the Oviedo cloth, just as he had from the Shroud. What he found was pollens representative of Israel, North Africa and Spain, exactly in accord with the cloth's known history. And among those Israel pollens was, yet again, *Gundelia tournefortii*.

In fact, pollens are by no means the only potentially tell-tale elements to be found in the samples of the Shroud's dust trapped on the Frei and

ABOVE: *The excitement of reflectance spectroscopy scientists Roger and Marty Gilbert on discovering an unusually strong signal in the region of the man of the Shroud's heel. On-the-spot microscopic analysis quickly revealed the cause as dirt, far stronger in this area than anywhere else on the Shroud, and clearly consistent with the man of the Shroud having had dirty feet.*

RIGHT: *A detail of the region of the foot on the Shroud's back-of-the-body imprint, showing the heel region (arrowed) which registered the strongest 'dirt' signal.*

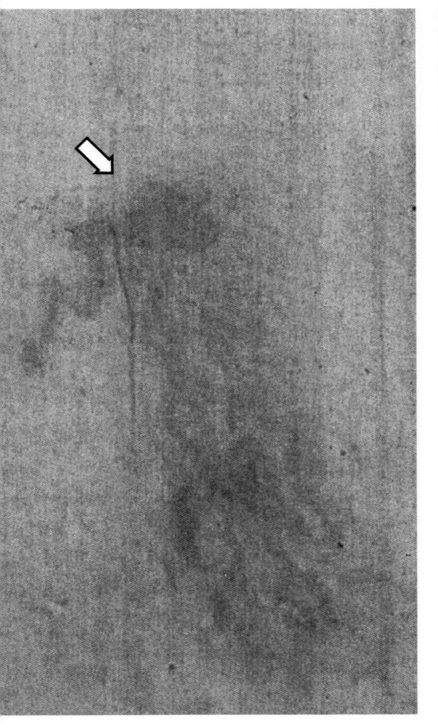

STURP sticky tapes. There is fly-ash from Turin's twentieth-century industrial pollutants. There are fibres from the red silk covering and blue satin surround. There are scraps from ecclesiastical vestments that once brushed against the cloth. There are silver, gold and iron particles from the various caskets in which it has been stored. There are paint fragments from the frescoed rooms in which it has been displayed, and from the artists' facsimiles pressed against it. All of these offer fleeting glimpses of moments in the Shroud's history through the centuries.

Perhaps the most tantalizing glimpse of all, however, came from reflectance spectroscopy work carried out by the husband-and-wife team Roger and Marty Gilbert in the course of the 1978 STURP examination. As they ran their equipment up and down the man of the Shroud's image the spectra they obtained proved relatively regular except when they reached the sole of the foot imprint on the back-of-the-body half of the cloth. Suddenly the spectra changed dramatically. Something in the foot area, and particularly around the heel, was giving a markedly stronger signal than elsewhere, but what? When optical physicist Sam Pellicori was summoned to view the area under the portable microscope the answer proved as chilling as it was obvious. Dead-pan, Pellicori pronounced, 'It's dirt!' As might have been expected in an individual who had had even his sandals taken away from him, the man of the Shroud had dirty feet. During the March 2000 Turin sacristy viewing I and others, even with the unaided eye, could see the Shroud is significantly dirtier at the soles of the feet than anywhere else on the cloth, this dirt very visible underlying the serum-haloed bloodstains that otherwise coat the same soles. So had the Gilberts stumbled upon the very dirt from the streets of Jerusalem that had blackened the feet of Jesus of Nazareth two thousand years ago?

In fact analysis of particles of limestone also found adhering to the Shroud have been identified by optical crystallographer Dr Joseph Kohlbeck as travertine aragonite that spectrally has a 'signature' strikingly similar to limestone samples from ancient Jerusalem tombs, taken by archaeologist Dr Eugenia Nitowski.[21] From such a variety of different directions, there is therefore the most striking evidence that rather than being a 'cunning painting', some time in its history the Shroud really was used somewhere in the environs of Jerusalem to wrap the dirty and bloody corpse of a man who had just been crucified.

Yet, even if this is the case, there is one fundamental question that needs to be tackled before we can try to reconstruct what that history might have been before the Shroud's known emergence in northern France some time in the mid-1350s. Even if all that we have seen so far throws some serious doubts on the Shroud being simply the work of a medieval French forger, how could three world-class radiocarbon laboratories have got their findings so seriously wrong?

Edward Hall (left), Michael Tite (centre) and Robert Hedges at the British Museum after revealing their findings on the shroud.

Turin Shroud shown to be a fake

By **Michael Sheridan** in Rome and **Phil Reeves** in London

CARDINAL Anastasio Ballestrero of Turin yesterday confirmed what newspaper readers around the world have known for weeks: that tests on the Turin Shroud have shown it to be of medieval origin.

The shroud, believed by many to carry the imprint of Christ's face and body when laid in the tomb, has attracted devout pilgrims to Turin for centuries. Leaks of the results of modern carbon-dating tests had infuriated the archdiocese of Turin and the shroud's Italian custodians who spoke darkly of foreign plots against Italy, anti-Catholic prejudice and the like.

Yesterday it was at last official: the tests had established a 95 per cent likelihood that the 14-foot linen was made between 1260 and 1390 AD. There is no chance that it dates back to the time of Christ.

Cardinal Ballestrero pointed out that the church had never claimed that the shroud represented Jesus but had honoured a tradition of piety rooted in centuries past.

"Considering the results of the scientific tests, the church reiterates her respect and her veneration for the shroud," he said.

The tests were carried out in laboratories at Oxford University and in Arizona and Zurich. They were based on counting the number of radioactive carbon 14 atoms in a fragment of the shroud about the size of a postage stamp.

However, they did not resolve the icon's origin, or the mystery which surrounds the blood-stained image on the shroud, resembling a photographic negative, of an apparently crucified man.

The Shroud of Turin: exposed as a fake.

Professor Edward Hall, the director of the Oxford research laboratory involved, gave his theory: "There was a multi-million pound business in making forgeries during the fourteenth century. Someone just got a bit of linen, faked it up, and flogged it."

Professor Hall, 64, who said he had a file full of mostly "cranky" letters from believers in the shroud's authenticity, added that some people would probably continue to regard it as genuine, "just as there is a Flat Earth Society". But he was utterly convinced his findings were right.

Modern Catholic teaching holds that relics are an aid to devotion. They divide into three classes: a first-class relic is either an instrument of the Passion, such as the Turin Shroud, or bones of the saints.

A second-class relic is an object which has touched one of these, and a third-class relic is an object which has touched a second-class relic.

The disappointment to believers in the shroud is unlikely to deter enthusiasts for the tens of thousands of relics, many of them the products of medieval tricksters, which repose in gilded cases and cushioned jewel-boxes in churches throughout Italy.

In Rome, one may view a feather from the Archangel Gabriel at the church of Santa Croce in Gerusalemme.

Other examples include vials containing the last breath of Saint Joseph, several heads of Saint John the Baptist, innumerable splinters from the True Cross, and two thorns from the crown.

In Naples, a vial containing the blood of Saint Januarius miraculously liquefies each year. In 1980, when it failed to to do, the city was struck by an earthquake.

CHAPTER 7

'I promise you . . . the presence of the biofilm . . . will dramatically change the radiocarbon date'

(Microbiologist Professor Stephen Mattingly)

IN 1986, two years before the Shroud radiocarbon dating, the Hong Kong-based archaeologist Bill Meacham wrote that among both scientists and laymen 'there appears to be an unhealthy consensus approaching the level of dogma . . . that C14 will settle the issue once and for all time.' He went on: 'This attitude sharply contradicts the general perspective of field archaeologists and geologists, who view possible contamination as a very serious problem in interpreting the results of radiocarbon measurement.'[1]

Yet when on 13 October 1988 the scientists who radiocarbon dated the Shroud announced their 1260–1390 result, to the world at large it was as if all previous research on the subject, however scientific and well founded, had immediately to be swept aside as of no consequence. Within minutes of the announcement BBC TV's science correspondent, James Wilkinson, was asking me how it felt to have the Shroud proved a fake. My all too shaky response was to deny that the matter was proven and to suggest that some undetermined factor might have skewed the result. This provoked Wilkinson to snort: 'But aren't you clutching at straws?'

And I freely admit that on that gloomy October day it certainly felt like clutching at straws. For the Shroud's radiocarbon date to have been even four or five centuries astray from the decade of Jesus' crucifixion might not have been too disturbing. Discrepancies of this proportion are not uncommon in the general run of archaeological work, and such a date would at least have supported the view of the Shroud as significantly older than the 1350s. But 1260–1390 was unthinkable. As a Shroud researcher for nearly a quarter of a century, it violated everything that I thought I knew about the cloth. As an historian, it was also totally at variance with my understanding of the Middle Ages and of what people of that time and later were capable of technically and artistically. The result simply did not make sense.

Across the other side of the world, Barrie quite independently had a similar reaction. From his study of the Shroud's image properties, coupled with so much other scientific evidence, he had long before become convinced that it was not by a medieval artist. But, like so many who accepted the validity of the radiocarbon dating, he abandoned his interest in the

FACING PAGE: *A typical example of one of the newspaper stories that followed the announcement of the Shroud radiocarbon-dating results on 13 October 1988. This particular example, from Britain's* Independent *newspaper, likened the Shroud to notorious relics such as a feather from the Archangel Gabriel, which is preserved at Rome's Basilica of Santa Croce in Gerusalemme, and a vial of the last breath of St Joseph.*

Shroud temporarily in favour of other projects, at the same time thinking that it made the Shroud mystery greater than ever.

That high personal respect for the science upon which the dating result had been based was very much my difficulty also. Invented in the 1940s by Chicago physicist Willard F. Libby, radiocarbon dating is founded on the principle that all living things, while they are alive, take in the very mildly radioactive isotope carbon 14 which 'decays' at a steady rate on death, relative to the stable carbon 12. Libby's achievement was to develop a form of Geiger counter to measure this 'decay' in samples of ancient organic material, whether the skin and bones of a body or the flax of linen fabric, and thereby read when the original living organism had died, rather in the manner of reading an atomic clock. Although the need for certain adjustments of this clock became evident when datings of ancient wood samples were checked against tree-ring dating, these re-calibrations have long been routine for every test conducted.

Further, the last two decades have seen the invention and development of the accelerator mass spectrometry (AMS) version of radiocarbon dating, which can date samples hundredths of the size originally needed by the Libby method; in the case of linen cloth the size was reduced from pocket handkerchief to fingernail. This, therefore, made it the ideal choice for the Shroud. As a result of its minimally destructive properties AMS has steadily been taking over from its older counterpart, and radiocarbon dating in general has become a thoroughly well-established technology called upon whenever archaeologists around the world seek hard dates for ancient materials that they have unearthed.

Indeed, such was my personal confidence in the technique that as long ago as the late 1970s, in my first book on the Shroud, I unequivocally advocated the AMS version of radiocarbon dating, which was then just emerging, for the Shroud. At around this same time I also struck up an amicable acquaintance with some of the leading scientists in the field, among them Dr Bob Otlet of the Atomic Energy Research Establishment (AERE) Harwell, who had done a great deal to refine the Libby 'proportional counter' method, Prof. Harry Gove of Rochester, New York, who pioneered the small sample AMS method, Prof. Paul Damon of the Arizona AMS laboratory, Prof. Teddy Hall of the Oxford AMS laboratory and Dr Michael Tite of the British Museum's laboratory. All the last three would ultimately take part in the Shroud carbon dating. During the run-up to the sample-taking for this in April 1988, also during the nail-biting months while the result was awaited, I was in cordial touch with these men, all highly respected, world-class experts in their field. So, when I learnt of their findings, blithely to reject them out of hand because they conflicted with my long-held understanding of the Shroud's date was simply not an option. While the knee-jerk reaction of many European Shroud researchers was to vilify the radiocarbon-dating scientists, accusing them

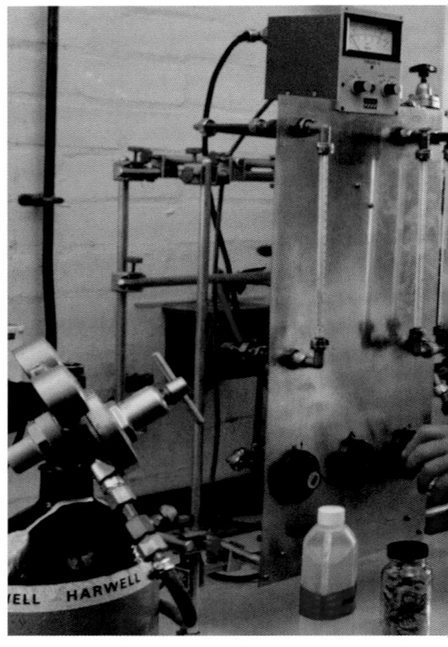

ABOVE LEFT: *Purification equipment at Britain's Harwell radiocarbon-dating laboratory, which used a 'stretched' version of the original Libby 'proportional counter' method of radiocarbon dating. One of seven laboratories originally chosen for the Shroud dating, it was dropped from the shortlist.*

ABOVE RIGHT: *The Oxford laboratory, one of the three Accelerator Mass Spectrometry (AMS) laboratories chosen for the Shroud radiocarbon dating.*

BELOW: *Lindow Man. The Harwell laboratory dated him to* c. *AD 500, Oxford to* c. *AD 100, yet both claimed accuracy to within a hundred years.*

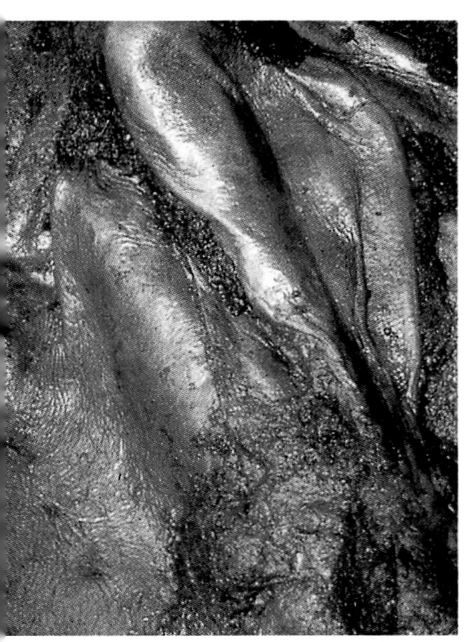

(and particularly the amiable Dr Tite), of every kind of mismanagement and duplicity, mine was positively to decline to join this unedifying clamour.

Mindful, though, of Bill Meacham's words describing contamination as 'a very serious problem in interpreting the results of radiocarbon measurement', I did begin to look out for examples of radiocarbon-dating anomalies in the case of other objects. And to my genuine surprise, these proved rather more frequent than I had expected, and often very difficult for the radiocarbon-dating scientists to explain away.

For instance, a classic example, which arose even before the Shroud dating, concerned Lindow Man, an ancient British human sacrifice victim whose remarkably preserved body was found in 1984 at Lindow Moss, a Cheshire peat bog. From samples taken from Lindow Man's tissues, and also from the peat immediately surrounding him, Dr Bob Otlet's highly experienced Harwell laboratory consistently dated him to *c.* AD 500. Professor Hall's Oxford laboratory, on the other hand, consistently dated his tissues to *c.* AD 100, and Dr Michael Tite's British Museum laboratory dated him to *c.* 300 BC. Despite each laboratory claiming that its findings were accurate to within a hundred years or so, even after they swapped samples with each other and cross-checked, each stuck to its own guns, insisting that it was right and the others wrong. As the journal *Current Archaeology* commented at the time: 'The archaeological world waits with bated breath to see how this problem is resolved.'[2] Yet the plain fact is that in all the years since, the problem never has been resolved.

A similar case, this time particularly pertinent to the suitability of linen for radiocarbon dating, concerns the Manchester Museum's Egyptian mummy number 1770, that of a girl in her early teens. Because 1770's provenance and dating were largely unknown to the Museum's curators, and her condition was relatively poor, she was chosen in the late 1970s as an ideal candidate for a scientific examination that was intended to be the most exhaustive ever carried out on an Egyptian mummy. As part of this exercise, in the early 1980s Manchester's head of Egyptology, Dr Rosalie David, took samples from 1770's body tissues and linen bandages and submitted them to Dr Michael Tite's British Museum radiocarbon-dating laboratory. When the result came back, to everyone's astonishment it showed that her linen wrappings were apparently eight hundred to a thousand years younger than her body.[3] This gave rise essentially to two alternative explanations. Either mummy 1770 (so far as anyone is aware, a girl of no special status), was specially rewrapped in fresh bandages some time up to a thousand years after she was first mummified, or there was something about her linen bandages that skewed the radiocarbon-dating reading. And even the scientifically cautious Dr David has never been particularly inclined towards the former view.

Yet, despite a number of such examples, and also an inter-comparison trial of thirty-eight radiocarbon laboratories that was conducted by Britain's Science and Engineering Council and showed the laboratories to be considerably less accurate than they claimed, any serious, well-founded explanation of how such errors might occur, in the case either of the Shroud, or of any other artefact, has taken a long time to emerge.

Among Shroud enthusiasts one widely favoured suggestion has been that the Chambéry fire of 1532 – during which the Shroud was tightly confined inside a sealed container and 'cooked' to dangerously high temperatures before being rescued – might have 'enriched' or 'rejuvenated' the cloth's radiocarbon content. Had it done so, any testing would, of course, furnish a radiocarbon date much more recent than its true origin. This so-called 'fire model' hypothesis was first mooted and supposedly tested by a Russian, Dr Dmitri Kouznetsov.[4] Some researchers, such as the Italian Mario Moroni claim to have partially replicated Kouznetsov's findings, and the former STURP leader Dr John Jackson is one of several leading Shroud researchers who continue to favour them. However, there has yet to appear a 'fire model' experiment that convincingly 'rejuvenates' a first-century cloth to give it a fourteenth-century radiocarbon date, and until that happens scepticism remains the order of the day.

A potentially much more viable explanation has been pioneered by Mexican-born Dr Leoncio Garza-Valdes of San Antonio, Texas who, although a paediatrician by occupation, has had a life-long passion for microbiology. At a Shroud conference in Rome in 1993 he presented a paper suggesting that a natural, plastic-like biofilm, comprising millions of micro-organisms, had accumulated on the Shroud's surface, much in the manner of the build-up of a coral reef.[5] Although little studied except by

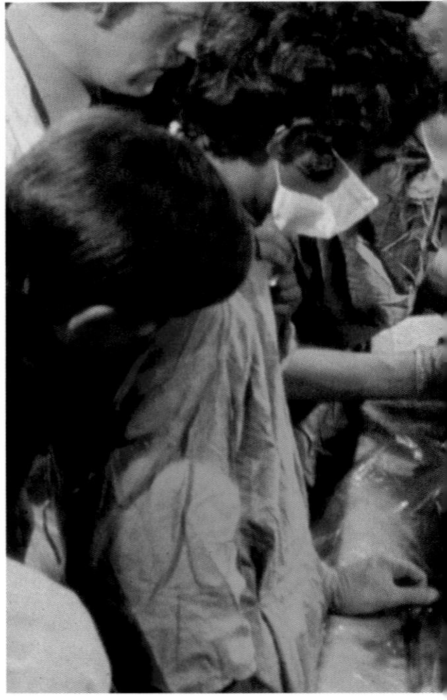

TOP: *Egyptologist Dr Rosalie David and pathologist Dr Tapp work on ancient Egyptian Mummy no. 1770. Radiocarbon dating showed the mummy's linen bandages to be a thousand years younger than the body they wrapped.*

ABOVE: *Dr John Jackson, who argues for the Shroud radiocarbon date having been skewed by the 1532 fire.*

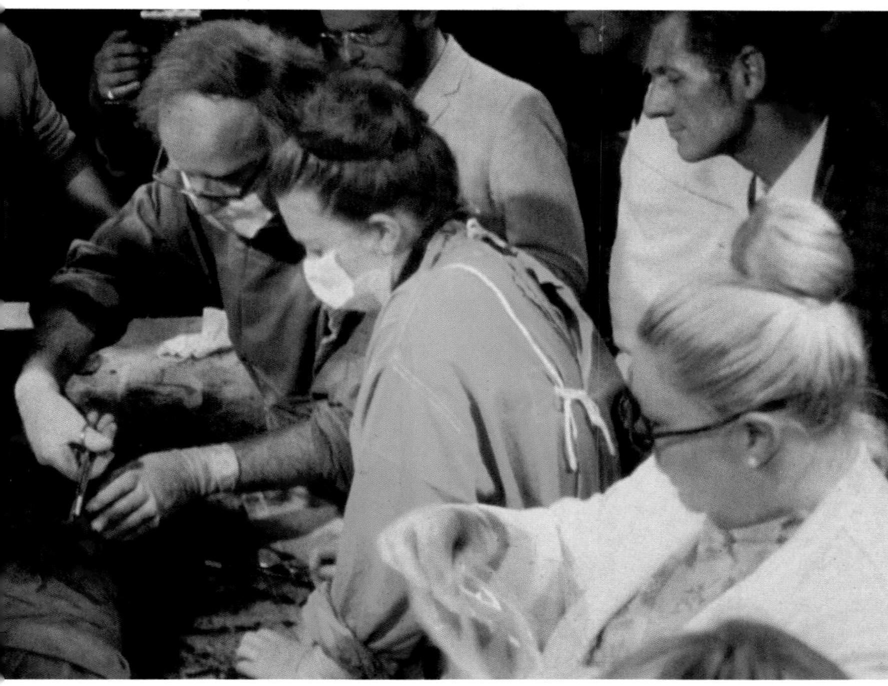

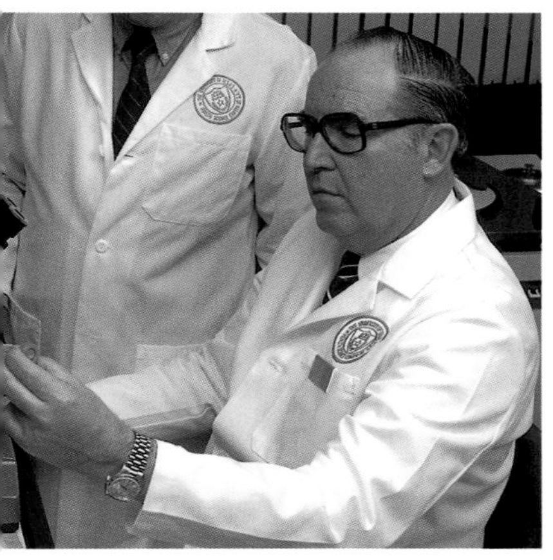

TOP RIGHT: *An ancient Mayan jade known as the Itzamna Tun. Radiocarbon dating of this showed it to be genuinely ancient, yet supposedly some five hundred years younger than its iconography indicated. Dr Leoncio Garza-Valdes (above), discovered that a still partly living 'biofilm' of tiny micro-organisms was responsible for this dating anomaly.*

professional microbiologists, such biofilms unquestionably exist very widely on innumerable surfaces in nature, including our skins, our intestines and even inanimate rock in the form of the so-called 'desert varnish' that covers weathered boulders. Garza-Valdes' startling suggestion was that, because many of the micro-organisms comprising the Shroud's biofilm remain alive, their mass could easily have skewed the radiocarbon dating, thereby giving a much too recent reading.

Unlikely though such a hypothesis might sound, Garza-Valdes had good reason for advocating it. As a collector of ancient Mayan jades, he had discovered a very similar biofilm on one specimen in his collection, the Itzamna Tun, which had been used in Mayan blood-letting rituals. When scrapings of the blood were sent for radiocarbon dating, the laboratories' pre-treatment or cleaning procedures should have removed any contamination, but, as Garza-Valdes discovered, the living bacteria coating these and the rest of the jade successfully resisted the solvents, as a result of which they caused the Itzamna Tun to be radiocarbon dated as some seven centuries younger than its true age as reliably known from its artistic style.

Inevitably, such a finding led him to consider its possible relevance to the Shroud carbon dating. Accordingly in April 1993 he visited Turin, where he met up with Professor Giovanni Riggi, the microanalyst who had been responsible for cutting off the sliver of the Shroud for carbon dating in 1988. As Garza-Valdes discovered, Riggi had personally retained some excess fragments which he had trimmed off from the sample of the Shroud that was divided between the radiocarbon-dating laboratories. And, when he viewed these fragments under the microscope, he immediately found himself staring at much the same biofilm as he had observed on the Itzamna Tun blood, except in this instance significantly thicker. As he was keenly aware, if such a film had not been removed prior to the radiocarbon-dating process, then it might easily have skewed the Shroud's dating, exactly as had happened with his Mayan jade.

Riggi gave him some Shroud fragments to take back to the United States, and he accordingly tried on them the very same chemical cleaning procedures that the official *Nature* scientific report on the Shroud dating[6] described the radiocarbon-dating laboratories as having used on their Shroud samples. As he discovered, even when the cleaning solvents were used at extra strength, they hardly affected the contaminating 'plastic' biofilm, instead doing rather more damage to the linen itself. And, although the radiocarbon-dating laboratories have calculated that for the Shroud's date to have been skewed by thirteen centuries a contamination layer amounting to an astonishing 60 per cent of the entire sample is needed, Garza-Valdes regards this sort of proportion as perfectly feasible.

For it is a matter of firm record that the sliver of Shroud that was taken for the 1988 radiocarbon dating was snipped from its top left-hand corner, one of the two corners by which it was traditionally held up for exposition over the centuries. In countless engravings of Shroud expositions back through history, bishop after bishop can be seen clutching the Shroud at this very point. Now, as microbiologists are fond of demonstrating, microbes from even the cleanest hand will grow impressive colonies in an agar dish in a matter of days. So, if there is any point on the Shroud on which the maximum amount of microbiological contamination could be expected to have accumulated, it would have to have to have been these corners.

Be this as it may, this does not, of course, represent proof that it was by contamination of this kind that the Shroud radiocarbon dating actually was skewed (if it was skewed), although certainly amongst microbiologists the possibility is now beginning to be considered very seriously indeed. This is particularly true in explaining how some of the other radiocarbon-dating anomalies, apart from that of the Shroud, came to occur. In a pilot experiment using the mummy of an ancient Egyptian ibis (a creature which, though sacred to the Egyptians, it is most unlikely that anyone would have rewrapped), Garza-Valdes first studied the microbiological film coating the mummy's wrappings. Noting that this was significantly thinner than that on the Shroud, he predicted that in any radiocarbon dating the discrepancy between the mummy body and its wrappings was likely to be around five hundred years. When the mummy and its wrappings were independently radiocarbon dated, the reading for the wrappings proved to be 550 years younger than that for the mummy. To

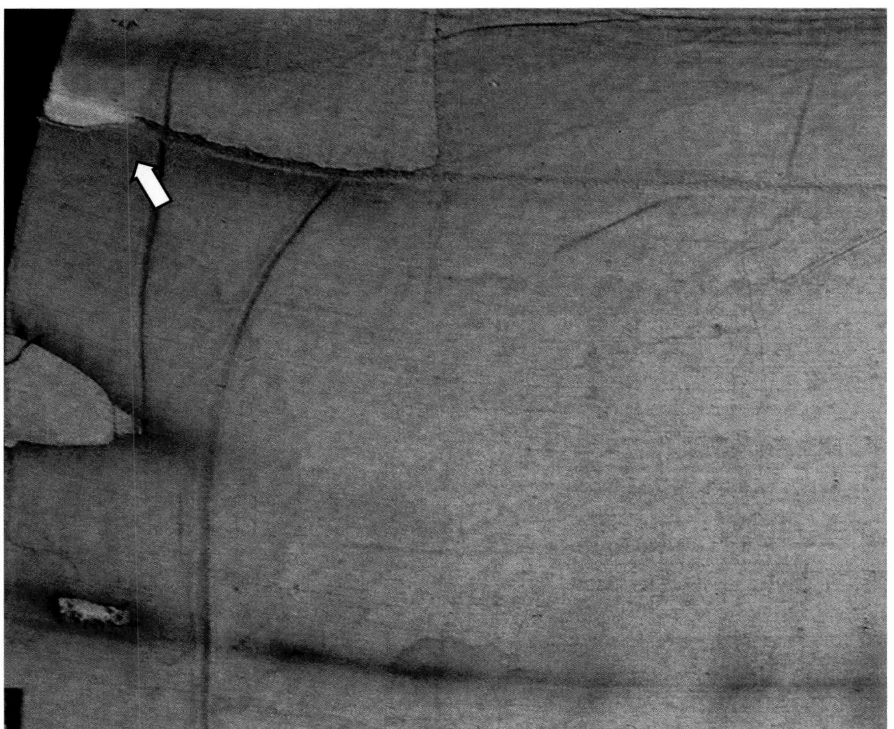

ABOVE LEFT: *Professor Giovanni Riggi extracting a thread sample from the Shroud.*

ABOVE RIGHT: *The corner area of the Shroud (arrowed) from which the radiocarbon-dating sample was taken in 1988. This can only have been heavily contaminated from repeated handling.*

RIGHT: *A detail from a sixteenth-century engraving of a Shroud exposition, showing the cloth typically held up by the very corner from which the carbon-dating sample would be taken.*

Garza-Valdes this, on top of his previous findings, all but proved his biofilm hypothesis.

Although most scientists would rightly feel that this was over-optimistic, the highly respected microbiologist Prof. Stephen Mattingly, of the University of Texas Health Science Center at San Antonio, having similarly studied the Shroud samples under the microscope, shares much of Garza-Valdes' optimism. While careful not to become too embroiled in the Shroud debate, he fully supports the view that a substantial microbiological biofilm is present: 'There is no doubt that the Shroud has a major layer of microbial contamination on and within the cellulose fibres.'[7]

Mattingly further supports Garza-Valdes' contention that this contamination was not removed by the laboratories' cleaning procedures, pointing out that the radiocarbon laboratories left themselves wide open to their result being challenged by their failure to perform either a preliminary or a post-test chemical analysis of the samples that their AMS radiocarbon-dating process had to destroy. In Mattingly's words, 'This is the first step in quantitative analysis in college chemistry. I can remember my lab instructor sending me back to the bench because the recovery mass of my unknown did not agree with the known value.'

Had the radiocarbon-dating laboratories performed such a chemical analysis, then the presence of contaminating material to the tune of 60 per cent would have become very readily apparent in a way that no optical method could provide. But, focused as they were on their own science of nuclear physics, they assumed that they were testing pure Shroud and nothing else, and therefore worked blind. Although Professor Hall said in 1989 that he would be amazed if even 1 per cent contamination remained on the cloth, Mattingly rejoins:

> I can assure you that you cannot look at any object and assume that it is appreciably free of microbial contamination. You might be surprised to know that every square millimetre of your skin is coated with a substantial layer of micro-organisms. They are contributing, along with your gut microbial flora, in a significant way to your overall body mass.[8]

Were a proper chemical analysis of Shroud samples conducted, certainly any from the area sampled for radiocarbon dating, what should be revealed is the presence of muramic acid. In Mattingly's words, 'If it is present, this is proof that bacteria are present. Muramic acid is only found in nature in the cell walls of bacteria. It is widely used as a marker for the presence of bacteria. The quantitative level of muramic acid can then be used to estimate the mass contribution of bacteria to the overall mass of the linen.'[9]

Mattingly's overall assessment is that, since micro-organisms make up 80 per cent of the mass of living organisms on the earth today, 'why they

Prof. Stephen Mattingly (right), head of the microbiology department at the University of Texas Health Science Center, San Antonio, Texas. He heavily criticizes the radiocarbon-dating laboratories for their failure to make a proper chemical analysis of their Shroud samples before destroying them by the

radiocarbon-dating process. Fully supportive of the 'biofilm' hypothesis of Dr Garza-Valdes (seen at left), Mattingly argues that it can only be a matter of time before the radiocarbon-dating laboratories will be obliged to admit that their 'proof' of the Shroud's medieval date was nothing of the kind.

should not comprise more than 50 per cent of the weight of a centuries-old linen should not be a major leap in credibility'. To demonstrate this, shortly before the March 2000 Symposium he cultured his own skin bacteria in his laboratory, concentrated these in pellet form and then repeatedly smeared the mixture over a 1 gram square of linen until the combined weight of linen plus bacteria reached 2.30 grams. Having thereby achieved a 57 per cent degree of contamination, he heated the bacteria to render them harmless, then sent the result to Drs Adler, Jackson and myself, together with an untreated sample as a 'control'. As he pointed out in a covering note, because of the coating's artificial and now sterile nature it cannot be considered a replication as such of that on the Shroud. Instead the clear message of his samples is that a 57 per cent layer of coating is nothing like as obvious and obtrusive as non-microbiologists expect it to be. And, because the radiocarbon laboratories failed to conduct a proper chemical analysis of the samples they destroyed, no one can deny that such a coating *could* have been present and have seriously affected the dating result.

In the light of Prof. Mattingly's comments, the confident claims made by the radiocarbon-dating laboratories in their *Nature* report of 1989 that they had 'conclusively' shown the Shroud to date from the Middle Ages may be considered effectively to lie in tatters. As was pointed out, even before the radiocarbon dating, by Dr Bob Otlet of the Harwell Laboratory, Oxford and its two companion AMS laboratories had had little experience of dating linen before they worked on the Shroud. Furthermore linen, because of the huge surface area presented by its multitudinous fibres, appears to be peculiarly subject to contamination that can seriously skew its dating, as is evident from the Egyptian mummy linen anomalies, quite apart from the Shroud. So the whole phenomenon of contamination peculiar to linen undoubtedly needs to be further explored, not least in the interests of archaeology in general, as well as those of the Shroud. Then, when the technology has been found to eliminate microbiological biofilm satisfactorily from any radiocarbon-dating reading, hopefully there can be a fresh dating of the Shroud, using a sample held back in 1988 for this very purpose. If and when this can be done, Mattingly confidently predicts: 'I promise you the presence of the biofilm [once removed] will dramatically change the radiocarbon date.'

In the meantime, now that the field can once more be considered clear to countenance at least the possibility of the Shroud being twenty as opposed to six centuries old, the question arises: can it be traced back through those twenty centuries? In the light of the botanical findings of pollens from Israel and Turkey, can at least a plausible history be reconstructed for it in the Near East prior to its mysterious emergence in France in the 1350s?

Ο ΑΥΓΑΡΟΣ ΠΡΟΣ ΤΟΝ ΚΥΡΙΟΝ: ΤΟΝ ΑΝΑΝΙΑΝ ΑΠΟΣΤΕΛΛΕΙ ?
Ο ΑΝΑΝΙΑΣ ΤΟΝ ΚΥΡΙΟΝ ΜΗ ΔΥΝΑΜΕΝΟΣ ΙΣΤΟΡΗΣΑΙ ?
ΤΟΝ ΑΓΙΟΝ ΜΑΝΔΗΛΙΟ

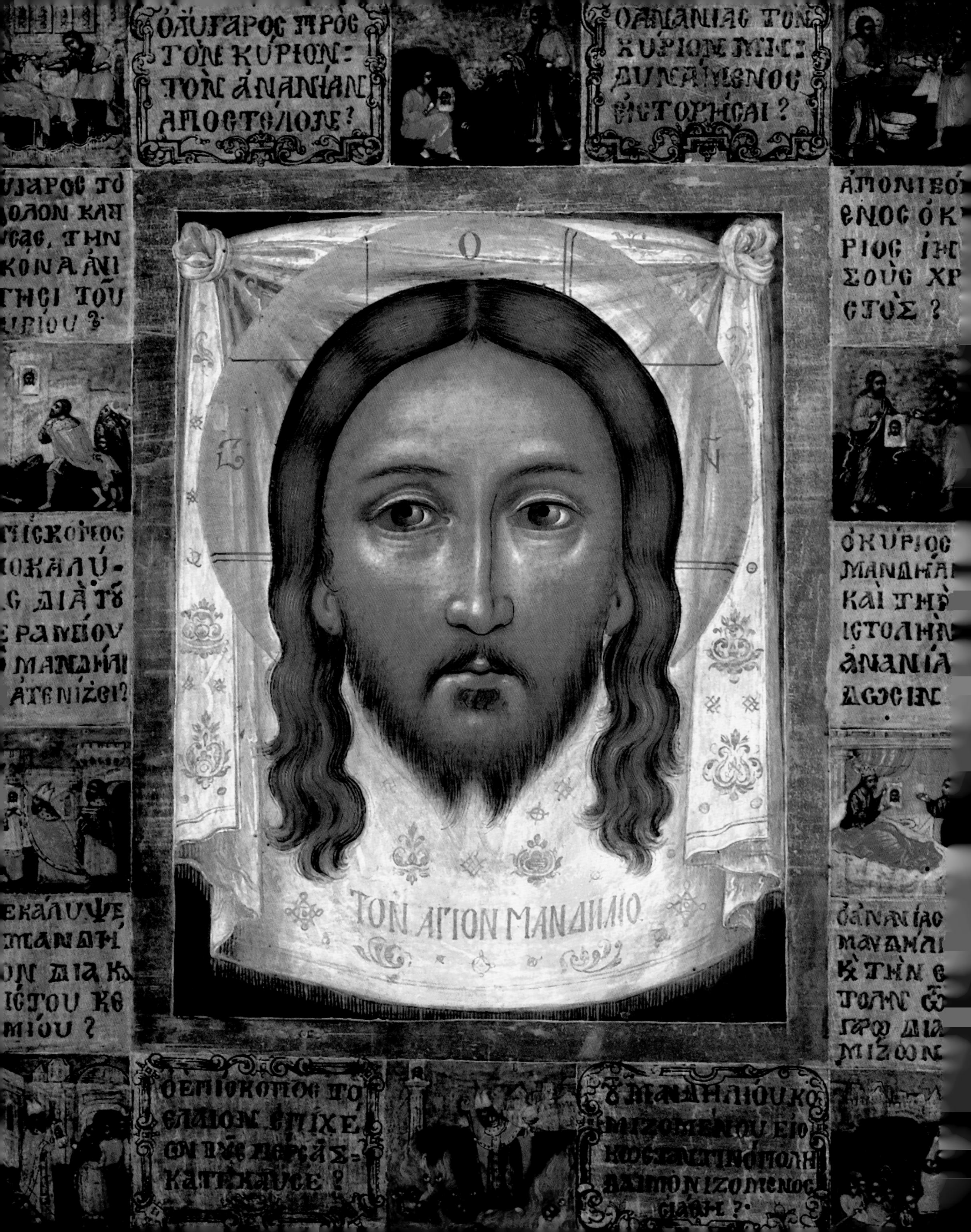

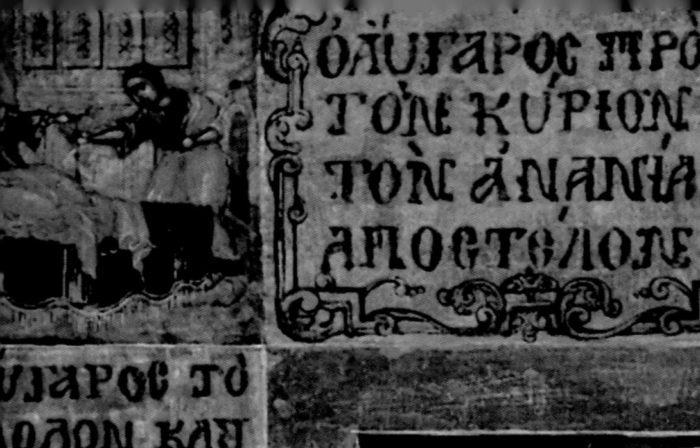

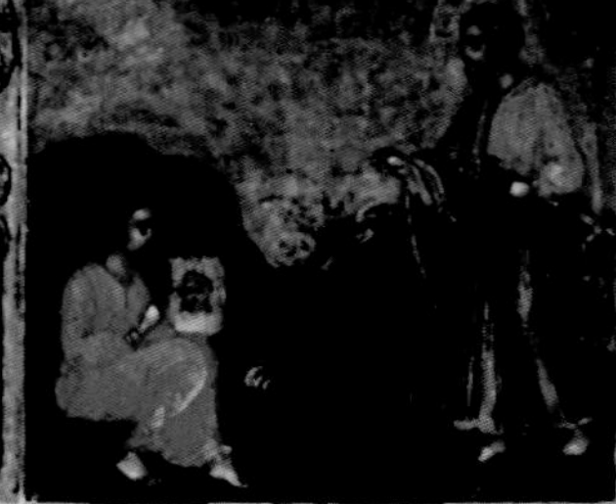

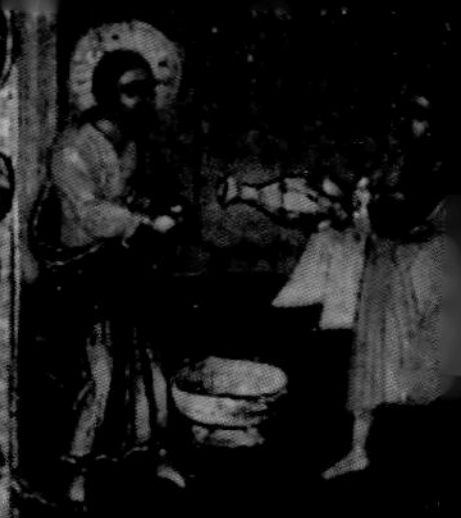

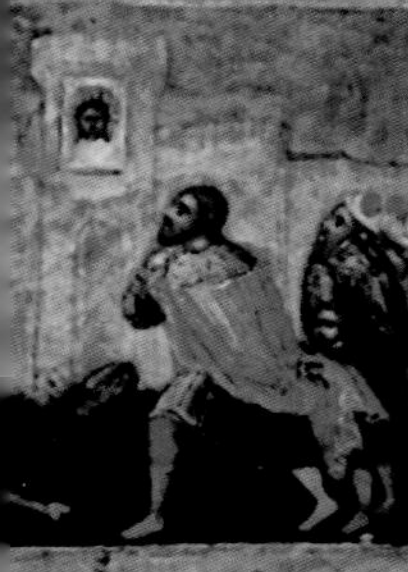

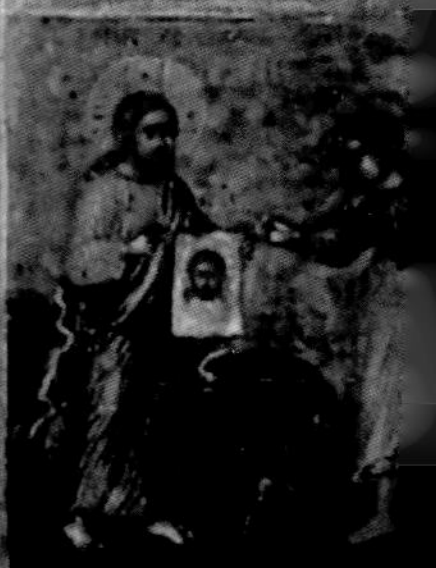

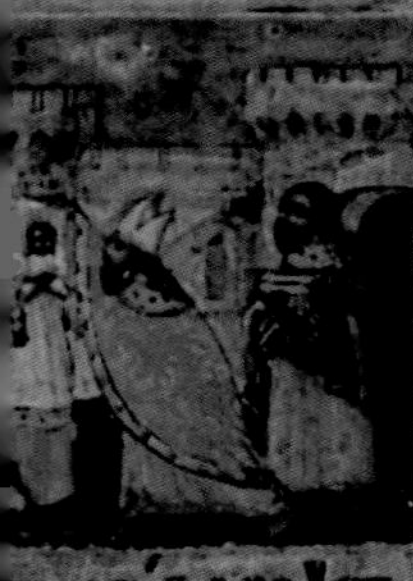

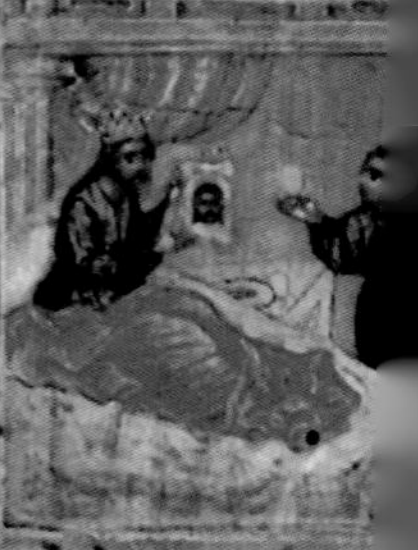

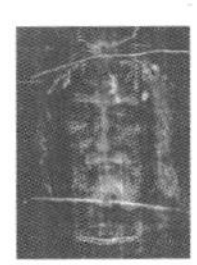

CHAPTER 8

'That the Saviour's features were imprinted on the cloth . . . is agreed by all'

(Anonymous Byzantine historian, *c.* AD 944[1])

BELOW: *A detail of the face from the Shroud, with (left), Buckingham Palace's icon depicting the mysterious, supposedly lost cloth of Edessa and scenes of its long and colourful history, including in Edessa and also Jerusalem. This history neatly matches the Frei/Danin findings concerning the geographical origins of the pollens so far identified on the Shroud. The icon is merely seventeenth-century, but faithfully preserves Eastern Orthodox traditions concerning a cloth already lost to them for several centuries.*

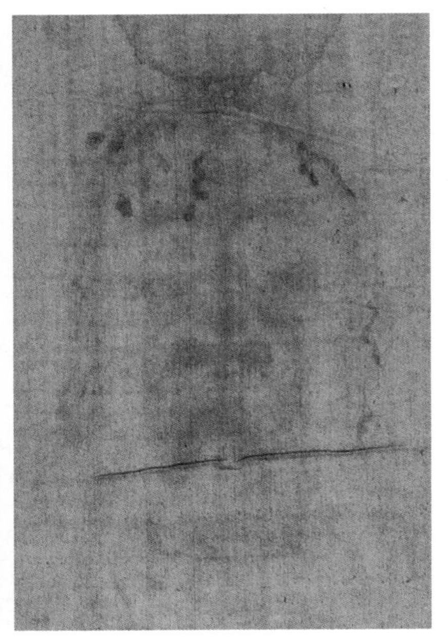

ONE POINT about the Shroud that cannot be over-emphasized is its singularity as bearing a meaningful human imprint. Human bodies, whether they are alive or dead, do not normally create photographic-type imprints of themselves on cloth; in all history this idea is unique to Jesus Christ. So if the Shroud really were an inspired forgery of the radiocarbon-dated 1260–1390 period, then we might expect the earlier centuries to be entirely silent about any cloth of this description.

Yet, whatever the validity of the carbon-dating findings, the historical facts are that this is far from the case. The idea of Jesus imprinting his likeness on a cloth is richly documented with absolute certainty at least as far back as the sixth century, historical sources further attesting to the existence of an actual object of this description back to this time. And by implication both the idea and this associated relic can be traced five centuries further back still to Jesus' Jerusalem.

Particularly meaningful in elucidating this is a quaint-looking icon that once hung in HM Queen Elizabeth II's private chapel at Buckingham Palace,[2] before being transferred to Hampton Court.[3] Acquired by the Queen's great-great-grandfather Prince Albert, the icon itself is not particularly old, being probably seventeenth- or eighteenth-century, though with earlier Eastern Orthodox antecedents, particularly in Russia and in Genoa[4]. But it has two prime fascinations.

First, its central feature is the face of Jesus imprinted on cloth, one that has all the hallmarks of being a distant echo of the facial area on the Turin Shroud. Although apparently only the face is represented, there is the same frontality, the same disembodiedness, the same monochromatic tonation.

Second, all around the icon's sides are depicted scenes from this Jesus-imprinted cloth's long and colourful history, scenes that place it in the Byzantine capital Constantinople (today Istanbul), and before then in Edessa (today the picturesque provincial town of Urfa in eastern Turkey). Both locations correspond to Dr Max Frei's finding of the pollens of Turkish plants on the Shroud. Then, before Turkey, the cloth is depicted in Jerusalem, redolent of Professor Avinoam Danin's finding of pollens from plants peculiar to the environs of that city.

As the icon's pictorial sequence runs, in the time of Jesus an ailing king of Edessa called Abgar sent a messenger to Jerusalem to ask Jesus to come to cure him (scene 1). In the course of this mission the messenger tried to paint Jesus' likeness (scene 2), but before he could do so Jesus miraculously imprinted his features on a piece of cloth (scene 3) and instructed him to take this back to Abgar (scene 4). When Abgar saw this cloth he was promptly cured and converted to Christianity (scene 5). Ordering Edessa's pagan idols to be overturned, he had in their stead Jesus' image set up over the gate of his city (scene 6). But a successor reverted to paganism and persecuted the Christians, whereupon the image over the gate had to be taken down and the miraculously imprinted cloth hidden away (scene 7), a cavity above the gate being the chosen hiding place. There it remained until the sixth century, by which time Edessa had once again become Christian, and part of the Byzantine empire. At this point a bishop rediscovered it (scene 8) and invoked its divine protection to overcome a siege of Edessa by the Persians (scene 9). In 944 the cloth was transferred, amid much joyful celebration, to the Byzantine capital Constantinople (scene 10), where it stayed as part of the Emperors' relic collection until it disappeared without trace during the sack of Constantinople by the Crusaders in 1204.

This story unmistakably shows signs of having acquired some legendary accretions, as indeed do the surviving supporting texts, some from the fourth century AD and even earlier, that tell the story in words. Indisputably, however, the Jesus-imprinted cloth in question, whatever its true nature, was a genuinely historical object from its rediscovery in Edessa in the sixth century, through to its well-documented transfer to Constantinople and thereupon to its disappearance from that city in 1204. Equally indisputable is that those living in the sixth century believed that the cloth originated in Jerusalem and that its image had been imprinted by Jesus himself.

Of course, from the Hampton Court icon, from other representations and from related texts, the Edessa cloth seems to have been just a face-only cloth created while Jesus was alive, rather than a full-body burial shroud. But, given the features it shares with the Shroud as bearing Jesus' imprint, and the striking match of its known history with the Shroud pollen evidence, if it could be identified as being the same as the Shroud, then the mystery of the latter's thirteen missing centuries of history would be explained at a single stroke.

So just what are the hard facts behind the story of the Jesus-imprinted cloth as told on the Hampton Court icon? First, it is a matter of firm historical record that there was a King Abgar of Edessa contemporary with Jesus. He was Abgar V, who reigned from AD 13–50. Although there is no contemporary evidence of this Abgar's conversion to Christianity, there was definitely a custom in his and neighbouring Parthian-affiliated

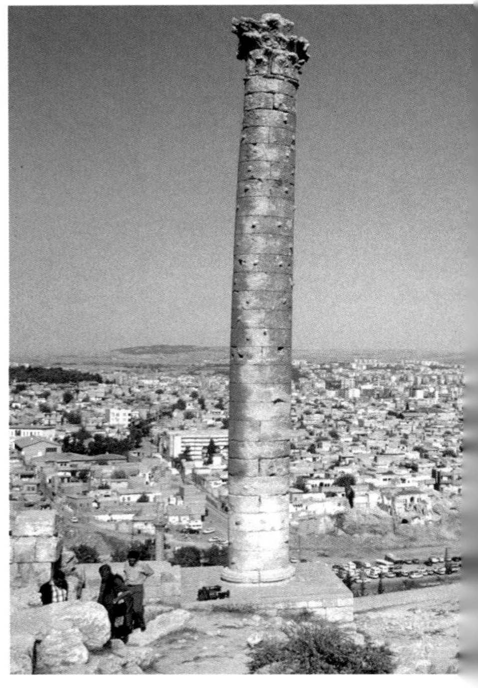

BELOW: *Today Urfa, the former Edessa, is notable chiefly for its mosques. Throughout much of the first millennium, however, it bristled with Christian churches, harking back to its very early evangelization and its famous Jesus-imprinted cloth. The two columns overlooking the city (top) date from the time of the city's rule by pagan members of the Abgar dynasty.*

ABOVE RIGHT: *A detail from a seventeenth-century Russian icon of the cloth of Edessa in the Verkhospassky Cathedral, Moscow, showing the discovery of the Edessa cloth in the sixth century, hidden in a niche above one of the city's gates. It was immediately identified as having been hidden there at a time when Edessa reverted to paganism.*

territories for the setting up of 'god' images over city gates, exactly as depicted in the icon's scene 6. Furthermore, a contemporary chronicle refers to a flood damaging a clearly tolerated church in Edessa in AD 201[5], so the city must have received Christianity very early. It is notable that Abgar VIII, the King at that time, is the first monarch in all history to be depicted on coins with the Christian cross on his tiara. In further support of this, the very scholarly church historian, Bishop Eusebius of Caesarea, who flourished around AD 300, insisted that he had seen in Edessa's highly esteemed record office the lost original Syriac documentation concerning Edessa's conversion during the time of the Abgars, as 'preserved from then until now'.[6]

From the fact that Eusebius says nothing about it, the Jesus-imprinted cloth seems to have long been hidden away by *c.* AD 300, exactly as the icon's pictorial cycle describes. Likewise a fourth century version of the story, the *Doctrine of Addai*, merely describes it as an image created 'with choice paints', arguably attesting to the extent to which it had been forgotten while its whereabouts lay unknown at this early period. Altogether more authoritative, however, is the report that upon the cloth's rediscovery in the sixth century – thought to have occurred during rebuilding work after a major flood at Edessa in AD 525 – its image became unhesitatingly hailed as *acheiropoietos*, or not made by human hands, suggesting that, once found and scrutinized, it was immediately recognized as bearing some kind of imprint rather than having been painted by an artist. Later Byzantine texts likewise describe it in a most Shroud-like way as a 'divinely wrought'

A *12th century*

B *11th century*

C *8th century*

D *6th century*

E *5th century*

F *4th century*

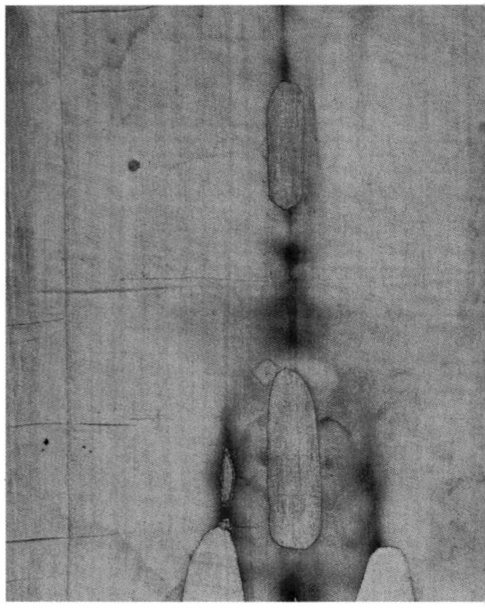

LEFT: *The striking change that occurs to the portrait of Jesus in art, as apparently caused by the rediscovery of the Edessa cloth in the early sixth century. Looking back in time, the authoritative bearded likeness automatically associated with Jesus today (A–D) traces back only to the sixth century, the time of the Edessa cloth's discovery. Many of the earlier Christ portraits (E and F) depict Jesus as an Apollo-like, beardless youth, and St Augustine, writing in the fifth century, reported that no one of his time had any idea of Jesus' human appearance. Clearly the impact on art of the Edessa cloth imprint was profound.*

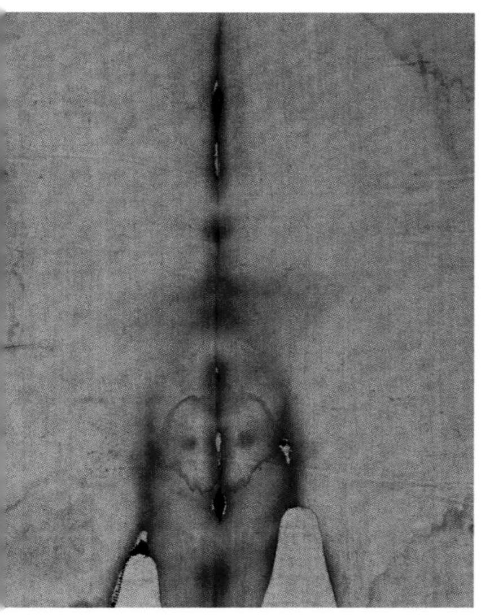

ABOVE RIGHT: *One of the earliest surviving depictions of the Edessa cloth's appearance, from a Byzantine fresco dating to the tenth or eleventh century, which decorated the top of an arch in a tiny church at Sakli in Cappadocia. This is relatively close to Edessa/Urfa. The fresco shows the imprint of Jesus' face as front-facing and seemingly 'disembodied' on a landscape-aspect cloth, strikingly resembling the equivalent area on the Turin Shroud (above left). The burn marks visible on the Shroud would not have been present at any time prior to 1532.*

image and an 'impression' comprising 'a moist secretion, without colouring or painter's art'.

From sources in the sixth century and those immediately following we learn that the Edessa cloth's material was 'linen',[7] the various Greek words used for describing it also including *sindon*, the very word used for Jesus' Shroud in the three synoptic gospels. And the earliest direct depictions of it, such as in a fresco at Sakli in Cappadocia, which date from the tenth century onwards, show it as a sepia-coloured, disembodied, front-facing 'face' on a landscape-aspect cloth looking most strikingly similar to the equivalent area on the Turin Shroud.

Nor is this all. When we look at the history of the likeness of Jesus as this has quite independently come down to us in art we find something very curious. The relatively few portraits of Jesus that date from before the sixth century are mostly very nondescript and unconvincing, often depicting him as a beardless, Apollo-like youth. A similar vagueness extends even to the few more credible ones that show him as Jewish-looking and with a beard. Consistent with this, St Augustine, writing in the fifth century, went on record as remarking, 'We do not know of his [Jesus'] external appearance, nor that of his mother.'[8]

But in the sixth century, and therefore synchronous with the Edessa cloth's rediscovery, something quite remarkable happens to the portraits of Jesus. They suddenly take on a highly distinctive character, often rigidly front-facing, and exhibiting all those long-haired, long-nosed, fork-bearded characteristics that to this day we 'recognize' as being Jesus' likeness. As if by invisible decree the Jesus portrait that we know today comes into being, and the logical explanation is that the Byzantines now had an authoritative reference for what Jesus looked like in the form of the cloth of Edessa.

Nor is even this all. For when the Jesus portraits which are influenced by the Edessa cloth are examined closely, many of them exhibit certain oddities that recur time and again. As early as the 1930s these oddities particularly struck a French scholar, Paul Vignon, who assembled a list of some fifteen that he considered particularly significant.[9] These included a raised eyebrow, a 'topless square' between the eyebrows, a small 'triangle' below this, heavily accentuated eyes, an enlarged nostril, exaggerated cheek markings and the hairless gap between lip and beard. And to Vignon the explanation seemed to lie unmistakably in the Shroud, since all the oddities could be traced to blemishes and quirks on its surface that the early artists had seemingly worked into their Jesus portraits. A classic example is an eighth-century Christ Pantocrator fresco in the Ponzianus catacomb in Rome, in which the artist has painted a very unnatural-looking topless square between Christ's eyebrows. When the equivalent area on the Shroud face is studied, there is this same topless square, telling us more strongly than any words that someone, somewhere, somehow knew of the Turin Shroud's existence back in the eighth century AD.

What Vignon was not able to explain satisfactorily was how the Shroud could have had such a profound influence on art so far back, when its existence as a historical object was not correspondingly frequently mentioned. But, if the Byzantine world knew our Shroud, not as a shroud but as the cloth of Edessa, then all such difficulties evaporate. For during the centuries before 1204 the Jesus-imprinted Edessa cloth received precisely the kind of historical documentation that is very largely absent for the cloth that we know as the Turin Shroud. So for what became known as the Turin Shroud after the 1350s to have been one and the same as the cloth known before 1204 as the cloth of Edessa would make a great deal of sense.

Though, in my opinion, this Vignon-inspired argument concerning the facial markings is highly compelling, nothing in Shroud studies is ever straightforward. A very valid objection that has been raised by some specialist scholars is that both in the great majority of documentary sources and in artists' copies the Byzantines clearly understood the cloth of Edessa to have been an imprint of Jesus' face only, not of his whole body.[10] They also understood it to have been made by Jesus while he was alive, not dead in the tomb. So how could it have been one and the same as our Turin Shroud?

For me a crucial breakthrough in overcoming this objection surfaced in the 1960s, when I noticed how a sixth-century Greek version of the Abgar story, the 'Acts of the Holy Apostle Thaddaeus', describes the Edessa cloth as a *tetradiplon*.[11] In all the corpus of Greek literature *tetradiplon* is an extremely rare word, and totally exclusive to the Edessa cloth. Yet, because it is a combination of two common words, *tetra* meaning 'four' and *diplon* meaning 'two fold' or 'doubled', its meaning is actually very clear:

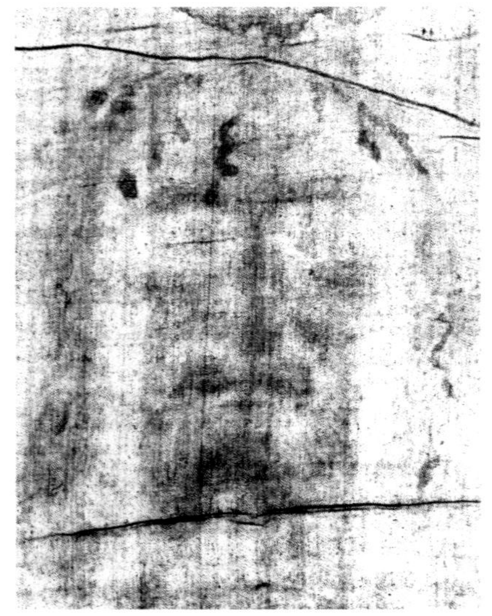

FACING PAGE: *The facial imprint as it appears on the Shroud (top), with (centre), a highlighting of some of the so-called Vignon markings that repeatedly occur in Byzantine portraits of Christ, as if copied from these anomalies to the Shroud face: (1) two strands of hair; (2) transverse streak; (3) 'topless' square; (4) 'V' shape; (5) raised eyebrow; (6) heavily accentuated eyes; (7 and 8) accentuated cheeks; (9) enlarged nostril; (10) line between nose and lip; (11) line under lower lip; (12) hairless area; (13) forked beard; (14) line across throat; (15) left sidelock longer.*

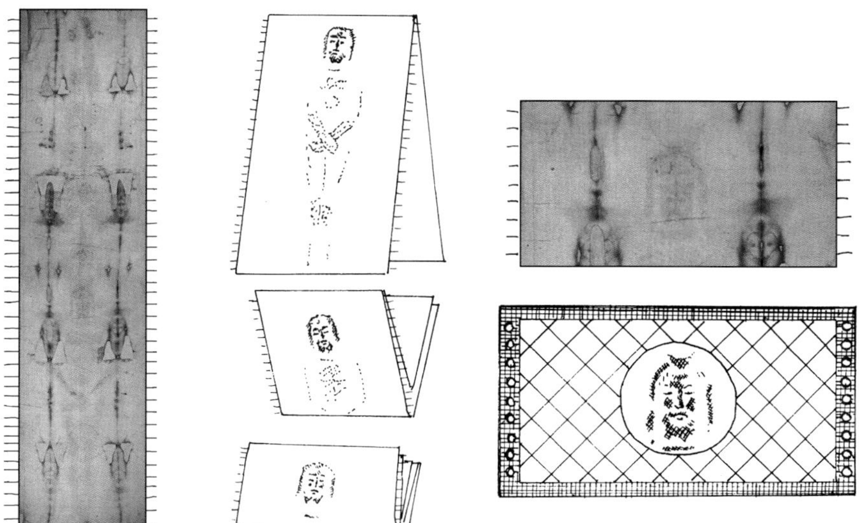

ABOVE RIGHT: *How during the first millennium the Shroud was arguably 'doubled in four' and mounted on a board so that only the face was visible.*

'doubled in four', suggesting four times two folds. This immediately raised the thought: 'What happens if you try giving the Shroud four times two folds?'

When I tried this, using a full-length photograph of the Shroud, I was dumb-founded by the result – as I continue to be today. There was the Shroud face, front-facing and disembodied-looking on a landscape aspect cloth, exactly as on the earliest artists' copies of the cloth of Edessa. Whenever the Shroud is presented in this manner – and it is a very logical way to present and make manageable a 437 cm length of cloth – its nature as a 'shroud' is in fact subordinated to its rather more socially acceptable nature as a 'portrait'. And historically such an arrangement finds ready support in the description of the Edessa cloth, on its arrival in Constantinople, as 'fastened to a board and covered with the gold which is now to be seen'.[12] It therefore readily explains the many centuries of silence about an image-bearing 'shroud' as such.

Furthermore, when the man of the Shroud's eyes are viewed on the cloth itself, as the Edessans and Constantinopolitans might have viewed them, rather than on the photographic negative that we tend to be more familiar with today, they appear open and staring, just as if he was alive, thus readily corresponding to this aspect of the Abgar story. And when we further learn that in the tenth century, when the cloth of Edessa was transferred to Constantinople, the Byzantines rewrote the story of the cloth's origins to suggest that it may have been created by Jesus' 'bloody sweat' in the garden of Gethsemane (Luke: 22 44), this also fits. It is just the sort of interpretation that anyone might come to when, ignorant of the Shroud's nature as a shroud, they noted on the forehead watery-looking bloodflows that we, from our perspective, now understand to have been from the crown of thorns.

FACING PAGE: *(Below) An eighth-century portrait of Christ from the Ponziano catacomb, Rome, showing a particularly striking example of the 'topless square' between the eyebrows.*

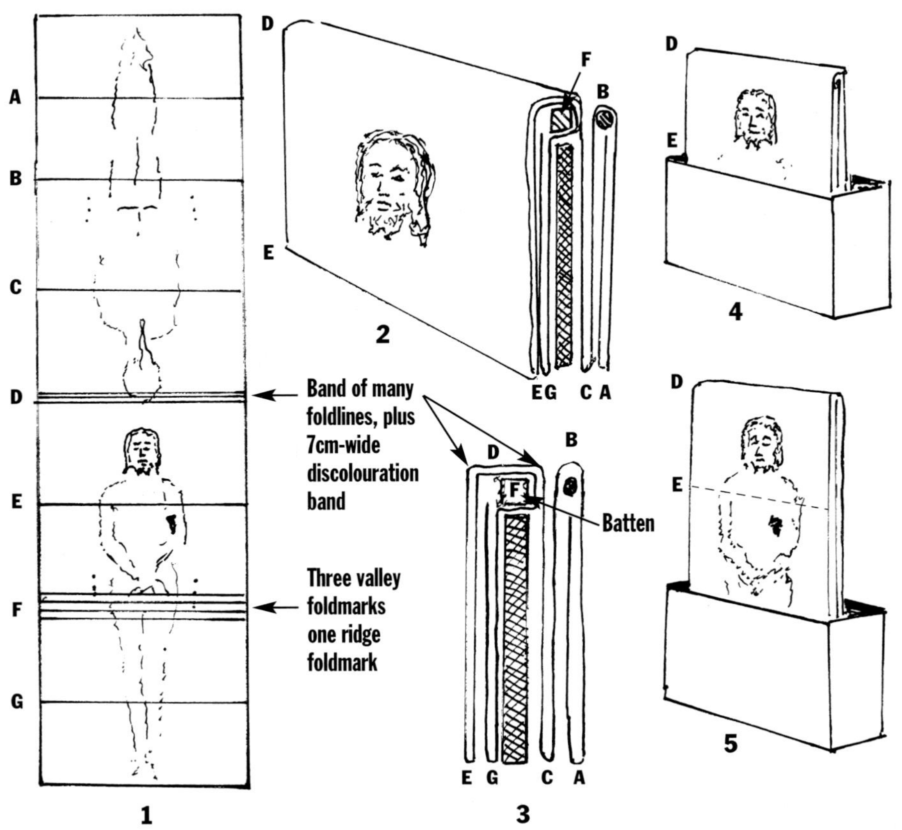

LEFT: *How the Shroud may have been made to 'stand upright' from its casket, for very privileged showings during the last years of its possession in Constantinople. The 'doubled-in-four' crease lines identified by Dr John Jackson (lettered A–G on diagram 1) and the particularly pronounced set of lines at point F indicate a folding arrangement around an apparatus as indicated in diagrams 2 and 3. The cloth could then have been made to rise upright, as in 4 and 5. The Byzantines delighted in the kind of gadgetry that the crease lines seem to indicate.*

Clearly a crucial component of this theory is that the Shroud should bear signs of its once having been folded, for some significant length of time, in the 'doubled in four' manner postulated. When the STURP team worked on it in 1978, at my urging they specifically included in their test programme raking light photography to show up as clearly as possible the innumerable ancient and not-so-ancient creases that criss-cross its surface. When Dr John Jackson carefully analysed these creases to gauge whether there were any significant and long-established fold-marks consistent with the 'doubled-in-four' theory, he found that indeed they were there. He even found that the way they fell, with two particularly pronounced concentrations – one at the level of the topmost part of the back of the head, the other just below the crossed hands – indicated that the cloth had at one time been stored so that, if it was pulled upwards, the imprint of the man of the Shroud would appear to rise up from whatever casket in which it was stored.

This was a particularly remarkable discovery because it made perfect sense of an isolated and otherwise puzzling description by a French Crusader, Robert de Clari, who toured Constantinople in 1203, just months before the city's ruthless sack by his fellow Crusaders the following year. In his memoirs of this tour de Clari wrote that among

FACING PAGE: *(Left) An Eastern Orthodox icon, preserved at Meteora, Greece, showing a 'Christ of Pity' or 'Extreme Humility' figure appearing to rise out of the tomb in a strikingly Shroud-like fashion. Although this particular example dates from the seventeenth century, it is one of many depictions of this scene in Eastern and Western art, some dating back to the twelfth century, which seem to embody a memory of special occasions in which the Shroud was made to 'rise up' from its casket in precisely this manner.*

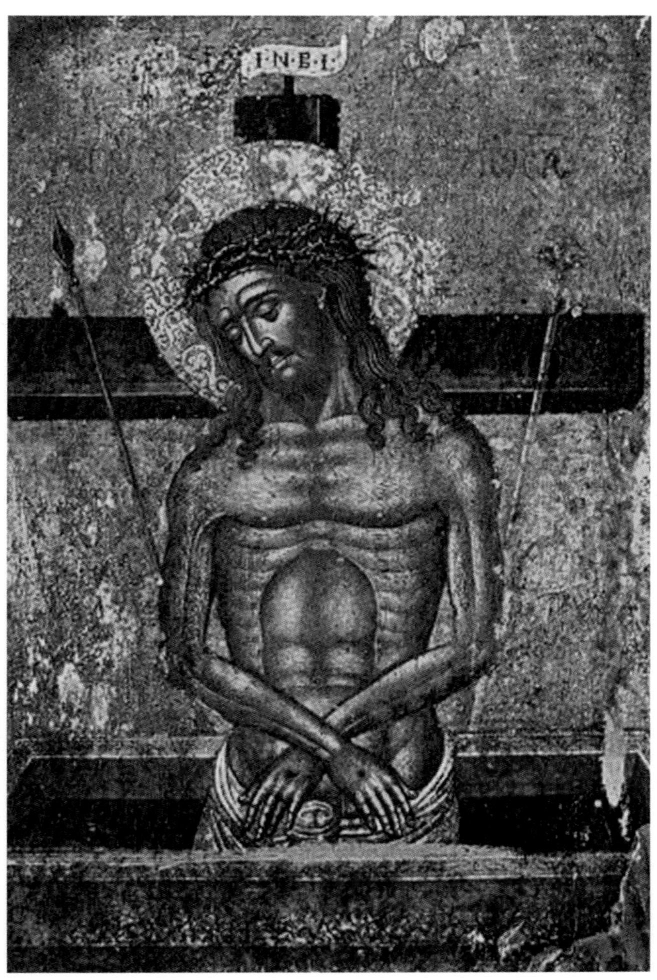

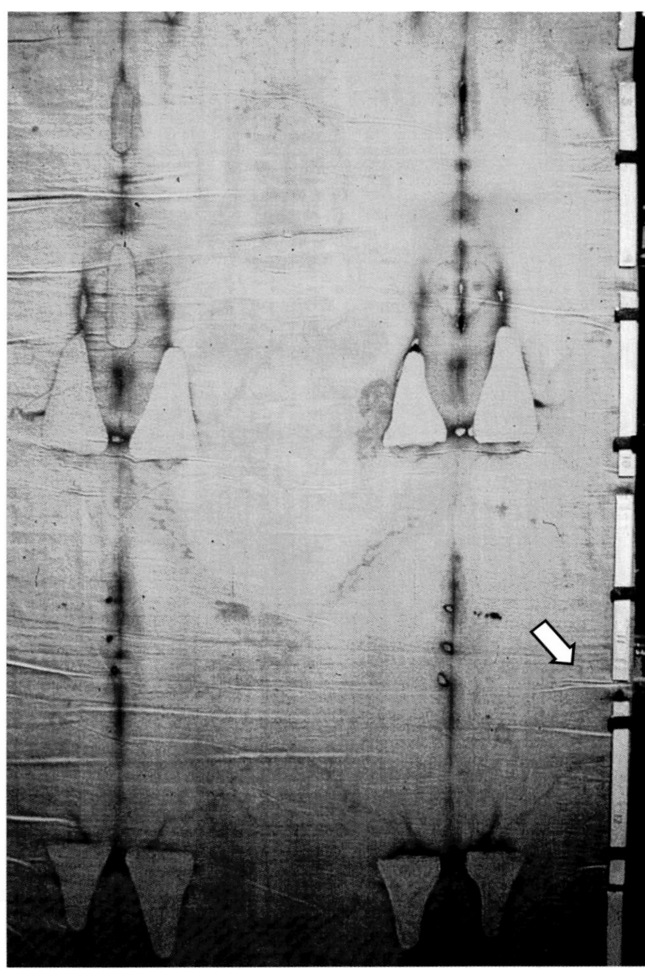

ABOVE RIGHT: *Raking light photography showing up innumerable creases on the Shroud's surface. Note the particularly pronounced band of lines (arrowed) at Dr John Jackson's fold point F, which he identifies as deriving from the folding apparatus used in the Byzantine period.*

Constantinople's many marvels, 'there was another church which was called My Lady St Mary of Blachernae, where there was the shroud in which Our Lord had been wrapped, which every Friday *raised itself upright*, so that one could see the figure of Our Lord on it.'[13]

This, it should be noted, comprises a clear, eyewitness account of a shroud of Jesus with a full body imprint on it being exhibited in Constantinople over fifty years before the earliest date ascribed to the Shroud by radiocarbon dating (1260). Historically, the problem with this reference has always been that it stands isolated, with no supportive references of earlier, similar showings of this shroud in Constantinople, nor any information concerning how and when it arrived in the city. This is disturbing, since the latter tended to be well documented even in the darkest of the Dark Ages. The arrival of the Edessa cloth in Constantinople in AD 944, for instance, was marked by much rejoicing, elaborate ceremonial and the institution of a feast day on August 16, which the Eastern Orthodox Church celebrates to this very day.

But, if the de Clari 'shroud' with its 'figure of Our Lord' was the same as the cloth otherwise recorded as the Edessa cloth, all makes perfect sense. It also accords well with versions of the Abgar story dating from after the Edessa cloth's transfer to Constantinople which suddenly and otherwise inexplicably describe Jesus as having 'impressed . . . a most beautiful imprint of . . . [his] *entire body*' on the Edessa cloth.[14] As first noted by the Italian scholar Gino Zaninotto, and corroborated by French Dominican Père Dubarle of Paris,[15] another account, by the tenth-century church official Gregory Referendarius, specifically refers to the Edessa cloth as including Jesus' lance-wound among its imprints – totally illogical *unless* the cloth was a shroud.

Effectively it is as if, not long after the Edessa cloth's arrival in Constantinople, its 'doubled-in-four' arrangement was undone and the full Shroud body imprint revealed. Arguably the cloth was then remounted so that on very special occasions, and normally before only a very privileged few (for in Byzantine thought the body of Christ was not for everyday viewing), it could appear to rise from its casket. This would readily explain the popularity, both during the later Byzantine period and in the early Middle Ages, of icons and panel paintings variously entitled the 'King of Glory', the 'Christ of Pity' or 'Man of Sorrows' which depict Jesus rising from a casket-like 'tomb'. Several of these represent him with his hands crossed over the genitals in the characteristically Shroud-like manner. It is also notable that from this later period the Byzantine Easter liturgy began to include so-called *epitaphioi* cloths sumptuously embroidered with very Shroud-like representations of Jesus laid out in death, a particularly fine example of which is preserved in the Museum of the Serbian Orthodox Church in Belgrade. As has been pointed out by American Shroud researcher Fr Kim Dreisbach, and developed by Indiana history professor Dan Scavone, some of these embroideries even reproduce the Shroud's otherwise rare and distinctive herringbone weave.[16]

ABOVE: *A thirteenth-century Eastern Orthodox* epitaphios *of King Milutin Uros, suggesting a retained memory of the Shroud's one-time ownership by the Byzantines of Constantinople (below).*

The Los Angeles artist Isabel Piczek has further noted that many later Byzantine full-length depictions of 'Jesus Enthroned' seem to embody further oddities to those noted by Paul Vignon, as if they were done by artists who now had some awareness of the Shroud's full-length figure. Thus she has noted how example after example features a raised shoulder, the very first feature that, it may be recalled, caused me discomfort on my adopting the Shroud man's burial pose. Intriguingly, according to St Bernard of Clairvaux (1090–1153), Jesus' 'greatest unrecorded suffering' was an injury to his shoulder, assumed to have been from carrying the cross.[17] Several Byzantine works also feature the markedly distended abdomen that we earlier noted was demonstrably caused by the crucifixion process, and which Isabel Piczek sees on the Shroud.

Perhaps most pertinent of all, however, is a discovery made by the distinguished French medical expert the late Prof. Jérôme Lejeune[18] from

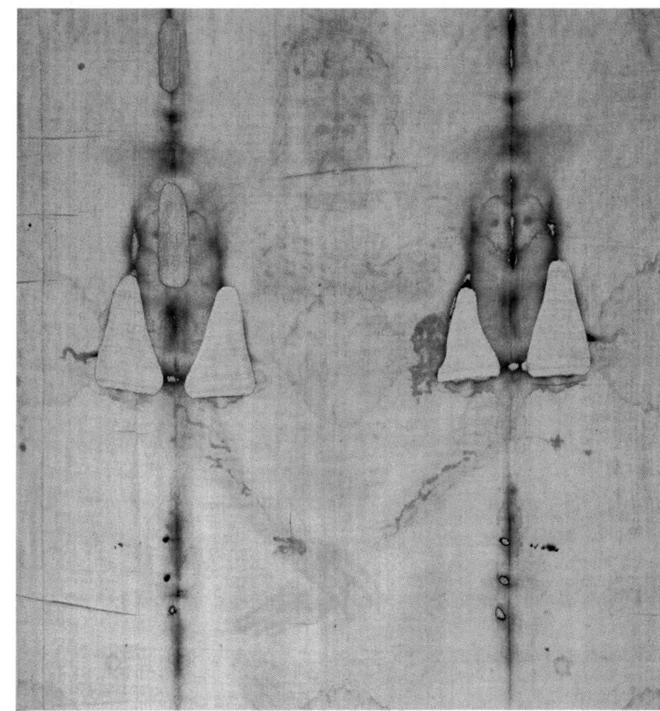

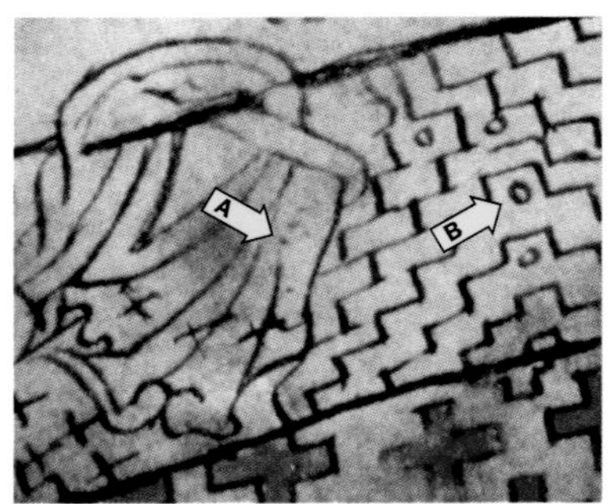

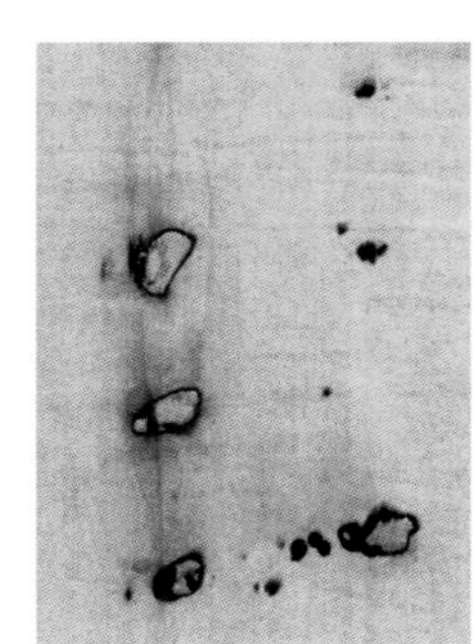

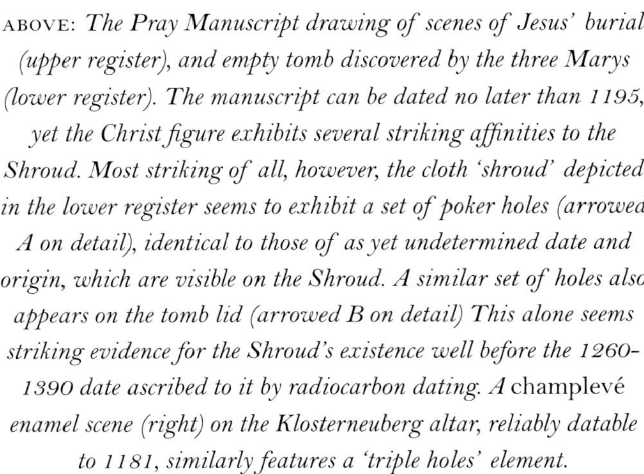

ABOVE: *The Pray Manuscript drawing of scenes of Jesus' burial (upper register), and empty tomb discovered by the three Marys (lower register). The manuscript can be dated no later than 1195, yet the Christ figure exhibits several striking affinities to the Shroud. Most striking of all, however, the cloth 'shroud' depicted in the lower register seems to exhibit a set of poker holes (arrowed A on detail), identical to those of as yet undetermined date and origin, which are visible on the Shroud. A similar set of holes also appears on the tomb lid (arrowed B on detail) This alone seems striking evidence for the Shroud's existence well before the 1260-1390 date ascribed to it by radiocarbon dating. A* champlevé *enamel scene (right) on the Klosterneuberg altar, reliably datable to 1181, similarly features a 'triple holes' element.*

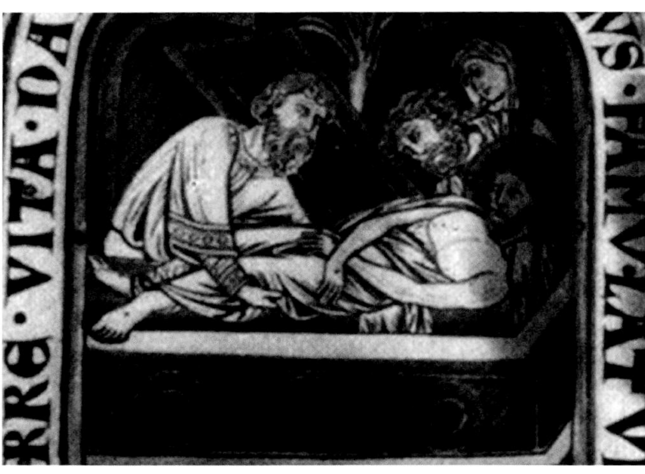

LEFT: *The Shroud-like Templar panel painting discovered at Templecombe, England, during the Second World War. This represents the prime clue that the Knights Templar may secretly have owned the Shroud during the period immediately following the capture of Constantinople and up to their suppression in 1307.*

FACING PAGE ABOVE: *The Templar Order's two highest dignitaries, Grand Master Jacques de Molay and Master of Normandy Geoffrey de Charny, being burnt at the stake in 1314. It was one generation later that the Shroud as we know it today mysteriously emerged in the possession of another Geoffrey de Charny, a French knight whose son Geoffrey II de Charny is depicted in the drawing (below right) of his tombstone at Froidmont, destroyed during the Second World War. Geoffrey II de Charny was reported to have exhibited the Shroud with his own hands, claiming it as the true Shroud of Jesus.*

studies of a very Shroud-like figure that is one of the illustrations in a Hungarian manuscript, the so-called Pray Manuscript of Budapest, datable to *c.* 1192–5.[19] I had first come across this manuscript illustration in the 1960s and had immediately been struck by the figure's very accurate Shroud-like pose and similarly Shroud-like total nudity. I had also seen in the 'Discovery of the Empty Tomb' illustration below this that there was a cloth depicted on the tomb lid, clearly intended to represent Jesus' shroud discarded after the Resurrection. But it was Prof. Lejeune who on a personal visit to the National Szechenyi Library in Budapest, where the manuscript is housed, spotted several crucial features that had escaped me.

First, the Shroud-like depiction of Jesus' dead body features four fingers, but no thumbs, exactly as on the Shroud. Second, just over the dead Jesus' right eye in the manuscript illustration is a single bloodstain in exactly the same position as the distinctive three-shaped one on the Shroud. Third, and not least, the 'shroud' cloth lying on the tomb lid clearly bears a group of holes that are just like the Shroud's so-called 'poker holes' – damage marks that, whatever their causation (we noted that Dr Mechthild Flury-Lemberg suggested some liquid spillage), would have been the Shroud's most distinctive feature prior to the 1532 fire. And another, similar set of marks can be seen on the tomb lid, along with a pattern again distinctively reminiscent of the Shroud's herringbone. As a pointer to the Shroud's existence as early as the twelfth century, the evidence of the Pray Manuscript is therefore strong.

If, then, the Turin Shroud was indeed the same as the 'face-cloth' of Edessa which, on its passing to Constantinople, gradually became revealed as a full-body shroud, then, despite the radiocarbon dating, we have a

credible history for the Shroud from the death of Jesus around AD 30 to its disappearance from Constantinople in 1204. This leaves just the period from 1204 to its appearance in the hands of the de Charny family in the 1350s to be explained.

There are some compelling clues. For instance, during the Second World War a most Shroud-like panel painting was found enigmatically hidden in the ceiling of the outhouse of a cottage at Templecombe in south-west England. Since Templecombe was a stronghold of the rich and secretive Crusader Knights Templar, who are independently credited with having worshipped some kind of bearded male head at secret chapter meetings, one inference is that the Shroud had fallen into the hands of this order, and the Templecombe panel painting was a copy of the original Shroud which they held, for a period at least, in France.

Buttressing this, when the Templars were suppressed by France's King Philip the Fair on idolatry and other charges in 1307, one of their two highest dignitaries is recorded to have been a Geoffrey de Charny, Templar Master of Normandy, an individual whom King Philip ordered to be burnt at the stake in Paris seven years later, along with the Order's Grand Master, Jacques de Molay. As may be recalled, the Shroud's first known European owner, one generation later, was another Geoffrey de Charny.

Although surviving records are insufficient to establish a definite family link between these two men, certainly an inheritance in such highly charged circumstances would explain the relatively humble de Charny family's reluctance to explain exactly how they had come to acquire the Shroud. For it cannot be emphasized enough what unlikely owners they were. In the thirteenth century King Louis IX of France built the magnificent Sainte Chapelle, Paris, to house a very uninspiring twist of thorn branch reputed to have been Jesus' crown of thorns. By contrast, Geoffrey I de Charny, the Shroud's first known owner, was the squire of a tiny village who, when captured by the English, could not afford to pay his own ransom. And he had to get a grant from his king to fund the building of a very modest wooden church that was the Shroud's first known European home. It was unheard of for so relatively lowly an individual to own so priceless a relic, hence the utter disbelief – among the normally relic-gullible people of the Middle Ages – which the first showings of the Shroud are known to have aroused.

Overall, then, although the reconstruction just outlined is very far from proven, the Shroud's history before the 1350s is hardly the blank that we might expect if it really had been 'cunningly painted' some time between 1260 and 1390 as indicated by the radiocarbon dating.

But in any event the Shroud history, or lack of it, is not its most daunting mystery. That is the question of how its image got there. For if the key to the Shroud's history hangs on just one hypothesis, around the nature of its image there revolve literally dozens.

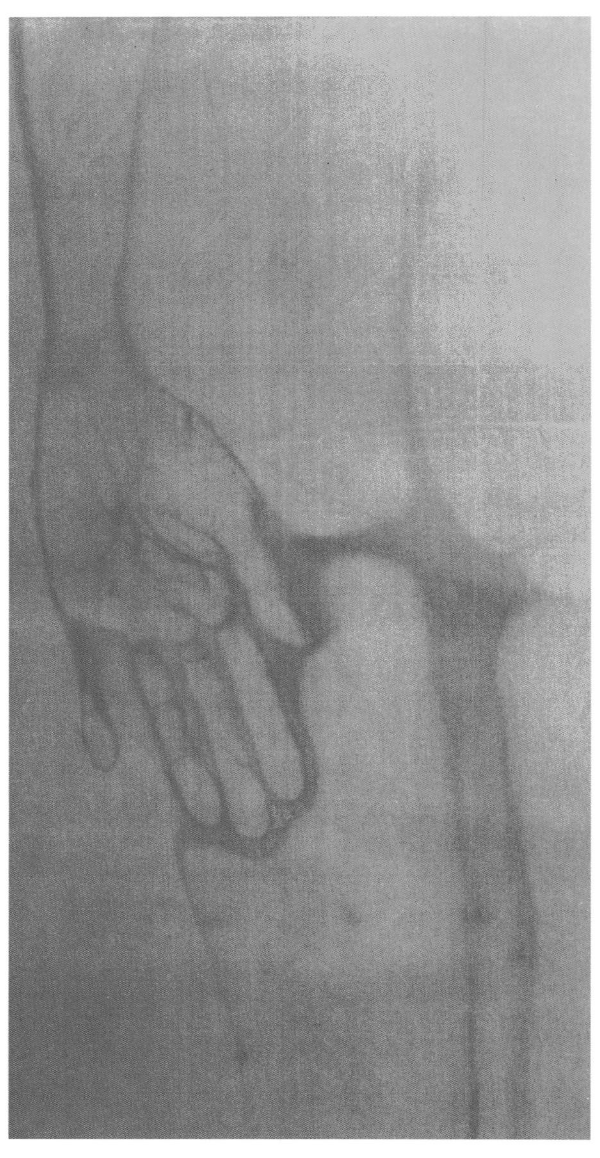

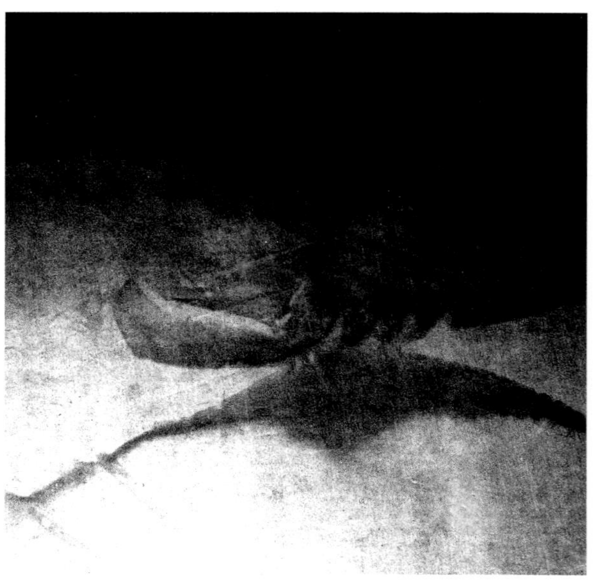

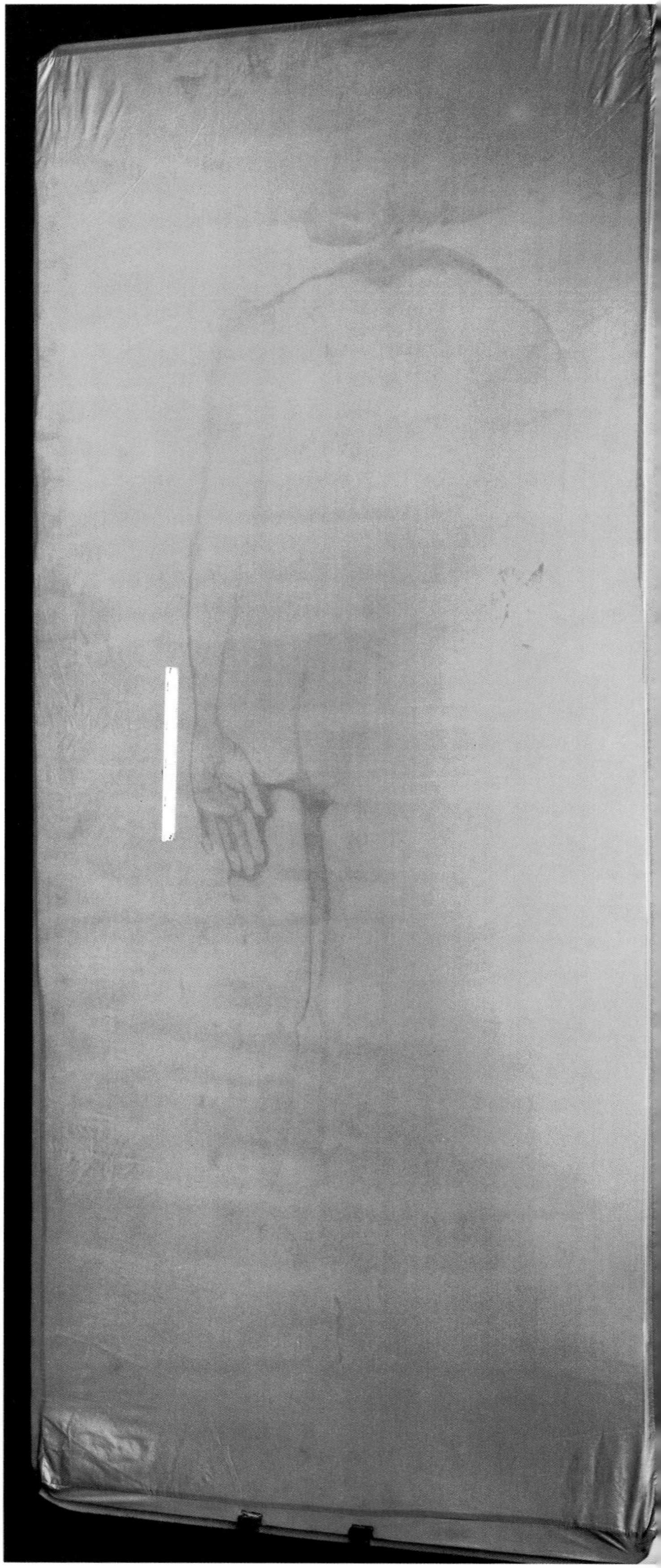

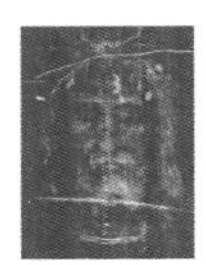

CHAPTER 9

'How the image got there remains a mystery.'

(STURP scientists Larry Schwalbe and Ray Rogers, 1982[1])

As NOTED at the beginning of the last chapter, human bodies, whether they are alive or dead, do not normally create meaningful imprints of themselves on cloth. Not least of the difficulties raised by the Shroud, therefore, is its lack of any obvious parallel, ancient or modern, to which it can be related – bar one *partial* modern-day exception that at least deserves mention.

That exception appeared on the morning of 9 March 1981, in the otherwise unexceptional setting of an English suburban hospice, Jospice International's facility at Thornton, on the outskirts of Liverpool. In the early hours of that morning, after a stay of just eleven days, there died of cancer of the pancreas a pleasant, forty-four-year-old called Les Hunter. In accordance with normal practice, the undertakers took his body away in the hospital sheet on which he had been lying, after which it fell to hospice nurse Patricia Oliver to tidy up. Discarding the pyjamas that Les had been wearing, and noticing what looked like a stain on the nylon cover to his mattress, she tried scrubbing at it without success, then suddenly went cold with disbelief.

For, as she looked more carefully, she saw that in fact the stain was the image of a hand, palm upwards, but so precisely imprinted on the taut fabric that she could even discern its crease lines. To its right, even clearer, was the divide of naked buttocks and the upper part of legs, while winding upwards from it was the outline of an arm and shoulders, topped by the shadow of a jaw, distinctively Les's jaw, awkwardly twisted face downwards. One of many weird features was that, although Les had died wearing his pyjamas, the image was quite unmistakably of his naked body. Furthermore there had been a sheet between his body and the mattress cover, and in death his head had rested on a pillow. Yet to all appearances something of him had passed through the sheet, pyjamas and even the thickness of the pillow to imprint with striking clarity on the mattress cover. Impossible?

FACING PAGE: *Detail of the imprint of hospice patient Les's hand (far left above) that appeared on the nylon cover of the mattress (main picture) on which he had been lying at the time of his death in March 1981. A detail of Les's lower jaw (far left below), which seems to have been awkwardly facing backwards, into his pillow, at the time of his death. The fringes of hairline can also be seen. As noted by Fr O'Leary (above), who has retained the cover, the image is clearly more linear than that of the Shroud.*

As an imprint created by a dead body, the Jospice mattress cover is by no means a perfect parallel to the Shroud. Not least, it is less complete, more linear, its stains are of the body's shadows rather than its highlights, and it lacks photographic negative-type tonal subtleties. But of its authenticity there can be no possible doubt. At the invitation of the hospice's founder, Fr Francis O'Leary, I personally examined it in May 1986, subsequently introducing Fr O'Leary to the leading British pathologist James Malcolm Cameron, Professor of Forensic Medicine at the London Hospital Medical School, and also to the American medical examiner Dr Fred Zugibe. Despite exhaustive tests, and the scrutiny of a BBC television programme,[2] no comprehensively meaningful explanation of the imprint was ever arrived at.

Another phenomenon which parallels the Shroud image is the Volckringer-type plant images mentioned in Chapter 6. Despite the fact that there are many specimens in herbariums all over the world, and these are far more accessible than the Shroud, exactly how their surprisingly photographic imprints form remains far from perfectly explained. Whatever the nature of the Shroud, the authenticity of the Shroud-like images that dead plants create of themselves is beyond dispute.

These examples aside, any explanation of how the Shroud's image was formed depends greatly upon what prior opinion is held by those doing the explaining. As is generally understood from examinations such as that by STURP, the Shroud image's key characteristics are a monochromatic coloration, the semblance of a 'photograph' (particularly when seen in negative), some semblance of X-ray properties, an absence of brushstrokes, no signs of its having been painted or dyed, a lack of any directionality to the lighting, 'true' three-dimensionality when seen via VP-8 and relative stability when subjected to water, heat and some chemicals. Whether the Shroud is authentic or a forgery, these characteristics somehow need to be accounted for in any explanation which is offered, though an immediate difficulty is that not all the characteristics are universally accepted.

Thus, as we noted in Chapter 5, the Chicago microanalyst Dr Walter McCrone continues to insist that paint particles are responsible for what the eye sees as the Shroud's 'body' and 'blood' images. In his explanation for how the Shroud image was formed, McCrone wholeheartedly agrees with the fourteenth-century bishop of Troyes, who claimed that the Shroud was 'cunningly painted', envisaging that the unknown mediaeval painter:

> . . . carefully studied the New Testament, sources of information on the crucifixion and other artists' paintings of Christ. He then thought about a shroud image in terms of a dark tomb. Instead of the usual portrait with normal light and shadow, he assumed that the image could only be produced by body contact with the cloth. He painted directly on the cloth to image the body-contact points (forehead, bridge of nose, cheekbones, moustache, beard, etc.), over the entire body, front and back. This automatically creates a negative image; areas that normally catch available light and appear bright, like the bridge of the nose, would instead all be dark with a paint.

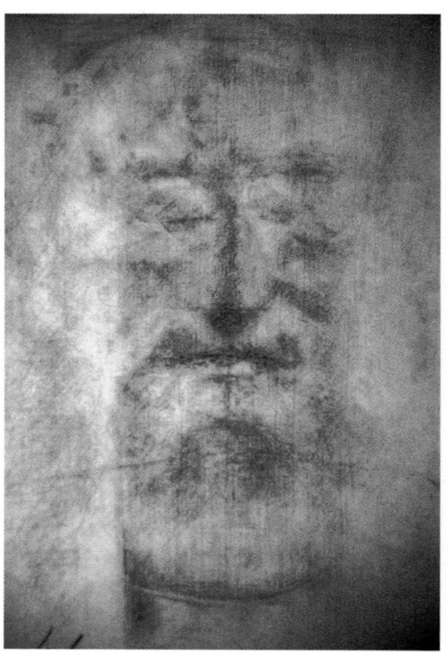

ABOVE LEFT: *Replication of the Shroud face as painted for Dr Walter McCrone by professional artist Walter Sanford, with (above right) how this appears in negative, and the true Shroud negative (right) for comparison purposes.*

LEFT: *The imprint of a pressed plant from the author's collection, as discovered in a guidebook of the 1970s. The plant has been displaced from its original position to show that it has imprinted either side of the sheets of paper covering it.*

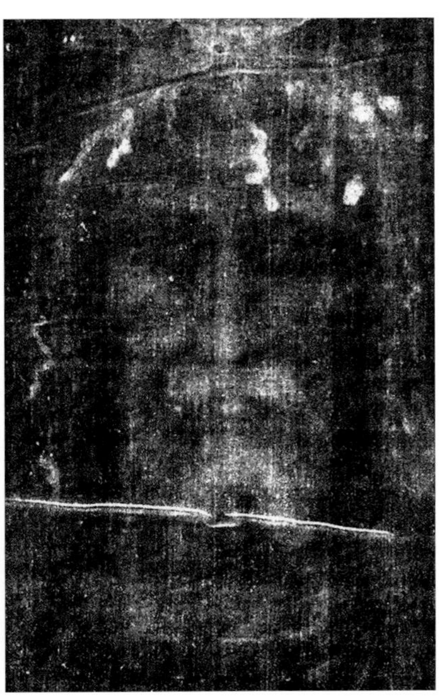

However, those areas appear bright on a photographic negative. He decorated the body with blood-stains as required by the New Testament descriptions. These he rendered dark on the Shroud, hence they form a photographic positive image superimposed on the otherwise negative Shroud body image.[3]

However straightforward and plausible this might sound when expressed just in words, when anyone is confronted with the actual task of creating on 437 cm of untreated linen an image with the Shroud's tonal subtleties it is an entirely different matter, as I can confirm from my own very limited attempts. Nor is this just my experience. When in the late 1970s the British artist John Weston was given the task of copying the Shroud tone by tone for the TV documentary *The Silent Witness* he found himself so deeply impressed that he became convinced of the Shroud's genuineness. The crudity of the dozens of life-sized copies of the Shroud painted during centuries after the fourteenth century show just how difficult otherwise competent artists of the Renaissance and later eras found performing this task.

In order to demonstrate his claims Dr Walter McCrone specially commissioned an artist, Walter Sanford, to paint just the Shroud face the way that he thought a medieval artist might have done it. Because it was painted in iron oxide, the painting's coloration is significantly redder than that of the Shroud's image,[4] and despite the artist's best efforts to emulate the Shroud's tones, it still looks humanly created. Furthermore, although his lavishly illustrated *Judgement Day for the Turin Shroud*,[5] did not show how Sanford's version might look in negative, Barrie and I are able to do this here. You must judge this for yourself, but be assured that, had the Shroud's 'hidden negative' been of anything like this mediocrity, then neither of us would ever have given the subject a second glance.

None the less, in support of McCrone's 'medieval artist' hypothesis, and in an attempt to account for the Shroud's 'blood' stains' medical accuracy, Baltimore art professor Gary Vikan has recently suggested that these latter stains might have been inspired by lay brotherhoods of *penitentes*, medieval imitators of St Francis of Assisi, who went to great extremes mortifying themselves, even to the extent of self-crucifixion.[6] To support this idea Vikan has cited a bloody crucifix that was carved for Spanish American *penitentes* by the late nineteenth- and early twentieth-century sculptor José Benito Ortega. The problem is that not only does this crucifix date from six centuries later than the period of the Shroud's possible forgery, its anatomy and its bloodflows are so crude that not even a six-year-old child would have been deceived by them.

Arguably one of the best-considered hypotheses in favour of the 'painting' scenario has come from the Kentucky forensic anthropologist Dr Emily Craig, who favours the medieval artist having used what she calls a 'dry transfer' technique.[7] Having listened to a lecture on the Shroud by Tennessee textile expert Professor Randall Bresee, Craig became inspired to create on ordinary white drawing paper a charcoal portrait of a fellow graduate student's face, working with a dry brush to indicate in shades of dark those areas that she would normally have left light, and vice versa.

Thus far her methodology was little different from that of McCrone's Walter Sanford. But then, taking a piece of cloth the same size as the paper sketch, she laid this face down on the cloth and proceeded to rub the back of it in much the same way that transfers and Letraset-type lettering are created. Onto the cloth there was duly transferred a left-to-right reversed imprint that had lost all indications of her original brush-strokes. Having obtained this, Craig did what McCrone omitted: she photographed the imprint in order to see what it would look like in negative. In her opinion the result represents a 'perfect' parallel to the Shroud's hidden 'photograph', one which she went on to make even more so by repeating the procedure using iron oxide instead of charcoal.

But just how 'perfect' is it? Certainly, as a 'transfer', it lacks obvious brush-strokes, but even as a face only, as distinct from all the double-imprint complexities of the Shroud proper, it echoes Sanford's version in exhibiting all those modelling and contour infelicities that betray the hand of a human illustrator. The coloration is also again too red. Barrie also points out that, because of Craig's background as a professional medical illustrator specializing in reconstructing faces from skeletal remains, she has far more knowledge of medical matters and 3-D properties than anyone in medieval times could possibly have had. She is also unable to offer any tenable explanation for how the Shroud's bloodstains could have got onto the cloth before the body imprint.[8]

But what about someone in the Middle Ages perhaps having temporarily 'invented' a pioneering form of photography in order to make a convincing fake of the Shroud image? In 1994 the London journalist Lynn Picknett, in partnership with systems analyst Clive Prince,[9] created quite a stir by suggesting that Leonardo da Vinci faked the Shroud by this means. The small fact of history that the Shroud was being exhibited a hundred years before Leonardo was born, was overlooked by the media who had great fun with the theory. (As I was told by one British TV researcher, 'But it's such a good story!'). As for their version of 'how Leonardo did it' Picknett and Prince used a sculpted head to produce a facial imprint on cloth, then daubed this with fake 'blood', and since it looked passably photographic when viewed in negative, *voilà*, that must have been how Leonardo made the Shroud.

A British artist, Caroline Rye, went one further, by building a three-section, room-sized box, 'The Turin Machine', 9 m long and billed as 'the largest pinhole camera in the world'. First presented publicly at Bristol's

TOP LEFT: *The dry powder sketch that is the starting point of the replication by Emily Craig (seen demonstrating at far right) of how the Shroud image was 'cunningly painted' by an artist.*

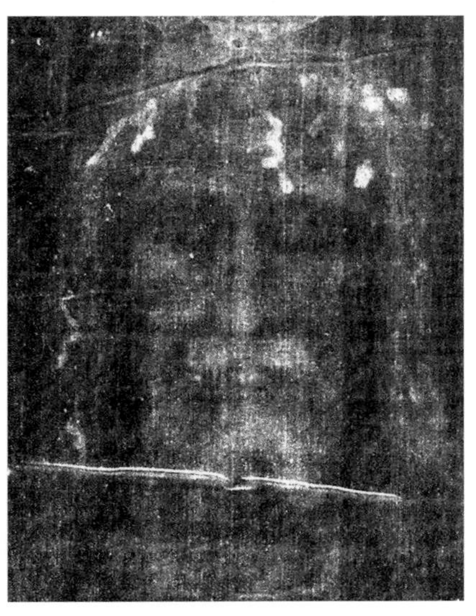

TOP RIGHT: *The image created on cloth when the original powder drawing is burnished onto this, dry-transfer style. The resultant image has some of the Shroud's characteristics, such as lack of outlines, but, when seen in negative (below left), clearly lacks the photographic qualities of the Shroud negative seen above.*

RIGHT: *Proof that the Shroud was not produced by Leonardo da Vinci in 1492. A pilgrim's amulet of the 1350s, datable from the two coats of arms, clearly depicts an exposition of the same Shroud we know today.*

Arnolfini Gallery in December 1996, and currently ongoing, this comprises a brilliantly lit first section in which Rye stands naked, coated in white stage paint, for up to six hours at a time, while in a second section, totally dark except for a pinhole, a light-sensitized cloth (or 'shroud') gradually 'receives' her upside-down image through this. In the box's third, similarly darkened, section spectators are invited one by one to view what they can of this interesting process. The venture is funded by the English and Scottish Arts Councils and Rye insists that its purpose is 'solely . . . art', using 'a live body, modern photographic chemicals, polyester material and electric light', rather than its being concerned 'with proving or disproving how an image might have been created on the Turin Shroud.'[10] None the less it at least has the merit of producing a full-frontal body image on a cloth 'negative' that translates into a convincing-looking positive 'photograph'.

Altogether the most authoritative approach to the idea of the Shroud's image having been made using some lost medieval photographic method has come from a South African art professor, Nicholas Allen.[11] Basing his method on a life-sized, light-proof room or 'camera', not dissimilar to Caroline Rye's 'Turin Machine', Allen has posited the use of quartz for a lens, silver salts for photographic emulsion and urine or ammonia for a fixative, all materials readily enough available during the Middle Ages. According to Allen's scenario either an actual dead body or a plaster cast of one was suspended for several days in strong sunshine in front of the light-proof room, while inside this room hung a 'Shroud' coated in silver salts and folded in two. Upon the room's quartz lens being opened up, the image first of one side of the suspended body would have been projected onto one half of the cloth. Then someone would have had to enter the room to 'expose' the cloth's second half to the lens, while at the same time the body outside would have had to be turned to face the opposite direction. Over a further period of days the image of the back of the body would thereby have been chemically received on the cloth likewise. All that then remained would have been for someone to enter the still light-fast room and 'fix' the two images using the urine/ammonia fixative, after which an image-bearing 'Shroud' would then have been ready for showing to the world.

Based on this method, Professor Allen, to his very considerable credit, has produced an undeniably convincing-looking 'negative' on cloth of the two sides of the body, one that represents by far the best replication of the Shroud's hidden 'photograph' that anyone has come up with to date. Yet even so, it nowhere near establishes that this was how the Shroud actually was produced in the Middle Ages. As Barrie points out, images that have been created using light as the imaging mechanism, as in any type of photographic process, display a lighting directionality obvious to even the least experienced viewer. In Allen's 'negative' there are deep shadows

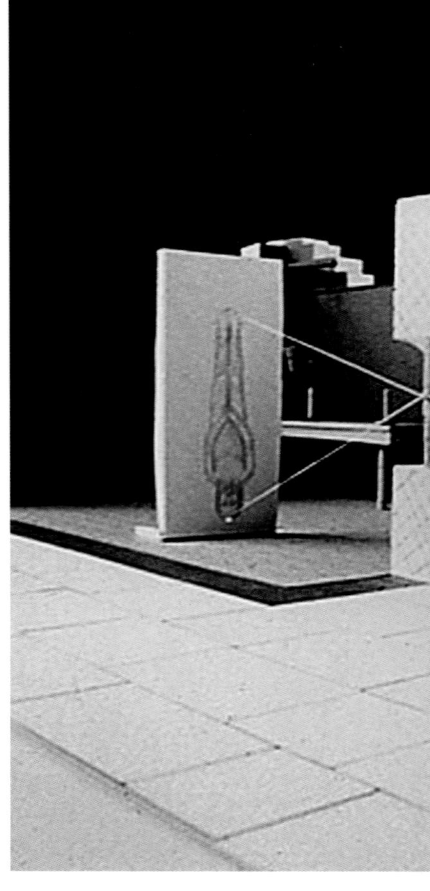

ABOVE: *Prof. Nicholas Allen's reconstructed 'camera' for producing the Shroud image, using basic 'photographic' materials and knowledge that would have been available in the Middle Ages. These included a light-proof room, or 'camera obscura', a quartz 'lens' set into an 'aperture' of this room, and a cloth coated in light-sensitive silver salts. In effect, the Shroud was the 'film' inside the camera obscura.*

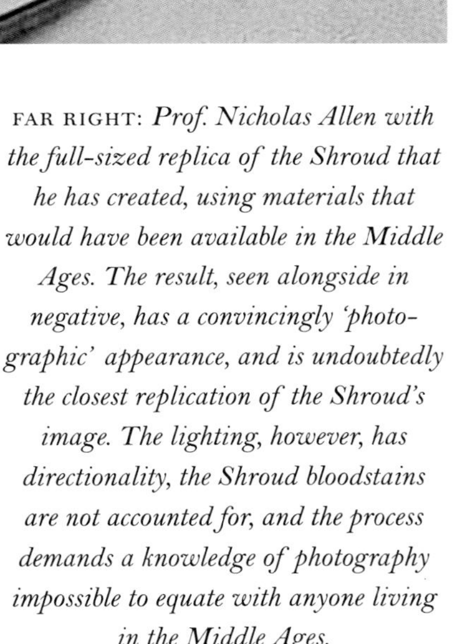

FAR RIGHT: *Prof. Nicholas Allen with the full-sized replica of the Shroud that he has created, using materials that would have been available in the Middle Ages. The result, seen alongside in negative, has a convincingly 'photographic' appearance, and is undoubtedly the closest replication of the Shroud's image. The lighting, however, has directionality, the Shroud bloodstains are not accounted for, and the process demands a knowledge of photography impossible to equate with anyone living in the Middle Ages.*

under the nose and chin and in the eye sockets, from which it is clear that the light came from almost directly above the model's vertical image. Yet in the case of the man of the Shroud's image there is absolutely no directionality. Furthermore, whereas the edges of Allen's model are very distinct and sharp, as one would expect in a properly focused photograph, the Shroud man's body image has no such edges. Most importantly of all, Allen's version fails to exhibit the 3-D characteristics of the Shroud image which we noted earlier, characteristics which simply cannot be achieved using light or any other modern photographic means.

Even if all these serious difficulties were set aside, the Allen method demands a distance of 9m from 'body' to 'shroud'. This most certainly cannot account for the Shroud's 'blood' stains, which can only have been created either by direct contact with a crucified dead body or by being artificially daubed on. And in the latter case an impressive array of international expertise attesting to the fact that the blood flows are medically convincing would have to be tossed aside as mere moonshine.

A further difficulty in the Allen method is that after the requisite several days of exposure to strong sunshine, any actual body would have lost all post-mortem stiffness and begun serious decomposition. As Barrie points out, this would have meant a considerable change in shape, any image thereupon becoming more of a misshapen blob rather than the perfectly formed image on the Shroud. Allen's fallback explanation is that a plaster cast of a full-sized body might have been used, something admittedly just within fourteenth-century capabilities. Yet, even if this were possible, the Allen method demands additionally that someone in the Middle Ages had an extraordinarily highly developed understanding of photography's principles, principles which took decades to evolve among several different innovators even during the nineteenth century. For any single medieval forger to have hit upon these and successfully developed them in so highly creative a way for an object as large and complex as the Shroud, only to abandon them immediately, beggars belief.

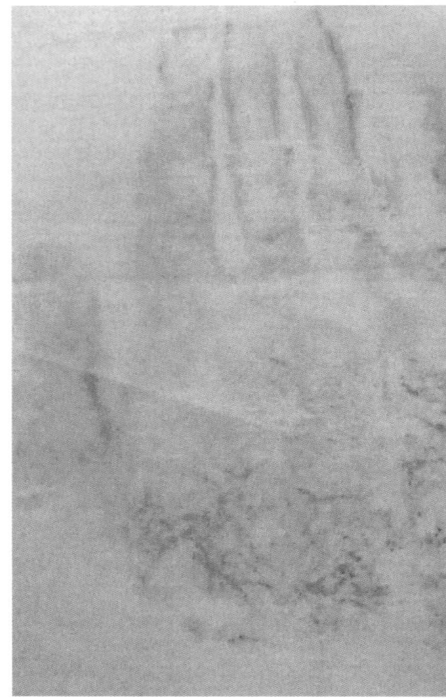

So, if these scenarios are the best that anyone can come up with in favour of the forgery argument, how much more convincing are the explanations of those who believe the image to have derived from a crucified body? It immediately needs to be made clear that there is one scenario by which both the Shroud's 1260–1390 radiocarbon dating and the pollen evidence indicative of its Near Eastern derivation can still be accepted. As conceived by the British physician Dr Michael Straiton,[12] a Crusader battling the Saracens in the Holy Land might have been captured, scourged and crucified in deliberate mockery of Jesus' crucifixion, and his body then wrapped in a sheet and left in hot sunshine. When the imprint that was thereby formed was discovered, the cloth was sold to the highest bidder. It is an interesting hypothesis, and if Straiton were able properly to demonstrate the image-making process, and if before 1260–1390 there were absolutely no record of the existence of any shroud-like imprint of Jesus, it might be the best available to us. But neither condition pertains. The same objection applies to the claim by authors Christopher Knight and Robert Lomas that the Shroud was used to wrap Templar Grand Master Jacques de Molay after his purported crucifixion as a mode of torture by the Inquisition,[13] a theory for which there is no historical substance whatsoever.

Rather more plausible, and in this instance neutral on the issue of the Shroud's date, is a suggestion by the respected British physicist, Dr Allan Mills of the University of Leicester. Intrigued by the Volckringer-type plant-image phenomenon, Mills hypothesizes that these images may have been generated by the release of a gas molecule, singlet oxygen, triggered by the trauma that the plant suffers through being cut and killed before its being 'enshrouded' between sheets of paper. From this it was but a short step for him to suggest that something of the same process may have happened to the body of the highly traumatized individual wrapped in the Shroud. He shares the opinion of the STURP team that the Shroud is no painting.[14]

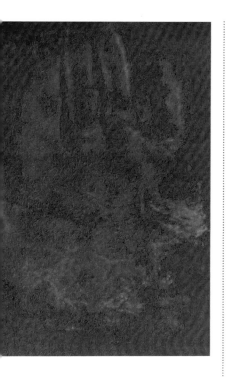

ABOVE: *A hand imprint created by Prof. Stephen Mattingly using a culture of skin bacteria. He suggests that the skin of anyone crucified would have been unusually 'rich' with skin bacteria. The method is, however, essentially a 'contact' one, failing to account for the Shroud's striking three-dimensionality.*

Intriguingly, this is not a million miles removed from a compelling new hypothesis for the Shroud's imprint, emanating from Prof. Stephen Mattingly of the University of Texas, whom we earlier described advocating a microbiological 'biofilm' as having skewed the Shroud's radiocarbon date (see Chapter 7). As we saw, even the cleanest hands are covered with bacterial micro-organisms that can migrate to fresh surfaces with every contact. In the case of the man of the Shroud, if his sufferings resembled the traumas described of Jesus in the Christian gospels, then we can be confident that his skin would have been anything but clean. The gospels and the Shroud alike attest to facial bruisings, pulpy contusions caused by the vicious scourging, abrasions from repeated falls in Jerusalem's streets, copious sweating from the suspension on the cross and much localized blood, serum and plasma from penetrative injuries to head, forearms, feet and chest. All these skin-surface traumas would have created what microbiologists term a 'rich culture medium', one causing the skin's ever-present bacteria to accelerate into reproductive overdrive and grow 'with the capacity for reproducing every thirty minutes or so'. As envisaged by Mattingly, the entire skin surface of the body laid in the Shroud would have been 'highly sticky' with such bacteria, with the accompanying unpleasantness of a bacteria-generated odour that Mattingly calls 'the smell of death'.

By way of demonstration of this hypothesis, Mattingly has taken small specimens of the skin bacterium *Staphylococcus epidermis*, grown them in a liquid culture medium[15] to replicate the man of the Shroud's skin condition, then painted six layers onto his own hand. After pressing his hand lightly onto a clean linen cloth and keeping it in position for thirty minutes, followed by some mild incubation, a clear yellowish imprint of his hand formed, needing only a quick 'cook' to kill off the bacteria and permanently fix it.

According to Mattingly, this imprint derives from fatty acids and pigments produced by the bacteria that had been on his hand before fixing killed them off, and although it is significantly yellower than the Shroud imprint as observable today, this is readily attributable to the sort of fading through time which is to be expected of organic matter. Why such imprints are not seen more often is because most people who die and get wrapped in shrouds have not been crucified and allowed to live for an extended period of time coated with their own body fluids. Furthermore, perhaps one of the experiment's most impressive features is that the imprint produced exhibits much of that same skeletal X-ray character of the Shroud's image. As Mattingly explains:

> As you cover your hand or whatever in a thick coating of your own skin bacteria . . . the skin becomes tight and shrinks around the bone. This becomes even more apparent when you remove the dried

linen from the skin. If we could suffer extreme dehydration, as did the Man of the Shroud, the outline of the underlying bones would be even more apparent.[16]

Yet, despite the undoubted impressiveness of Mattingly's experiment, as Barrie points out, it demands that there was some direct physical contact between the cloth and the body to allow the bacteria to transfer, whereas, as John Jackson's and other cloth-drape experiments have shown, parts of the Shroud image have registered as if transmitted by the body at up to 4 cm distance from any contact with the cloth's surface. Since only such a process, avoiding the distortions that would arise from direct contact, can account for the Shroud image's photographic tonality and convincingly three-dimensional characteristics, it suggests some kind of radiant energy emanating from the body, and acting at a distance, as the more cogent scenario.

The number of theories advanced and experiments undertaken to try to explain this have been legion. In the 1960s the British author Geoffrey Ashe, noting the Shroud image's scorch-like appearance, tried heating an ornamental brass and placing it close to a piece of linen, to create a passably convincing scorch imprint. At first sight this might suggest that the imprint could have been created from some super-heated statue, a hypothesis actually favoured by the Oxford laboratory's Prof. Hall.[17] However, it must be noted that the STURP scientific findings of 1978 conclusively showed that the Shroud imprint cannot be a simple scorch, since the indisputable scorch marks from the 1532 fire fluoresce whereas the body imprint does not.

So, given that one interpretation of Jesus' resurrection is a dematerialization of the atoms of his physical body, what about the Shroud's imprint having been caused by some kind of atomic radiation from this event? In the Second World War bombings of Hiroshima and Nagasaki, the intense light from the atomic bombs' fireballs imprinted eerie images of people and objects on walls. Yet, however compelling this might sound, it cannot be a valid parallel to the Shroud image, since in the bombing instances it was the people's bodies blocking the light which created permanent shadows on the walls behind them, whereas in the case of the Shroud the light would appear to have come from the body itself, which was responsible for its unique, non-directional, self-lighting characteristics.

Based on this kind of thinking, the Harvard physicist Dr Thomas J. Phillips[18], in the wake of the 1988 radiocarbon dating, made the intriguing suggestion that, had Jesus' claimed resurrection involved a radiation of neutrons, it could explain at a stroke both the Shroud's 'scorch' image and the skewing of its carbon 14 content. Dr John Jackson has elaborately theorized that the Shroud's image was formed when the cloth collapsed through a body that became 'mechanically transparent', arguably in the

ABOVE: *A 'flash' imprint of a hand-valve wheel left as a permanent shadow on the side of a gas tank, following the searing light of the atomic bomb dropped on Hiroshima during the Second World War.*

course of the resurrection of Jesus described in the Christian gospels, the body's internal structures thereby intervening to form the image.[19] Dr Thaddeus Trenn, director of the Science and Religion Course at the University of Toronto, Canada, has formulated a theory of 'weak dematerialization', whereby if some kind of energy were generated in the man of the Shroud's body to overcome the pion bonding holding the nucleons together, there would occur 'dematerialization associated with spontaneous pion decay'.[20] Former Kodak technician Kevin Moran, again favouring a 'resurrection' event, has spoken of the image-making process as the result of 'high-energy particles' being involved in a 'collision event at the absolute speed of light'.[21]

Yet the problem with all these 'nuclear' scenarios is that, invoking as they do Jesus' resurrection as a real historical event, they prompt such scientists as the Oxford radiocarbon-dating laboratory's Dr Robert Hedges to comment: 'If a supernatural explanation is to be proposed, it seems pointless to make any scientific measurement on the Shroud at all.'[22] Furthermore, as noted in Chapter 2, one of the Shroud image's additional properties seems to be that of X-ray characteristics, particularly in the case of the bones in the hands, as first observed in the early 1980s by Michigan chemistry professor Dr Giles Carter, followed in 1995 by Dr

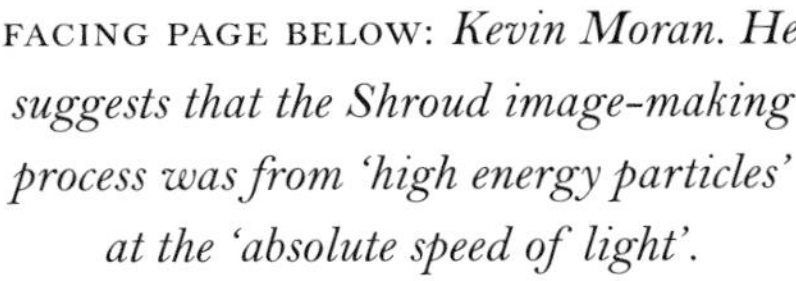

FACING PAGE BELOW: *Kevin Moran. He suggests that the Shroud image-making process was from 'high energy particles' at the 'absolute speed of light'.*

RIGHT: *One curiosity reported of Jesus is that even in life he appeared in some kind of brilliant light, as at the moment of transfiguration depicted here on a Byzantine mosaic.*

Alan Whanger and his wife. So what nuclear radiation process could possibly account for these as well as all the Shroud image's other properties?

At which point enter Dr August Accetta, a youthful physician based in Huntington Beach, California. So convinced of the Shroud's authenticity that he has founded a special Shroud Centre[23] to further Shroud researches and public education on the subject, Accetta has likewise been fired to go where no researcher has ever gone before on the subject, with a view to proving positively how the Shroud image could derive from some nuclear radioactive event. Using himself as a guinea pig, and working in collaboration with Dr Kenneth Lyons and Dr John Jackson, Accetta allowed himself to be injected with methylene diphosphate, a mildly radioactive compound with a six-hour 'half-life' that he routinely uses in his medical work to show up internal organs.[24]

Having allowed time for this compound to bind itself to his bones, tissues and body organs Accetta then assumed the Shroud pose, while a gamma camera was deployed to 'photograph' the photons radiating from his body. This was set to fire at timed intervals which Accetta and Lyons knew from their experience would register the body elements at different intensities relative to the degree of the methylene diphosphate's absorption and dispersal through them.

The results obtained proved quite astonishing, indeed little short of sensational. First, it was conclusively demonstrated that a full-body radiation image could be produced by this means, without the application of any paints or dyes, which replicated all the Shroud image's monochromatic characteristics. Second, the image had the same collimated, or straight-up, straight-down character as that of the Shroud's imprint, though in fairness it should be said that a collimator in the set-up ensured this, since otherwise the radiation would have spilled out at all sides. Third, apart from its being slightly more distinct against its background, the image had the same lack of outline as that on the Shroud. Fourth, the image shared the Shroud's otherwise seemingly unique lack of any light focus. Fifth, the Shroud's X-ray properties were strikingly replicated, spectacularly in the case of the hands, in which the metacarpal bones and phalange or finger bones could clearly be distinguished with a most compelling similarity to these same bones on the Shroud. Sixth, when viewed via the VP-8 Image Analyzer, Accetta's body exhibited the same three-dimensional properties as that on the Shroud imprint, the limbs being particularly similar.

One of the Accetta process's few differences from the Shroud was that it produced images of some of the body's internal organs, most notably the kidneys. Another difference was that Accetta's head, unlike the rest of his body, appeared very distorted on the VP-8 Image Analyzer, seemingly because of the high volume of radiation emitted from its lower two-thirds, a problem that he expects to eliminate in future experiments.

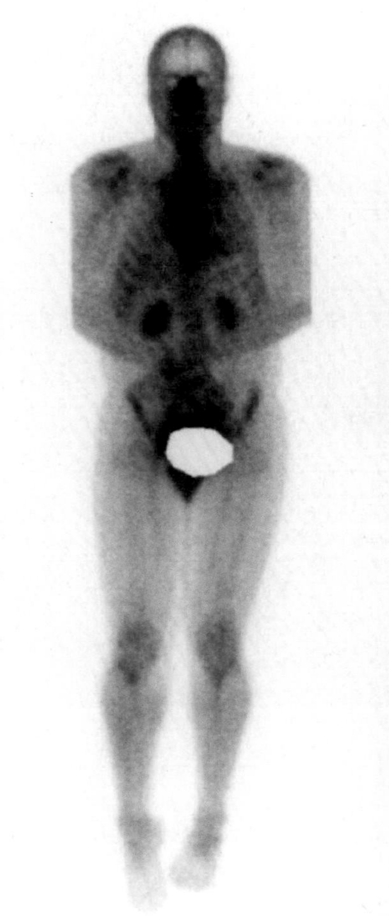

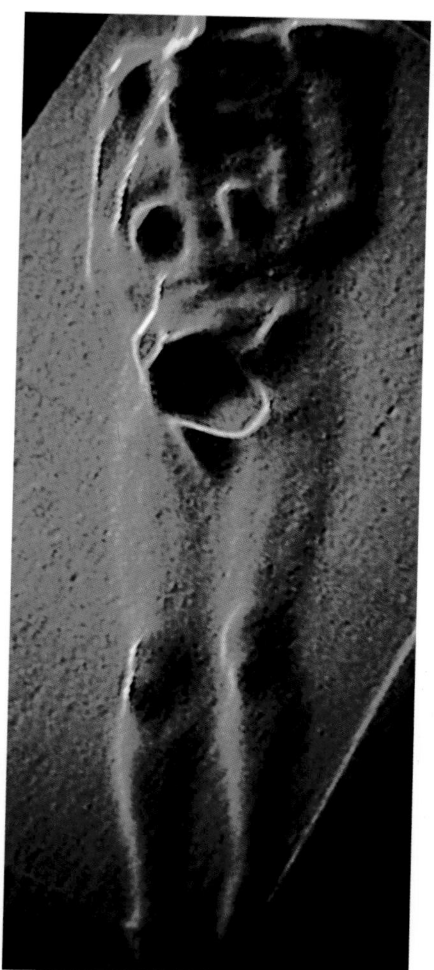

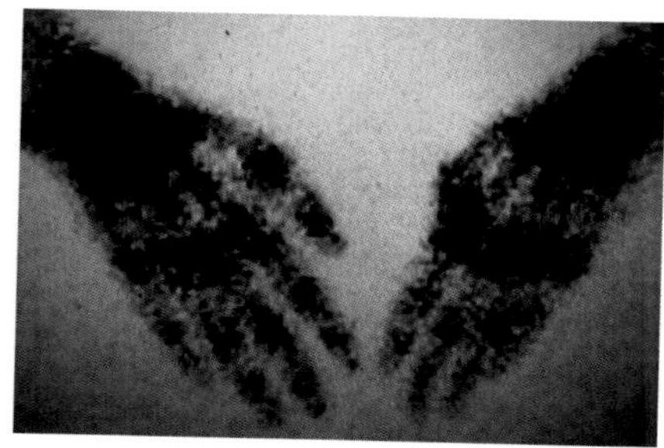
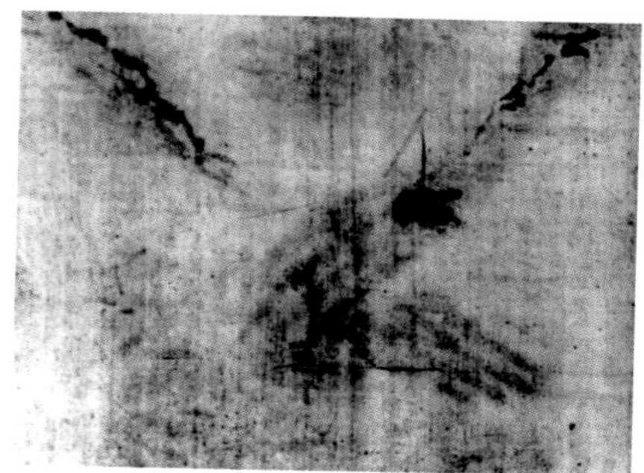
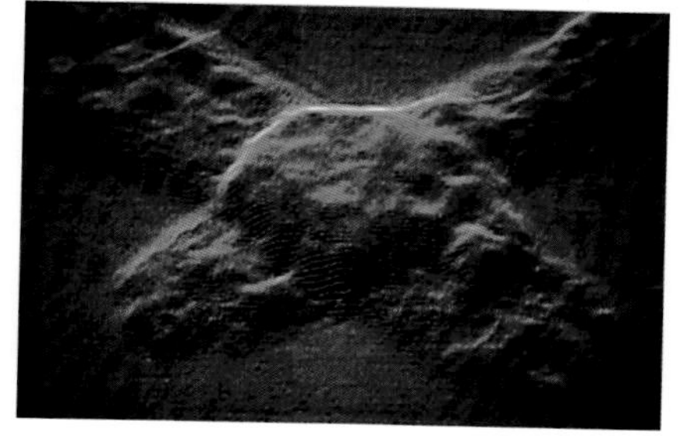

TOP LEFT: *A nuclear radiation image produced by Dr August Accetta (below left) after injecting himself with a weak radioactive substance. The 'V' shape in the genital area is a protective shield. The image has convincing VP-8 three-dimensionality, thereby replicating the Shroud. And particularly striking is the image of the hands, as seen at far right, top and bottom, compared to those on the Shroud, seen between them. Unlike in the case of the Shroud, the process showed up Dr Accetta's internal organs. Conceivably, therefore, the Shroud process was similar, though a mainly surface phenomenon only.*

As Accetta is the first to acknowledge, he cannot claim to have been able to replicate all the Shroud's characteristics exactly, nor indeed did he expect to. A quite spectacular achievement on his part, however, is that he very genuinely has been able to reproduce some of those characteristics sufficiently closely for some kind of nuclear radiation explanation for the Shroud's image to be considered seriously, more so than anyone might previously have dared contemplate.

In which regard, given that for the last two thousand years Christians having been claiming the historicity of such a resurrection event solely from the testimony of their written gospels, could it be that the scientific testimony of the Shroud, as increasingly understood by experiments such as Accetta's, might provide an additional, crucial beacon for them for the next two thousand? If so, exactly what further light might the burgeoning technologies of our exciting third millennium be able to shed on the mystery? And will the Roman Catholic Church, as the Shroud's owners since 1983, ever allow those new technologies to be applied?

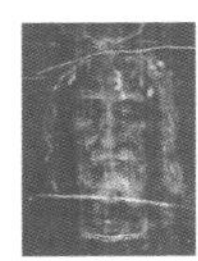

CHAPTER 10

What Should Happen Next?

ABOVE: *Prof. Edward Hall of Oxford. His verdict on the Shroud: 'Someone just got a bit of linen, faked it up and flogged it'.*

FACING PAGE: *STURP technician Bill Mottern making fine adjustments to what were state-of-the-art examination procedures in 1978. Now they have been greatly superseded by the latest technological advances.*

IT MAY BE RECALLED that at the October 1988 press conference at which the Shroud radiocarbon-dating results were released, the Oxford laboratory's Prof. Edward Hall, asked how he thought the Shroud had been forged, pronounced: 'Someone just got a bit of linen, faked it up and flogged it.' With the greatest respect to Prof. Hall's expertise as a nuclear physicist, such a sweeping statement, from the very moment it was uttered, showed disregard for those of equivalent calibre in other fields who have found the Shroud less easy to dismiss.

Let us allow Prof. Hall the benefit of the argument and try to build up a profile of the forger he postulated. According to Hall, he 'just got a bit of linen'. Well, as he would now be bound to concede, not quite any piece of linen. On the authority of his own colleague and successor, Prof. Tite, the Shroud is not a piece of linen commonly found in the Middle Ages. To my direct knowledge, Tite searched high and low to find a medieval parallel to it to serve as a carbon-dating control sample, even asking for my help in this quest. And he failed.

As a touch of quite extraordinary finesse for a medieval European faker, it also had to be a 'bit of linen' that had been in Israel. That much we have on the authority of the Hebrew University's Professor Avinoam Danin, who cannot by any stretch of the imagination be dismissed as a blinkered, born-again Christian, and who arguably knows his Holy Land flora every bit as thoroughly as Hall knows his protons and photons. Whatever the Shroud is, some time in its history someone directly laid on it fresh-cut flowering plants from the environs of Jerusalem – and he or she did so around the time of the year that Christians know as Easter.

According to Hall, this forger, having gone to the lengths of obtaining this rare piece of linen derived from the Holy Land, then just 'faked it up'. Well, perhaps not quite as easily as that. On the authority of Isabel Piczek, who has painted more feet of mural than Prof. Hall has had hot dinners, the Shroud is no painting. Or, if it is, it is unique in the history of art in bearing no outlines, exhibiting foreshortening before any artist discovered it, and being created as a 'photographic' negative five hundred years before photography itself had been invented – to name just some of its singularities.

Likewise, on the authority of a whole galaxy of distinguished medical specialists such as Bucklin of Los Angeles, Cameron of London, Zugibe of New York, Baima-Bollone of Turin, all professionally conversant with traumatic injuries, the bloodstains visible on the Shroud are positively not mere daubings added for artistic effect. Or, at least if they are, they exhibit a degree of a trained medical artist's knowledge, expertise and sophistication of rendition that would be near impossible to replicate even today.

To crown it all, according to Prof. Hall this multi-talented forger, after having produced the forgery of all forgeries, then just 'flogged it'. So who did he 'flog it' to? To the highest bidder? To some trillionaire French noble or rapacious cardinal wanting to use it to enrich his sumptuous new cathedral? Well, hardly. As we have learnt, and as must be accounted a hard fact of history, Geoffrey de Charny, historically the prime suspect as the Shroud's first known procurer, was a surprisingly modest sort of fellow – merely the squire of a very tiny French village, who could not even afford to pay his own ransom when he was captured by the English, and whose intended housing for the Shroud was a wooden hall that fell into serious disrepair within a few decades. Just as much as it was a matter of disbelief back in the Middle Ages that such a lowly individual could ever have come to own anything so spectacular as the genuine shroud of Jesus, so for us today it should be equally unbelievable that anyone of that kind and from that time could have made or procured such a spectacularly convincing forgery.

Accordingly, with the substantial withering of its credibility that the radiocarbon-dating verdict has undergone since 1988, there has arisen a curious stalemate. By any reasonable criterion of judgement the Shroud has absolutely not been proved a forgery sufficiently strongly for it to be locked away for ever as a disgrace to Christendom. The Church's decision to hold both the 1998 and 2000 expositions is testimony enough to that. Yet neither has it been sufficiently proved genuine for all Christendom to rally around its shadowy stains as a new twenty-first-century palladium of faith.

This inevitably gives rise to the key question: what should happen next to the Shroud? For particularly with the ushering in of a new millennium we can both look back on the limitations of the old approaches to it, among them the radiocarbon dating, and look forward to the opportunities presented by new ones. Just as the TV newsreels of moon landings now look dated from the perspective of thirty years later, so the STURP and other investigative work that was done on the Shroud back in 1978 has been greatly superseded by new scientific technology and markedly more conservationist-minded approaches.

For instance, in the 1970s the concentration was so much on proving whether the Shroud should be considered authentic or not, that relatively little thought was given to the potentially deleterious effect on the image of its cloth being bombarded with so many variations of the lighting spectrum – ultra-violet, X-ray and humanly visible light, including not

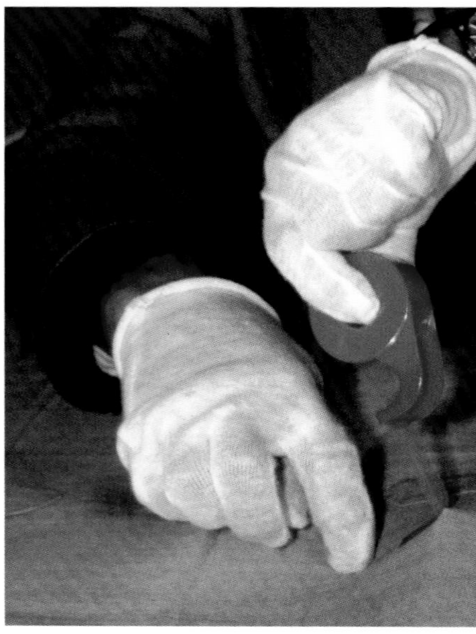

ABOVE: *Dr Max Frei's sticky-tape dispenser putting serious strain on the Shroud's surface during his sample-taking in October 1978. Reportedly the Shroud's surface is now showing discoloration in those areas to which he applied his tapes, apparently from gum residue left on the cloth's surface.*

least, the intense tungsten used for colour TV in 1973. As now warned by Dr Alan Adler and others, although the Shroud's 'body' imprints, instead of fading, have probably reached their maximum density, or strength of tone, the background, or off-image, areas have not.[1] These are slowly darkening with time and with every exposure to some fresh light source. The day must, therefore, come when the image and the off-image background will have the same tonal value, making the image invisible, as appears to have happened with Rome's 'Veronica' cloth.[2] This means that such considerations will need to be far more carefully borne in mind in any fresh approaches to the Shroud than they have been hitherto.

Likewise the technique of collecting forensic information from the Shroud by pressing pieces of sticky tape to its surface, used by both Dr Max Frei and the STURP team during the 1970s, now seems almost crude in its clumsiness and limitations. According to Dr Adler, who serves on a team that advises Turin's Archbishop on conservation matters, the examination of the Shroud after the 1997 fire revealed no fire damage, but

BELOW: *European scientists who worked alongside the American STURP team in 1978 saturating the Shroud's surface with intense lighting. Any future approaches are likely to be much more conservation-conscious than those allowed back in 1978.*

one very real point of concern was tell-tale discolorations on the cloth which seem to have appeared wherever Dr Frei applied his sticky tapes two decades before. By current thinking, the introduction of even the smallest traces of modern adhesives onto ancient cloth has to be considered undesirable. And so this approach is most unlikely to be permitted again.

Yet even the very latest conservation approaches can raise concerns, as for instance, with regard to the recent preparations for the Shroud's long-term storage flat in its new container, which involved it being very lightly smoothed out in order to eliminate as many as possible of its wrinkles and creases. Both Dr Jackson and I were concerned to note during our March 2000 viewing that, although the historically important 'doubled-in-four' foldmarks are still present, they are now significantly less visible than when photographically documented back in 1978.

Enter onto the Shroud scene, therefore, the technology of the twenty-first century. In only the last few years, the combining of computers, digital cameras and sensors has led to the development of a particularly sensitive and remarkable new technology, digital imaging spectroscopy. Based on the fact that every element in nature has its own unique spectrum or wavelength at which it reflects or absorbs light, this technique measures the spectral characteristics of whatever object is under examination. It is a method that can reveal a great deal about that object's composition without the slightest 'sampling' or other direct physical interference.

At which point, enter also Prof. Warren S. Grundfest, director of the Laser Research Technology and Development Laboratory at Cedars-Sinai Medical Center, Los Angeles, a long-term associate of Barrie Schwortz. In the course of this partnership, and with the support of a co-operative manufacturer, Grundfest and Barrie participated in the development of a digital imaging spectroscopy system that can easily be attached to a microscope or to exploratory medical viewing instruments of the kind that ophthalmologists and internal medicine specialists use. The system enables digital images of extraordinarily high definition and detail to be captured and stored in the computer. It also enables the full spectral characteristics of each image to be analysed on a pixel-by-pixel basis, meaning that it should be possible to determine the chemical constituents of even the tiniest detail.

The system would involve the Shroud being re-photographed under carefully controlled lighting conditions with a high-resolution digital camera that would capture a near unlimited number of images. These would range from large-scale, such as full-lengths of the front-of-body and back-of-body image; to medium close-up, such as homing in on the 'crown of thorns' blood flows, and ultra-close-up, such as details of blood drops, scourge marks, individual burn marks – and creases.

One great advantage of such a procedure is that it would not need the Shroud to be touched, let alone sampled, thereby immensely improving

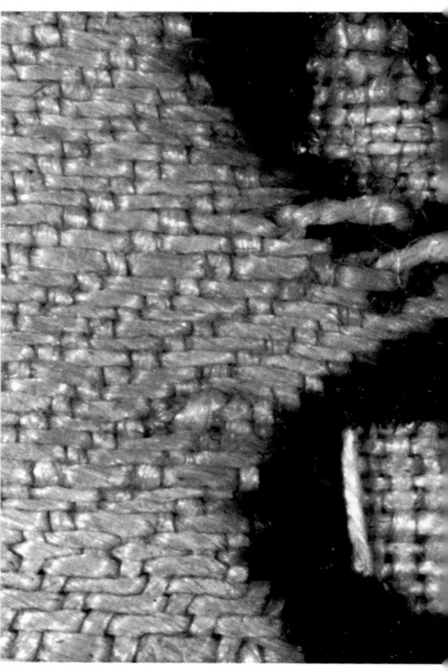

ABOVE: *A close-up of part of the Shroud's so-called 'poker-hole' damage. If the blackening derives from pitch or similar, spectroscopic analysis of its components could throw new light on the Shroud's early history.*

BELOW: *Prof. Warren Grundfest. His digital imaging spectroscopy method could revolutionize future scientific approaches to the Shroud.*

upon the five days of sampling, manipulation and cotton-gloved handling that it underwent in 1978. Another great advantage is that instead of individual scientists needing to plead for direct access to the Shroud, with all the concomitant security risks and conservation considerations, the digital images could be very economically reproduced in any quantity via the very popular CD-R disc format. They could, therefore, be made easily available to interested researchers anywhere in the world.

By far the system's greatest advantage, however, is its capacity to bring about a quantum leap in the research data available on the Shroud. For this, digital imaging spectroscopy's potentials are quite staggering.

Thus, without the application of a single new piece of sticky tape, it ought to be possible to resolve the deeply entrenched argument between Dr Walter McCrone on the one hand and 'Shroudies' such as Dr Alan Adler and Isabel Piczek on the other, concerning whether the Shroud's body image has or has not been painted on with iron oxide pigments. From the data obtained via digital imaging spectroscopy any researcher with the appropriate computer hardware and software should be able to dial up the wavelength for iron oxide, the computer thereupon displaying, highlighted and coloured in map form, the places where such pigments are to be found on the Shroud. If iron oxide were to show up in profusion and with a marked correlation to body image areas, then McCrone's 'medieval painter' argument would be well nigh overwhelmingly validated. If, on the other hand, the incidence of iron oxide particles was found to be sparse and random, as Adler and others insist, then this would heavily favour the view that the Shroud's image is no painting. It was via precisely this kind of quantitative appraisal, so very different from microanalysis of arbitrarily obtained direct samples, that McCrone's 'fake' judgement on the Vinland Map, as most confidently promulgated by him in 1973, was decisively overturned by the University of California's Crocker Laboratory in 1987, thereby reinstating the map as genuine after all.

Likewise, we may recall how there are differences of opinion concerning the causation of the Shroud's so-called 'poker-holes', my preference being for a red-hot poker dipped in pitch or boiling oil, while Dr Mechthild Flury-Lemberg favours the spillage of some liquid, and Barrie and others some accident with an incense burner. Since close-up photography of these holes clearly reveals intense blackening around their edges, digital imaging spectroscopy should enable firm identification of the substances present, thereby throwing most valuable new light on an early damage occurrence that history has otherwise not recorded. And this is but one among hundreds of potentially solvable Shroud mysteries. Overall, as Prof. Grundfest remarks, if digital imaging spectroscopy were deployed, 'today we could gather more data in five minutes than STURP was able to acquire in five days and nights'[3] during their 1978 examination of the Shroud.

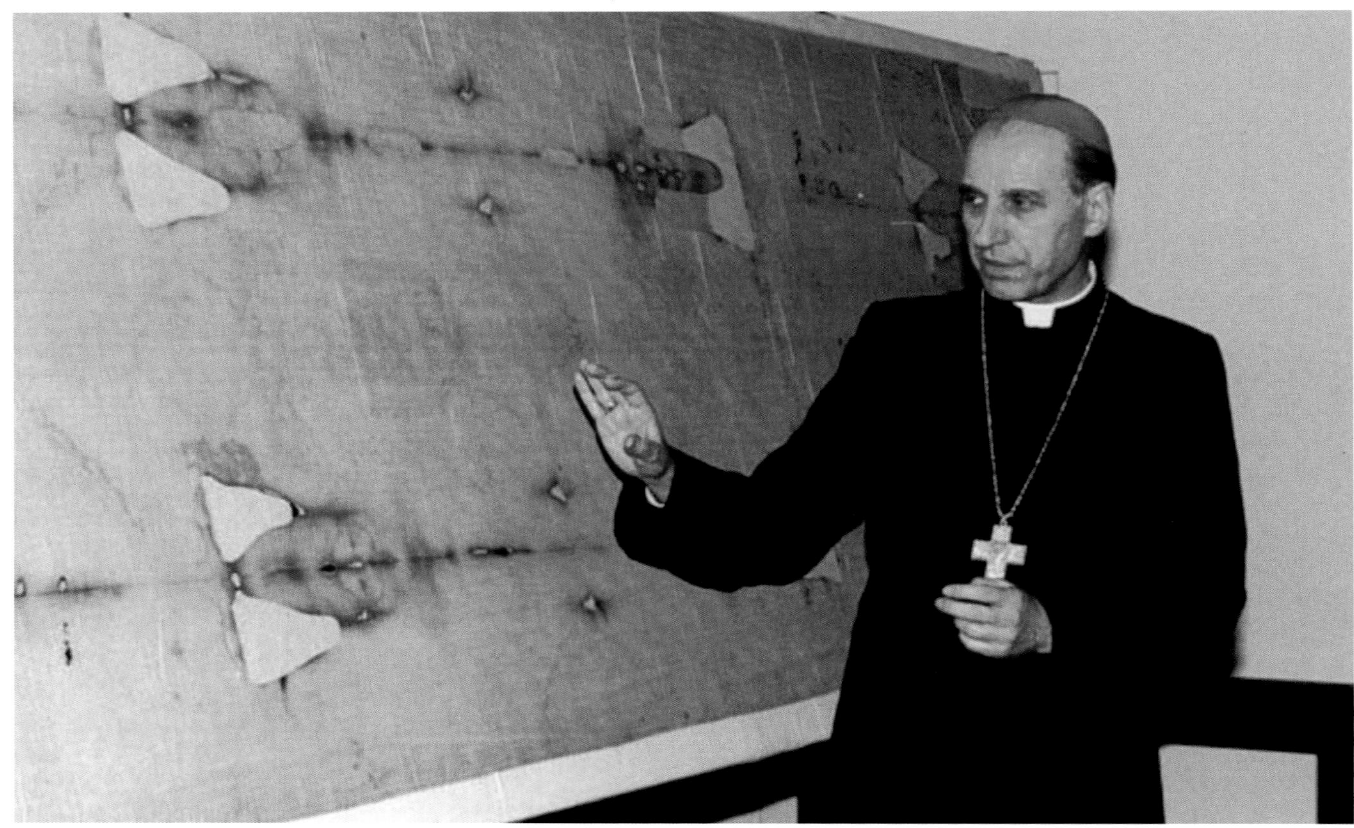

ABOVE: *Archbishop Severino Poletto of Turin speaks reflectively on the Shroud during the showing in the Cathedral sacristy, 3 March 2000, for those scientists and scholars who attended the special symposium.*

This raises the inevitable question: can we expect the Church's custodians actually to permit such procedures to be performed on the Shroud, and, if so, when? Pope John Paul II, in his Turin homily of 24 May 1998, remarked that the Church has 'no specific competence' to pronounce on the question of the Shroud's authenticity, and then went on expressly to state that the Church 'entrusts to scientists the task of continuing to investigate, so that satisfactory answers may be found to the questions connected with this cloth'. At the very least this makes clear that, under John Paul II's leadership (and he is formal owner of the Shroud), the Church is open to considering any responsibly thought out scientific initiatives on the subject.

But with the Pope in what can only be the swan-song years of his pontificate, it looked as if this might be little better than fine words until June 1999, when a most unexpected invitation went out to more than 30 scientists and scholars around the world to visit Turin between 2 and 6 March 2000 for a symposium specially called to deliberate on the Shroud's past, present and, most crucially, future. No one was more astonished to be invited than myself, a most pleasant further surprise being the so privileged second opportunity to view the Shroud in close-up, as described in the Introduction.

In the event, before the symposium could be held the Shroud's custodianship quietly passed from the genial Cardinal Saldarini, obliged to retire through ill health, to the vigorous Severino Poletto, formerly bishop of Asti, birthplace of Secondo Pia. Although Poletto was appointed Archbishop of Turin on 1 September 1999, at that moment becoming hands-on responsible for the Shroud, at the time of this book being finalized he still awaits the cardinal's hat that is normally automatic for the Turin archbishopric. But, as immediately became clear to those of us who attended the symposium, Poletto is not the kind of prelate to make a grand entrance, spend five minutes uttering bland generalities, then leave, in the manner of at least some of his predecessors. Though he has virtually no English (and some 50 per cent of the symposium's content was English-language), it was his habit throughout the four-day proceedings repeatedly to slip into the conference room, pick up one of the simultaneous-translation ear-pieces, and quietly listen for sometimes several hours at a stretch, such 'listening and learning' being his self-avowed priority at the present time.

And thanks to the symposium's firm direction under Turin University professors Piero Savarino and Silvano Scannerini, and its speakers' diversity of disciplines and countries of origin, Poletto was able to listen to some creditably balanced approaches to the subject. Challenging Dr Alan Adler's oft-repeated interpretations of the Shroud's 'body' and 'blood' images, the Italian Prof. V. Pesce Delfino argued noisily but unconvincingly

BELOW: *Author Ian Wilson (far right) discusses details of the Shroud with Dr Avinoam Danin on the same occasion.*

for the image having been created by a bas-relief. While French radiocarbon specialist Dr Jacques Evin of Lyon pleaded passionately in favour of radiocarbon dating's general reliability, Hong Kong archaeologist Bill Meacham pointed out how, in his experience, easily 20 per cent of all radiocarbon dates can seriously differ from those that the archaeologists expect, in which circumstances he and his fellow archaeologists have not the slightest hesitation rejecting them, and with none of the agonizing associated with the Shroud during the last twelve years.

Amid all these arguments it became clear that those in Turin most responsible for the Shroud's custody, beginning with Poletto himself, are now genuinely open to fresh scientific initiatives on the subject, probably more than at any previous time in the Shroud's history. Those of us who attended the symposium were explicitly encouraged to prepare within weeks concise recommendations for the fresh scientific approaches that we would like to see implemented, the availability of a 'hot-line' e-mail communications facility underlining a genuine sense of urgency. The meeting warmly approved the basic principle of non-invasive, digital imaging-type procedures by which a whole new database could be created, any ongoing uncertainties simply relating to choice of system. Likewise the basic principle of fresh, radiocarbon-dating work was also found broadly acceptable, with the proviso that its timing should depend on a better understanding being reached of how and why any spurious carbon 14 might have skewed the 1988 result.

Sometime within the next decade or so, therefore, the Shroud looks poised for the turning up of fresh scientific revelations potentially as intriguing as those of the last hundred years. But will those revelations ever ultimately prove its authenticity? Although Barrie Schwortz and I are often asked that question, it is also one that we always find hard to answer.

For just as Pontius Pilate reportedly asked of the human Jesus before him, 'What is truth?' (John 18: 38), so we must ask of the reader, 'What is proof?' Let us suppose that the Grundfest-Schwortz digital imaging spectroscopy procedure definitively refutes the McCrone contention that the Shroud was 'cunningly painted' using iron oxide. Let us also suppose that Prof. Mattingly, using the portion of Shroud conveniently held back from the 1988 radiocarbon dating, successfully demonstrates that the Shroud's surface is thickly coated with a still living biofilm and develops a certain way of removing it. Let us further suppose that the Church makes fresh samples from the Shroud available for a redating,[4] whereupon, when the coating is removed, the date that is arrived at is found to be *c.* AD 30, plus or minus fifty years. What will all that prove? However ecstatically the 'believer' might receive such findings, the avowed sceptic will no doubt point out that, since the Romans crucified thousands of people between 20 BC and AD 80 in what is today Israel, the cloth will still not be proved to have belonged to Jesus Christ. As Dr Alan Adler is ever fond of pointing

'We do not have a laboratory test for Christness . . .'

Dr Alan Adler

out: 'The hypothesis "Is this Jesus Christ?" is not experimentally testable. We do not have a laboratory test for Christness.'

So the search for proof on the Shroud is like a tantalus that is unlikely ever to be satisfied. Which is perhaps how the man of the Shroud has always wanted it, for ultimately there really is only one test of the Shroud, and that is the test of whatever it might speak to your heart. Perhaps you can look on that face, and that body with all its wounds, be totally unmoved by it, and wonder what all the fuss is about. But if, on the other hand, that image, and particularly that face, touches you as it does Barrie and me, then shutting your heart and your mind to it is simply not an option.

One of the most moving moments of my entire life was during that viewing of the Shroud on 3 March 2000, when Archbishop Poletto called for readings in Italian, English and Hebrew from the so prophetic 'Suffering Servant' passages of Isaiah chapter 53, as written several centuries before the human Jesus trod Israel's soil:

> Without beauty, without majesty we saw him . . .
> A thing despised and rejected by men
> A man of sorrows and familiar with suffering . . .
> We thought of him as someone punished,
> Struck by God and brought low.
> Yet he was pierced through for our faults
> Crushed for our sins
> On him lies a punishment that brings us peace
> And through his wounds we are healed . . .

It had, of course, to be Avinoam Danin, veteran of the struggle to create the new Israel and so unlikely a character to be standing in a northern Italian cathedral's sacristy, who read those passages in their original Hebrew. At which point the quite inescapable thought went through my mind: I wonder how many centuries it has been since the Shroud was last in the presence of words of Hebrew. Whereupon it became very, very hard indeed to hold back the tears . . .

NOTES AND REFERENCES

Introduction

1 Harry E. Gove, *Relic, Icon or Hoax? Carbon Dating the Turin Shroud*, Bristol and Philadelphia, Institute of Physics Publishing, 1996

2 Memorandum of Pierre d'Arcis, Bishop of Troyes, to the Avignon Pope Clement VII, translation by Rev. Herbert Thurston reprinted in Ian Wilson *The Turin Shroud*, London, Gollancz, 1978, pp.230–5

3 For the official scientific publication of the laboratories' findings, see P.E.Damon et al., 'Radiocarbon dating of the shroud of Turin', *Nature*, vol. 337, no.6208, pp.611–15.

4 This sermon was published in the Vatican newspaper *L'Osservatore Romano*, 27 May 1998.

Chapter 1

1 See John Beldon Scott, 'Seeing the Shroud: Guarini's Reliquary Chapel in Turin and the Ostension of a Dynastic Relic', *Art Bulletin*, December 1995, pp.609–637

2 This has the merit of showing the pre-1825 appearance, before the view from the nave was ruined by a massive glass partition, now utterly destroyed.

3 Measurements very kindly supplied to me by Dr Flury-Lemberg, November 1999, in advance of the paper she presented to the Turin Symposium, March 2000

4 From the closer inspection allowed by the March 2000 display arrangement, this feature seemed more likely to be discoloration from the Shroud having at some period been folded along that line – almost certainly the same period as that during which the so-called 'poker hole' damage occurred.

5 For an English translation, see Dorothy Crispino, 'The Report of the Poor Clare Nuns, Chambéry, 1534', *Shroud Spectrum International* 2, March 1982, pp.19–27

6 Such was the embarrassment over the fire that several early post-1532 copies omit to show the burns and patches, an example of how even in the artistically-competent sixteenth and seventeenth centuries, artists' so-called 'copies' are never to be entirely trusted.

7 Mechthild Flury-Lemberg, 'Die Leinwand des Turiner Grabtuches – Aussagen zu einzelnen ihrer Merkmale', paper presented to the International Scientific symposium 'The Turin Shroud, past, present and future', Turin 2–5 March 2000, in press.

8 Quoted in Nicholas Reeves, *The Complete Tutankhamun*, London, Thames & Hudson, 1990, p.155

Chapter 2

1 For the best English-language account of Secondo Pia's photographic work, also that of his successor, Giuseppe Enrie, see John Walsh, *The Shroud*, New York, Random House & London, W.H.Allen, 1963

2 Quoted in *Amateur Photographer*, 8 March, 1967

3 Dr John Jackson interviewed in the 1978 British-made TV documentary *The Silent Witness*

4 Peter M. Schumacher, 'Photogrammetric Responses from the Shroud of Turin', paper delivered at the Shroud of Turin International Research Conference, Richmond, Virginia, Friday, 18 June 1999

5 ibid

6 Giles F. Carter, 'Formation of the Image on the Shroud of Turin by X-Rays: A New Hypothesis' *ACS Advances in Chemistry*, no.205, *Archaeological Chemistry III*, Joseph B. Lambert, ed.,1984, pp.427–446

7 Alan and Mary Whanger, *The Shroud of Turin: An Adventure of Discovery*, Franklin, Tennessee, Providence House, 1998, chapter 10.

8 Barrie points out that he was using a well-known photographic edge enhancement technique for this.

Chapter 3

1 Mechthild Flury-Lemberg 'Die Leinwand des Turiner Grabtuches - Aussagen zu einzelnen ihrer Merkmale', paper presented to the Shroud Symposium at the Villa Gualino, Turin, 2 March 2000

2 See D. Barag, M. Hershkovitz et al (eds.), *Masada IV: Lamps, Textiles, Basket, Wood and Ballista Balls*, vol 4 of the final reports of the Masada excavations., Jerusalem, Israel Exploration Society, 1994

3 Jean M. Glover, 'The Conservation of Medieval and later Shrouds from Burials in North West England', in Sonia A. O'Connor and Mary R. Brooks, *Archaeological Textiles, Occasional Papers no.10*, proceedings of the conference 'Textiles for the Archaeological Conservator held by the UKIC Archaeology Section, York, April 1988, pp.51-4

4 Solomon Gansfried, *Code of Jewish Law (Kitzur Shulchan Aruch)*, trans Hyman E. Goldin, New York, Hebrew Publishing Company, 1927 vol IV, ch. CXCVII. Laws pertaining to Purification (Tahara), nos. 9 & 10, pp.99–100.

5 Up until very recently I held the view that the body of the man of the Shroud cannot have been washed, since such a procedure would automatically have removed the bloodstains that are so eloquent evidence of crucifixion. However the New York forensic pathologist Dr Fred Zugibe, who was at my side when I studied those same bloodstains during the March

2000 showing, has gone some way to persuading me that they derive from blood that continued to seep from the body after this had been hurriedly sluiced immediately prior to burial. This should not affect the use of a *sovev*, which would still have been necessary since Jesus' clothing had been commandeered by his executioners

6 Werner Bulst and Heinrich Pfeiffer, *Das Turiner Grabtuch und das Christusbild*, Frankfurt, Knecht, 1987, p.38

7 Lynn Picknett and Clive Prince, *Turin Shroud: In Whose Image? The Shocking Truth Unveiled*, London, Bloomsbury, 1994

8 Some regard even this as too tall, because of the prevalence of the idea that people in antiquity were much shorter than us. However the reality is that human height has changed relatively little during the last several thousand years, for instance, one of ten adult skeletons in a Jerusalem cemetery from Jesus' time was found to have been a six-footer.

9 Fully justifying this posing experiment has been the appearance, just as this book was being prepared for press, of Keith Laidler's *The Divine Deception: The Church, the Shroud and the Creation of a Holy Fraud*, published by Headline of London, March 2000. In this Laidler claims, echoing Picknett and Prince, that 'the head of the figure on the Shroud is unnaturally low, confirming the conclusion that it is in an impossibly incorrect position and has been artificially attached to the body on the Shroud.' Had Laidler taken up the Shroud burial pose himself, and with due consideration to the principles of foreshortening, he might have reached a very different conclusion.

10 See Gabriel Barkay, 'Burial Headrests as a Return to the Womb - A Re-evaluation', *Biblical Archaeology Review*, March 1988, pp.48ff, with useful bibliography on p.50

Chapter 4

1 Gary Vikan, 'Debunking the Shroud: Made by Human Hands', *Biblical Archaeology Review*, November/December 1998, pp.27–9

2 W.O.Hassall, *The Holkham Bible Picture Book*, London, Dropmore Press, 1954.

3 Pierre Barbet, *The Passion of our Lord Jesus Christ*, Dublin, Clonmore & Reynolds, 1954, p.152

4 These were areas that had been beyond my close-up viewing range in 1973, because the vertical mode of display on that occasion meant that the entire back of the body image was way above my head

5 Frederick T. Zugibe, 'Pierre Barbet Revisited', *Sindon*, December 1995, p.118

6 Leoncio Garza-Valdes, *The DNA of God?*, New York, Doubleday, 1999, pp. 190–2

7 For example, Quintilius Varus crucified two thousand after the riots that followed the death of Herod in 4 BC, while in the late 60s AD Titus crucified 500 a day around Jerusalem's walls during his siege of the city prior to crushing the Jewish Revolt.

8 Zugibe, op.cit., p.112

9 Nicu Haas, 'Anthropological Observations on the Skeletal Remains from Giv'at ha-Mivtar', *Israel Exploration Journal*, vol 20, no.1-2, 1970, pp.38–59

10 Joseph Zias and Eliezer Sekeles, 'The Crucified Man from Giv'at ha-Mivtar: A Reappraisal', *Israel Exploration Journal* vol. 35, no.1, 1985, pp.22–7

11 'Crudelissimum eterrimumque supplum', quoted in Frederick T. Zugibe, *The Cross and the Shroud: A Medical Examiner Interprets the Turin Shroud*, New York, Angelus, 1982, p.37

12 Josephus, *The Jewish War*, trans. G.A. Williamson, revised E. Mary Smallwood, Harmondsworth, Penguin, 1981, pp.389–90

13 Quintilian, *Declamationes*, 274

14 Among the exponents of the idea have been Hans Naber, alias Kurt Berna, alias John Reban, *Inquest on Jesus Christ: Did He Die on the Cross?*, London, Leslie Frewin, 1967; Rodney Hoare, *The Testimony of the Shroud*, London, Quartet, 1978, and Holger Kersten and Elmar Gruber, *The Jesus Conspiracy: The Turin Shroud & the Truth about the Resurrection*, Shaftesbury, Element, 1994

15 Zugibe, *The Cross and the Shroud*, p.151

16 ibid., p.165

17 Isabel Piczek, 'Is the Shroud of Turin a Painting?', *Actes du Symposium Scientifique International*, Rome, 1993, A.A.Upinsky (ed.), Paris, François-Xavier de Guibert, 1995, p.269

Chapter 5

1 For an authoritative scientific summary of the main approaches, see E.J.Jumper et al., 'A Comprehensive Examination of Various Stains and Images on the Shroud of Turin', *ACS Advances in Chemistry*, no. 205, *Archaeological Chemistry III*, Joseph B. Lambert, ed., pp.447-76, 1984

2 W.C.McCrone, 'Light Microscopical Study of the Turin "Shroud" I & II', *The Microscope* 28, 1980, pp.1–13

3 Quoted in Domenico Leone, *El Santo Sudario en España*, Barcelona, Biblioteca Sindoniana, 1959, pp.47–56.

4 For a popular account, see John Heller, *Report on the Shroud of Turin*, Boston, Houghton Mifflin, 1983

5 Alan Adler, 'The Shroud Fabric and the Body Image: Chemical and Physical Characteristics', paper presented to the International Scientific Symposium 'The Turin Shroud, past, present and future', Villa Gualino, Turin, 2–5 March 2000. In press.

6 Kevin E. Moran, 'Microscopic Observations on the Max Frei 1978 Samples', private communication, 25 June 1995

7 Alan Adler, 'Chemical and Physical Characteristics of the Blood Stains', paper presented to the International Scientific Symposium 'The Turin Shroud, past, present and future', Villa Gualino, Turin, 2–5 March 2000. In press.

8 Walter McCrone, *Judgement Day for the Turin Shroud*, Chicago, McCrone Research Institute, 1996

9 T.A.Cahill et al., 'The Vinland Map Revisited: New Compositional Evidence on its Inks and Parchment', *Analytical Chemistry* 15 March 1987, 59, pp.829–33

10 That Vikings genuinely discovered America before Columbus has further been confirmed by the archaeological discovery of a Viking settlement of *c.* AD 1000 at L'Anse aux Meadows on the northern tip of Newfoundland. See Anne Stine Ingstad and Helge Ingstad, *The Norse Discovery of America*, vols. I and II, Oslo, Norwegian University Press, 1985
11 Isabel Piczek 'Is the Shroud a Painting?' *Actes du Symposium Scientifique International*, Rome,1993, A.A. Upinsky, (ed.), Paris, François-Xavier Guibert, 1995 p.266
12 Baima-Bollone, P., M.Jorio, A.L.Massaro, 'Identification of the Group of the Traces of Human Blood on the Shroud', *Shroud Spectrum International* 6, March 1983, pp.3–6, after an article in the original Italian *Sindon* 31
13 Leoncio Garza-Valdes, *The DNA of God?*, New York, Doubleday, 1999
14 Mark Guscin, *The Oviedo Cloth*, Cambridge, Lutterworth Press, 1998.
15 Alan Adler, 'Updating Recent Studies on the Shroud of Turin', in Mary Virginia Orna (ed.), *Archaeological Chemistry: Organic, Inorganic and Biochemical Analysis* American Chemical Society Symposium Series No.625, p.226

Chapter 6

1 *La S. Sindone: Ricerche e studi della Commissione di Esperti nominata dall'Arcivescovo di Torino, Card. Michele Pellegrino, nel 1969*, supplemento *Rivista Diocesana Torinese* January 1976
2 For Rolfe this trip served as reconnaissance expedition for his subsequent award-winning film *The Silent Witness.*
3 As a preliminary, in June 1982, only months before his death, he published a summary 'Nine Years of Palinological Studies on the Shroud' in the US Journal *Shroud Spectrum*, no. 3, pp.2–7
4 Paul Maloney, 'The Current Status of Pollen research and Prospects for the Future', paper given at the Paris 'Symposium Scientifique International sur le Linceul de Turin', 7–8 September 1989
5 Joe Nickell, 'Pollens on the Shroud: A Study in Deception', *Skeptical Inquirer*, vol.18, summer 1994, pp.379–85. In fact, as Barrie points out, the gloves had been brought over to Turin from the United States, where they had been purchased, so they are unlikely to have been bearing Near Eastern pollens
6 For the facts on Frei's part in this, see Charles Hamilton, *The Hitler Diaries*, University of Kentucky Press, 1991. Oxford University history professor Hugh Trevor-Roper, ennobled as Lord Dacre, was chiefly responsible for the diaries' mistaken authentication, with Frei but one of several 'experts' called in to advise on the handwriting, a subject (unlike botany) not his specialist field.
7 From an article in the Whanger Newsletter CSST News July 1998
8 Mary and Alan Whanger, *The Shroud of Turin: An Adventure of Discovery*, Franklin, Tennessee, Providence House, 1998
9 In fact the evidence is ambivalent. Bunches of flowers have been reported in some secondary burials of the Second Temple period, as in the Giv'at ha-Mivtar excavations mentioned in chapter 4. Sceptics like Zias, however, attribute such flowers to natural vegetative growth invading the burial container.
10 J. Volckringer, *Le Saint-Suaire de Turin: le problème des empreintes devant la Science*, Paris, Procure du Carmel de 'Action de Graces, 1942
11 O. Scheuermann, *Das Tuch*, Regensburg, Verlag Pustet, Veritas, Linz-Wien, 2nd edition
12 Avinoam Danin, 'Pressed Flowers. *Eretz Magazine*, November/December 1997, p.37
13 Avinoam Danin, Alan D.Whanger, Uri Baruch, Mary Whanger, *Flora of the Shroud of Turin*, St Louis, Missouri Botanical Garden Press, 1999
14 Just over one third of all pollens proved impossible to identify positively, due to the optical limitations of the sticky tapes, restraints on removing them from their locations for better viewing, etc.
15 See *National Geographic* December 1967
16 Kupicha, F.K., 'Gundelia', in Davis, *Flora of Turkey*, Edinburgh, University Press, vol 5, pp.325–6
17 The three sticky-tape samples taken in the head region (6Bd, 6Ca and 5Ca) produced nine, five and three *Gundelia* pollens respectively.
18 V.D.Miller and S.F.Pellicori, 'Ultraviolet Fluorescence Photography of the Shroud of Turin', *Journal of Biological Photography*, 49, 3, 1981, pp.71–85
19 *Lomelosia (Scabiosa) prolifera* (L) Greuter et Burdet, *Cistus incanus*-type and *Cistus salvifolius*-type
20 Avinoam Danin, 'Micro-traces of plants on the Shroud of Turin as geographical markers' , paper presented to the International Scientific Symposium 'The Turin Shroud, past, present and future', Villa Gualino, Turin 2-5, 2000, in press.
21 Joseph A.Kohlbeck & Eugenia L.Nitowski, 'New Evidence May Explain Image on Shroud of Turin', *Biblical Archaeology Review*, July–August 1986, pp.18–29.

Chapter 7

1 William Meacham, 'On Carbon Dating the Turin shroud', *Shroud Spectrum International*, June 1986, pp.15–25
2 *Current Archaeology*, August 1986
3 Rosalie David, *Mysteries of the Mummies: The Story of the Manchester University Investigation*, London, Cassell, 1978
4 See Ian Wilson, *The Blood and the Shroud*, London, Weidenfeld, 1998, pp.219–23
5 Leoncio A. Garza-Valdes, 'Biogenic varnish and the Shroud of Turin', *Actes du Symposium Scientifique International Rome 1993*, A.A. Upinsky (ed.), Paris, François-Xavier Guibert, 1995
6 P.E.Damon et al., 'Radiocarbon dating of the shroud of Turin', *Nature*, vol. 337, no.6208, 16 February 1989, pp.611–15.
7 Stephen Mattingly, e-mail communication to Dr John Jackson, copied to the author, December 1999
8 ibid
9 ibid

Chapter 8

1 From 'Story of the Image of Edessa', quoted in translation in Ian Wilson, *The Shroud of Turin*, New York, Doubleday, 1978, p.236, after the Greek text in J.P.Migne, *Patrologia Graeca*, Paris, 1857-66, vol CXIII, cols. 423–54
2 Lionel Cust and Prof. E. Von Dobschutz 'Notes on Pictures in the Royal Collection: Article III The Likeness of Christ', *Burlington Magazine*, September 1904, p.517
3 Royal Collection Trust catalogue number HC 1567 403934. See Gabriele Finaldi *The Image of Christ: The Catalogue of the Exhibition 'Seeing Salvation'*, London, National Gallery Company Ltd., 2000, pp.98–101
4 C. Dufour Bozzo, *Il 'Sacro Volto' di Genova*, Rome, Istituto Nazionale d'Archeologia e Storia dell'Arte, 1974
5 For the relevant Syriac text in translation, and original source details, see J.B. Segal, *Edessa 'The Blessed City'*, Oxford, Clarendon, 1970, pp.24–5
6 Eusebius, *The History of the Church*, trans. G.A. Williamson, Harmondsworth, Penguin, 1965, p.66
7 'Story of the Image of Edessa', in Wilson, op.cit, p.236.
8 St Augustine, *De Trinitate* VIII, 4, 5, in J.P.Migne, *Patrologia Latina*, vol.42, 1801.
9 Paul Vignon, *Le Suaire de Turin devant la Science, l'Archéologie, l'Histoire, l'Iconographie, la Logique*, Paris, Masson, 1939, p.128ff.
10 Averil Cameron, 'The Sceptic and the Shroud', Inaugural Lecture, Department of Classics and History, King's College, London, 29 April 1980
11 For an English translation of the 'Acts of the Holy Apostle Thaddaeus' see Alexander Roberts and James Donaldson (eds.) *The Ante-Nicene Fathers, Translations of the Writings of the Fathers Down to AD 325*, vol. VIII, Grand Rapids, Michigan, Eerdmans, 1951, p.558–9
12 'Story of the Image of Edessa', in Wilson, op.cit, p.242
13 The Robert de Clari manuscript is preserved in the Royal Library, Copenhagen as MS. 487. The passage quoted in translation derives from fol 123b. The definitive modern-day edition of this text was prepared by Philippe Lauer, *La conquête de Constantinople*, Paris, Classiques français du moyen âge, 40, 1924, reprinted 1956
14 Gervase of Tilbury, *Otia Imperialia* III, from *Scriptores rerum brunsvicensium*, G. Liebnitz (ed.), Hanover, 1707, I, pp.966–7
15 A.M.Dubarle, 'L'homèlie de Grégoire le Référendaire', *Actes du Symposium Scientifique International, Rome 1993*, A.A. Upinsky (ed.), Paris, François-Xavier de Guibert, 1995, p.51
16 Dan Scavone, lecture, 'Evidence for the Shroud in Constantinople prior to 1204' Shroud of Turin Conference 'Multidisciplinary Investigation of an Enigma', Richmond, Virginia, June 18, 1999, In press
17 I am grateful to Michael Lente of Grants, New Mexico for notifying me of this tradition associated with St Bernard, which he found mentioned on the back of a prayer card
18 Jérôme Lejeune, 'Étude topologique des Suaires de Turin, de Lier et de Pray', *Actes du Symposium Scientifique International, Rome 1993*, A.A. Upinsky (ed.), Paris, François-Xavier de Guibert, 1995, pp.103–9
19 Ilona Berkovits, *Illuminated Manuscripts in Hungary, X-XVI Centuries*, trans. Zsuzsanna Horn, Shannon, Irish University Press, 1969

Chapter 9

1 'We seem to know what the image is chemically, but how it got there remains a mystery.' L.A.Schwalbe and R.N.Rogers, 'Physics and Chemistry of the Shroud of Turin', *Analytica Chimica Acta* 135 (1982), pp.3–49
2 QED's 'Riddle of the Turin Shroud', screened on BBC2, 17 October 1988
3 Walter McCrone, 'The Shroud of Turin: Blood or Artist's Pigment?', *Accts. Chem. Res.*, vol. 23, no.3, 1990, p.82
4 Any thought that the pigment's redness might have faded over time has to be discounted, since iron oxide is frequently found in ancient burials and essentially retains its coloration indefinitely.
5 Walter McCrone, *Judgement Day for the Turin Shroud*, Chicago, Microscope Publications (Division of McCrone Research Institute Inc.), 1996
6 Gary Vikan, 'Debunking the Shroud Made by Human Hands', *Biblical Archaeology Review*, November/December 1998, pp.27–9
7 Emily A.Craig and Randall R. Bresee, 'Image Formation and the Shroud of Turin', *Journal of Imaging Science and Technology*, January–February 1994, pp.59–67
8 See chapter 5, note 5
9 Lynn Picknett and Clive Prince, *The Turin Shroud: In Whose Image? The Shocking Truth Unveiled*, London, Bloomsbury, 1994
10 Letter to Ian Wilson, 23 February 2000, in which she refused to permit publication of the photographs by which she promotes showings of 'The Turin Machine'
11 Nicholas Allen, 'Verification of the Nature and Causes of the Photo-negative Images on the Shroud of Lirey-Chambéry-Turin, *De Arte* [Journal of the Department of Art History and Fine Arts, University of South Africa], April 1995, pp.21–35
12 Dr Michael Straiton, 'The Man of the Shroud: A Crucified Crusader?', *Catholic Medical Quarterly*, c.1989
13 Christopher Knight and Robert Lomas *The Hiram Key: Pharaohs, Freemasons and the Discovery of the Secret Scrolls of Jesus*, London, Century, 1996
14 Allan A. Mills, 'Image formation on the Shroud of Turin: the reactive oxygen intermediates hypothesis', *Interdisciplinary Science Reviews*, vol. 20, no.4, December 1995, pp.319–26
15 Trypticase Soy Broth or TSB
16 Professor Stephen Mattingly, personal communication to Ian Wilson, December 1999
17 Remark made by Professor Hall during Ian Wilson's visit to the Oxford radiocarbon-dating laboratory, summer 1988
18 Thomas J. Phillips, Letter to the Editor, *Nature*, 16 February 1989
19 John P. Jackson, 'Is the image of the Shroud due to a process heretofore unknown to modern science', *Shroud Spectrum International*, 34, March 1990
20 Thaddeus Trenn, 'The Shroud of Turin: Resetting the Carbon-14 Clock', *Facets of Faith and Science*, vol. 3, *The Role of*

Beliefs in the Natural Sciences, ed. Jitse M. van der Meer, Ancaster, Ontario, 1996.

21 Kevin E. Moran, 'Microscopic Observations on the Max Frei 1978 Samples', private communication 25 June 1995

22 Robert Hedges, Letter to the Editor, *Nature*, 16 February 1989

23 Shroud Center of Southern California, 18351 Beach Blvd, Suite B, Huntington Beach, California 92646

24 August Accetta, 'Experiments with Radiation as an Image Formation Mechanism', paper given at Shroud of Turin International Conference, Mary, Mother of the Church Abbey, Richmond, Virginia 18–20 June 1998

Chapter 10

1 Dr Alan Adler, remarks to the International Scientific Symposium 'The Turin Shroud, past, present and future', Villa Gualino, Turin, 2–5 March 2000

2 Legend has it that when Jesus was carrying his cross to Golgotha, a woman of Jerusalem, 'Veronica', wiped his face with her veil, whereupon an imprint was left on this. The legend is a late one, but a cloth bearing such an imprinted likeness (a '*vera icon*') is definitely reported in Rome from the eleventh century on, being probably an artist's copy of the Edessa cloth face, alias our Shroud. But, whatever the Veronica's origins, during the Middle Ages pilgrims trampled each other to get a glimpse of its facial imprint, whereas those who have viewed the cloth during the twentieth century (it is kept in one of the piers of St Peter's, Rome), have reported no visible image. For a full discussion, see Ian Wilson, *Holy Faces, Secret Places*, London, Doubleday, 1991

3 Dr Warren Grundfest, addressing the Shroud of Turin International Research Conference, Mary Mother of the Church Abbey, Richmond, Virginia, 18–20 June 1998

4 At the March 2000 Symposium Drs Jacques Evin and Bob Otlet jointly suggested using a sample of scorched material from under one of the patches, a thread from the seam that joins the side-strip to the main body of the Shroud, and a newly cut sample from a bottom corner (i.e. the opposite corners to the ones repeatedly handled when the Shroud has been publicly exhibited back through the centuries)

A WHO'S WHO OF SHROUD RESEARCHERS

Accetta, Dr August Californian physician. Has experimented with injecting his own body with radioactive material in order to research radiation as an explanation for how the Shroud's image came to be formed.

Adler, Dr Alan Emeritus Professor of Chemistry, Western Connecticut State University, USA, specializing in blood chemistry. In the wake of the 1978 STURP examination studied the sticky-tape samples taken from the Shroud 'body' and 'blood' imprint areas, concluding the 'blood' to be blood, and the body image to derive from some force that selectively degraded the cloth.

Allen, Prof. Nicholas P.L. Dean of the Faculty of Art and Design, Port Elizabeth Technikon, Port Elizabeth, South Africa. Experimented with creating a Shroud-like 'photograph' using materials that would have been available in the Middle Ages.

Ashe, Geoffrey British author. In the 1960s experimented with heating a horse brass and lightly applying a cloth to it to create a Shroud-like 'scorch' image.

Baima-Bollone, Prof. Pier Luigi Professor of Forensic Medicine, Turin University. Italy's leading medical expert on the Shroud. Identified the Shroud 'blood' as group AB.

Barbet, Dr Pierre (d. 1961) Chief surgeon at St Joseph's Hospital, Paris, during the 1930s. Viewed the Shroud in daylight displayed on the steps of Turin Cathedral in 1933. Deduced that the man of the Shroud had been nailed through the wrists, and experimented with cadavers to demonstrate this, and its accompanying physiological effects.

Baruch, Uri Specialist in pollen analysis for the Israel Antiquities Authority, Jerusalem, Israel. From the sticky-tape samples of the Shroud taken by Dr Max Frei has confirmed the presence of significant numbers of plants of Israel represented among the pollen grains found on the Shroud.

Bonnet-Eymard, Brother Bruno French priest of community at Sainte-Parres-les-Vaudes, France. Argues that the radiocarbon-dating findings in 1988 were the result of a conspiracy.

Bresee, Prof. Randall Associate Professor of Textiles, University of Tennessee, Knoxville. With Emily Craig developed the hypothesis that the Shroud image was created by an artist using a 'dust transfer' technique.

Bucklin, Dr Robert Retired head of the Forensic Medical Division, the Los Angeles County Coroner-Medical Examiner Office. One of the USA's most experienced and respected forensic medicine specialists, he is said to have inspired the *Quincy* TV series. A Shroud researcher since the 1950s, says of the Shroud, 'The markings on this image are so clear and so medically accurate that the pathological facts which they reflect concerning the suffering and death of the man depicted . . . are in my opinion beyond dispute.'

Bulst, Prof. Werner, SJ (d.1995) Jesuit theologian chiefly based in Darmstadt, Germany from the 1960s. Author of what was long the most definitive German-language book on the Shroud, *Das Grabtuch von Turin*, first published in 1955.

Cameron, Prof. Averil British classicist, Warden of Keble College, Oxford who made dismissal of the Shroud's identity with the cloth of Edessa the subject of her inaugural lecture.

Cameron, Prof. James Malcolm Retired Professor of Forensic Medicine, the London Hospital Medical School. Worked on Australia's famous 'Dingo baby' case. Foremost British advocate of the view that the Shroud is medically convincing.

Carter, Dr Giles F. Professor of Chemistry, East Michigan University. From the apparent 'bony' character of the Shroud man's body, hypothesized that the Shroud image was formed by X-rays coming from the bone and teeth, these X-rays then interacting with elements on the surface of the body to produce secondary, low-energy X-rays which caused the image to form.

Cheshire, Group Captain Leonard, VC (d.1992) World War II RAF hero who after the war pioneered raising awareness of the Shroud in the UK.

Craig, Dr Emily A. Forensic anthropologist, Medical Examiners Division, Frankfort, Kentucky. With Prof. Randall Bresee developed the hypothesis that the Shroud image was created by a medieval artist using a 'dust transfer' technique.

Damon, Prof. Paul E. Professor, Dept of Geosciences, University of Arizona, and co-director of the University's AMS radiocarbon-dating laboratory which was the first to carbon date the Shroud in 1988.

Danin, Prof. Avinoam Department of Evolution, Systematics and Ecology, the Hebrew University, Jerusalem. Identifies some Shroud stains as images of flowers of Israel.

Delage, Yves (d.1920) Professor of Comparative Anatomy, the Sorbonne, Paris. An avowed agnostic, he was the first twentieth-century scientist to recognize how medically convincing the Shroud imprint is as deriving from a real-life crucifixion.

D'Muhala, Thomas President, Nuclear Technology Corporation, Connecticut. Was responsible for much of the logistics which brought into being the 1978 STURP scientific examination of the Shroud.

Donahue, Prof. Douglas Professor of Physics, University of Arizona, and co-director of the University's AMS radiocarbon-dating laboratory. Was the first scientist in the world to know the radiocarbon-dating result in 1988.

Dreisbach, Fr Kim Founder of the Atlanta Center for the Continuing Study of the Shroud of Turin.

Dubarle, Père A.M. French Dominican monk, formerly of the École Biblique, Jerusalem. France's foremost authority on the Shroud's history, he has drawn special attention to the importance of the tenth-century Gregory Referendarius description of the cloth of Edessa as a reference to the Shroud.

Enrie, Giuseppe (d.1958) Turin professional photographer. In 1931 took the set of official black-and-white photographs of the Shroud that were to remain definitive for much of the rest of the century.

Ferri, Prof. Lorenzo (d.1975) Professional sculptor and Professor of Art, Studio of Sacred Arts, Rome. Researched the Shroud for over forty years, making life-sized drawings and sculptures of his reconstructions of the man of the Shroud's body.

Filas, Prof. Francis, SJ (d.1985) Professor of Theology, Loyola University, Chicago. Pioneered research on the perceived imprints of Romano-Jewish lepton coins over the eyes of the man of the Shroud.

Flury-Lemberg, Mechthild Head of the Textile Workshop of the Abegg Stiftung, in Switzerland, and a world-class textile conservation specialist. Removed the modern blue surround from the Shroud and prepared it for its present conservation case.

Fossati, Don Luigi Salesian priest based in Turin. Specialist in the Shroud's history during the centuries of its ownership by the Dukes of Savoy.

Frei, Dr Max (d.1983) For twenty-five years Director of the Scientific Department of the Zurich Criminal Police. Was investigator for the UN of the death of UN Secretary-General Dag Hammarskjöld. In 1973, while notarizing Shroud photographs taken in 1969, obtained permission to apply sticky tapes to the Shroud's surface with a view to sampling the cloth's dust. Took further samples alongside the 1978 STURP scientific examination. Determined the presence on the sticky tapes of significant numbers of pollens of plants from Israel and Turkey.

Garza-Valdes, Leoncio Paediatrician at the Santa Rosa Hospital, San Antonio, Texas. Discoverer of the still partly living biofilm coating to the Shroud's surface that is alleged to have skewed the radiocarbon-dating result.

Ghiberti, Don Giuseppe Biblical scholar and member of the Pontifical Biblical Commission. Priest of the Turin diocese. Appointed by Cardinal Saldarini, Archbishop of Turin, with special responsibility for the Shroud, and for its expositions in 1998 and 2000.

Gilbert, Roger and Marty Oriel Corporation. Husband and wife team who participated in the 1978 STURP scientific examination, pioneering a reflectance spectroscopy approach to the Shroud. Encountered unusually strong signals in the foot area of the Shroud, leading to the discovery that this derived from dirt.

Gonella, Prof. Luigi Professor of Physics (metrology) at the Turin Polytechnic. Was scientific advisor to Cardinal Ballestrero at the time of the 1978 scientific examination of the Shroud, and the 1988 radiocarbon dating.

Gove, Prof. Harry E. Emeritus Professor of Physics at the University of Rochester, New York, and co-inventor of the AMS radiocarbon-dating method used on the Shroud in 1988. Was present at the Arizona AMS laboratory when the first radiocarbon-dating result on the Shroud was obtained.

Green, Fr Maurus, OSB Ampleforth-educated Benedictine monk. Pioneered historical researches on the Shroud in the UK during the 1960s and '70s.

Grundfest, Dr Warren Director of the Laser Research and Technology Development Laboratory, Cedars-Sinai Medical Center, Los Angeles, and Clinical Professor of Surgery, University of California, Los Angeles. Proposes new digital imaging spectroscopy approach to the Shroud.

Guscin, Mark Translator and classical scholar, resident in La Coruña, Spain. Has shown possible links between the Shroud and the so-called cloth of Oviedo.

Hall, Prof. Edward T. Retired founder-director of the Oxford University Research Laboratory for Archaeology and the History of Art, the British AMS radiocarbon-dating laboratory which carbon dated the Shroud in 1988. A self-avowed 'total agnostic', firmly believes the Shroud to be a medieval fake.

Hedges, Dr Robert Senior scientist at the Oxford radiocarbon-dating laboratory who worked directly on the carbon dating of the Shroud in 1988. Firmly upholds the medieval date.

Heller, Dr John (d.1995) Professor of Internal Medicine and Medical Physics at Yale University, and later Director of the New England Institute, Ridgefield, Connecticut. With Dr Alan Adler, made extensive analysis of the sticky-tape samples of the Shroud's 'body' and 'blood' imprints as obtained during the 1978 STURP examination, concluding that the Shroud is no forgery.

Hoare, Rodney (d. 1997) British science lecturer. From consultation with pathologists in East Anglia, promulgated the theory that the man of the Shroud was still alive when laid in the cloth.

Jackson, Dr John P. Physicist, formerly an instructor at the US Air Force Academy, Colorado Springs, where in partnership with Dr Eric Jumper he began much of his pioneering research on the formation of the Shroud's imprint. This led directly to the discovery of the Shroud imprint's 3-D properties, and in turn to the formation of the Shroud of Turin Research Project (STURP), of which he was co-director. Under Jackson's leadership, this was the group that carried out the extensive scientific examination of the Shroud in Turin in 1978. In 1995, with his Jewish-born wife Rebecca, founded the Shroud of Turin Center of Colorado, at Colorado Springs as an education, research and resource centre for Shroud studies.

Judica-Cordiglia, Giovanni Battista First individual to photograph the Shroud in colour, during the secret preliminary examination authorised by Cardinal Michele Pellegrino in June 1969.

Jumper, Dr Eric Physicist who with Dr John Jackson conducted much pioneering research on the Shroud's imprint, and co-directed the STURP scientific examination of the Shroud in 1978. Unusually among the STURP team, has accepted the radiocarbon-dating findings of 1988.

Kohlbeck, Dr Joseph A. Specialist in optical crystallogaphic techniques with Hercules Aerospace in Utah, USA. With Eugenia Nitowski, made special study of limestone dust found on the Shroud's underside.

Lavoie, Dr Gilbert American physician specializing in internal and occupational medicine. Has made a special study of the Shroud blood flows, showing how they could have transferred to the cloth with such intactness.

Lejeune, Prof. Jérôme (d.1994) French physician specializing in congenital chromosome disorders. Vice-President of the

Pontifical Academy of Sciences. Made a special study of the evidence for knowledge of the Shroud as exhibited in drawings illustrating the Hungarian Pray Manuscript, reliably datable to 1192-5. His promising research into Shroud DNA was cut short by his untimely death.

Lynn, Donald J. Scientist at the US Jet Propulsion Laboratory, Pasadena. With Jean J. Lorre of the same laboratory, analysed the Shroud's imaging using some of the same computer technology used to study images of the surface of Mars sent back from the Viking Lander mission in 1976. Concludes that the Shroud's image has no 'directionality'.

McCrone, Dr Walter Chicago-based microscopy specialist. Founder of the McCrone Research Institute, devoted to the teaching of microscopy and crystallography. Achieved wide publicity in 1973 for declaring Yale University's Vinland Map a fake. From light microscope study of the sticky-tape samples taken from the Shroud by STURP scientists in 1978, concluded that the Shroud was the work of a medieval artist. In 1987 his Vinland Map findings were challenged by a new appraisal by the Crocker Laboratory of California, ultimately leading to his conclusion being overturned.

Maloney, Paul Former professor of Archaeology, Greek and Old Testament at Vennard College and United Wesleyan College, Pennsylvania. Arranged the transfer to the USA of the Frei collection of sticky-tape samples from the Shroud.

Marinelli, Prof. Emanuela Graduated in Natural and Geological Sciences at La Sapienza University, Rome. Has written several books on the Shroud, including, in English, with journalist Orazio Petrosillo, *The Enigma of the Shroud.* A leading promoter of the Rome-based Shroud group Collegamento pro Sindone.

Marino, Joe Former Benedictine monk. An indefatigable communicator of the latest findings and news relating to the Shroud.

Mattei, Prof. Luigi E. International artist based in Bologna. Has made a life-sized sculpture based on the man of the Shroud for a special exhibition in Bologna during the year 2000.

Mattingly, Prof. Stephen Head of Microbiology at the University of Texas Science Health Center, San Antonio. Supported Dr Garza-Valdes' pioneering microbiological approach to the Shroud's radiocarbon-dating problem. From recent experiments argues for a bacteriological cause of the Shroud's image.

Miller, Vernon Head of the Scientific and Industrial Photography Dept., the Brooks Institute of Photography, Santa Barbara, California. With Barrie Schwortz, was official photographer for the STURP scientific examination of the Shroud in 1978.

Mills, Dr Allan A. Senior Lecturer, Department of Physics and Astronomy, University of Leicester. Theorizes that the Shroud's image was produced by singlet oxygen lost from the Shroud man's body being carried upwards and promoting a long-term 'yellowing reaction' on the cloth.

Moran, Kevin Technology specialist and president of an engineering company. Has made detailed studies of Shroud imprint samples among the Max Frei collection of sticky-tape samples from the Shroud, currently housed in Durham, North Carolina.

Mottern, William Nuclear safeguards specialist with Sandia National Laboratories, Albuquerque, New Mexico. Was responsible for X-raying the Shroud as part of the 1978 STURP examination.

Nickell, Joe British instructor and sometime magician. Member of CSICOP(Committee For Scientific Investigation of Claims of the Paranormal). Claims the Shroud's image to have been created by a brass-rubbing technique.

Nitowski, Dr Eugenia L. American archaeologist. Made a definitive study of rock-cut 'rolling-stone' tombs of Jesus' time for her doctoral thesis. With Dr Joseph Kohlbeck worked on the analysis of limestone dust from the underside of the Shroud, finding it to be a strikingly close match to the limestone of Jerusalem's ancient tombs.

Orareo, Richard Based in Boston, has assembled America's finest private collection of books and other publications about the Shroud over the centuries. The collection includes what is probably the finest assemblage outside Italy of historical prints and engravings of Shroud expositions.

Otterbein, Fr Adam, CSSR (d.1998) Redemptorist priest. Founder of the American Holy Shroud Guild. Controlled US production and publication of the Enrie Shroud photographs and the Wuenschel Library of Shroud materials. Greatly encouraged and facilitated Shroud researches throughout the English-speaking world. Succeeded by Fr Fred Brinkman.

Pellicori, Samuel Optical physicist, Santa Barbara Research Center, Goleta, California. Has worked on various NASA space programmes. Made an ultraviolet fluorescence photography study of the Shroud during the 1978 STURP examination.

Pia, Secondo (d.1941) Piedmontese lawyer and politician. As a skilled amateur photographer was deputed to take the first-ever official photograph of the Shroud in 1898. Was the first to discover the Shroud's hidden 'photographic' characteristics when viewed in negative.

Picknett, Lynn London journalist. With systems analyst Clive Prince promulgated the theory that the Shroud image was created photographically in 1492 by Leonardo da Vinci.

Piczek, Isabel Los Angeles-based liturgical artist specializing in creating murals, mosaics and stained glass windows for churches and cathedrals. From her professional experience, and her exhaustive research with life models whom she employed to assume the Shroud pose, she argues for the impossibility of the Shroud being the work of a mediaeval artist.

Raes, Prof. Gilbert Director of the Laboratory for Textile Technology, University of Ghent, Belgium. Took a sample from the Shroud for specialist study in 1973.

Ricci, Monsignor Giulio, (d. 1995) Leading Italian researcher and lecturer on the Shroud, based in Rome. Made a particularly intensive and vivid study of the Shroud as a document of Jesus' sufferings prior to and during his crucifixion.

Riggi, Prof. Giovanni Turin microanalyst. Personally cut from the Shroud the sample divided between the radiocarbon-dating laboratories in 1988. Has made microanalytical studies of dust vacuumed from the Shroud's underside, discovering that virtually all the pollens from this underside have a limestone coating as if the Shroud had been laid on stone on this side.

Rinaldi, Fr Peter (d.1993) Italian-born Roman Catholic parish priest at Corpus Christi Church, Port Chester, New York. Acted as intermediary to bring about the STURP scientific examination of the Shroud in 1978.

Robinson, Dr John A.T. (d.1983), Anglican Bishop of Woolwich, England. Author of the controversial *Honest to God*, and one of Britain's most outstanding scholars of New Testament studies. Became one of the founders of the British Society for the Turin Shroud, describing the cloth and its image as unexpectedly compatible with the gospel descriptions of Jesus' burial, and as 'something that cannot easily be explained away'.

Rogers, Dr Ray N. Chemist at the Los Alamos National Laboratory. Participated in the 1978 STURP scientific examination of the Shroud, subsequently authoring a definitive *Analytica Chimica Acta* scientific paper on the Shroud's physics and chemistry.

Scavone, Prof. Daniel Emeritus Professor of History, University of Southern Indiana, Evansville. Foremost historian of the Shroud in the United States. Argues for the earliest versions of the Grail story to be based on the Shroud being taken to Edessa.

Scheuermann, Oswald German physics teacher. Produces by an instantaneous electrostatic process called corona discharge images on cloth which are claimed to be a parallel to the Shroud image.

Schumacher, Peter M. Electronics engineer. Inventor and developer of the VP-8 Image Analyzer by which the Shroud image's seeming 3-D characteristics were scientifically demonstrated.

Schwalbe, Larry Los Alamos National Laboratory, New Mexico. Participated in the STURP scientific examination of the Shroud in 1978. With colleague Dr Ray Rogers pioneered studies of the Shroud's physics and chemistry, concluding that the 'body' image was the product of some cellulose oxidation-dehydration reaction, rather than an applied pigment.

Schwortz, Barrie M. Los Angeles-based professional photographer. Official documenting photographer for the STURP scientific examination of the Shroud in 1978. Creator of the world's most encyclopaedic and respected Internet site for information on the Shroud, *www.shroud.com.*

Scott, Prof. John Beldon Professor of Art History, University of Iowa. Specialist in the architecture associated with the Shroud during the centuries that it has been kept in Turin.

Straiton, Dr Michael Physician resident in Surrey, England. Has put forward the theory that the Shroud is the imprint of a Crusader crucified by Saracens in the Middle Ages in mockery of the crucifixion of Jesus.

Tite, Prof. Michael Keeper of the British Museum radiocarbon-dating laboratory at the time of the Shroud carbon dating. Acted as invigilator/co-ordinator of the work of the three radiocarbon-dating laboratories, and in 1989 succeeded Prof. Hall as head of the Oxford laboratory.

Tryon, Dr Victor V. Director of Center for Advanced DNA Technology, University of Texas Health Science Center, San Antonio, Texas. He and his wife Nancy were the first Americans to determine the presence of DNA in 'blood' samples taken from the Shroud.

Vala, Leo London-based studio and fashion photographer. Intrigued by the possibilities of obtaining 3-D from a two-dimensional picture, produced the first-ever convincing 3-D representation of the head of the man of the Shroud during the 1960s, doing so by projecting the negative image onto a Plasticine-type mould , then working from information in the shadows.

Vial, Gabriel French specialist in the history of textiles, Centre International d'Etude des Textiles Anciens, Lyons, France. Attended the cutting from the Shroud of the radiocarbon-dating sample on 21 April 1988, and made technical studies of elements such as the seam-line between the so-called side-strip and the main body of the cloth.

Vignon, Paul (d.1943) Professor, Faculty of Philosophy, Institut Catholique, Paris. Developed a vaporographic explanation for the formation of the Shroud's image. Was accorded special examination of the Shroud during one night at the time of the 1933 exposition. Pioneered the iconographic theory that the Shroud influenced early Byzantine portraits of Christ.

Vikan, Gary Director of the Walters Art Gallery, Baltimore. Argues that the Shroud is a work of the Middle Ages inspired by the self-mortifying *penitentes* cult.

Volckringer, Dr Jean (d.1991) French pharmacist. During the 1930s a colleague of surgeon Dr Pierre Barbet at St Joseph's Hospital, Paris. Noting the Shroud image's similarities to the images created by pressed plants in botanical collections, assembled a collection of such plant images in the hope of shedding light on how the Shroud's image came to be formed.

Whanger, Dr Alan Professor of Psychiatry, Duke University Medical Center, Durham, North Carolina. Developer of the polarized image overlay technique for scientifically comparing the Shroud image with early Christ portraits. Identifies the imprints of numerous artefacts, also flowers of Israel, in the otherwise plain background to the Shroud's image.

Willis, Dr David (d.1976) Leading British medical researcher on the Shroud during the 1960s and early 1970s. Strongly contested the then widely promulgated non-medical arguments that the Shroud proved Jesus did not die on the cross.

Wilson, Ian A history graduate of Magdalen College, Oxford. During the 1960s, aided by Fr Maurus Green and Dr David Willis, he developed the theory that the Shroud was one and the same as the Jesus-imprinted cloth of Edessa, lost from Constantinople in 1204. With Bishop John Robinson and others, founded the British Society for the Turin Shroud in 1977, and continues to edit its newsletter.

Zaninotto, Gino Classical scholar based in Rome. First to discover the Gregory Referendarius description of the cloth of Edessa, which refers to this bearing, as on the Shroud, blood from the wound of the lance thrust into Jesus' side.

Zugibe, Dr Fred Chief Medical Examiner, Rockland County, New York. Leading medical proponent of the Shroud's authenticity in the eastern USA. Using volunteer subjects, has researched the physiological effects of crucifixion as indicated on the Shroud.

A PICTORIAL CHRONOLOGY OF THE SHROUD'S HISTORY

This chronology is based on the hypothesis that the Shroud is the same as the cloth of Edessa.

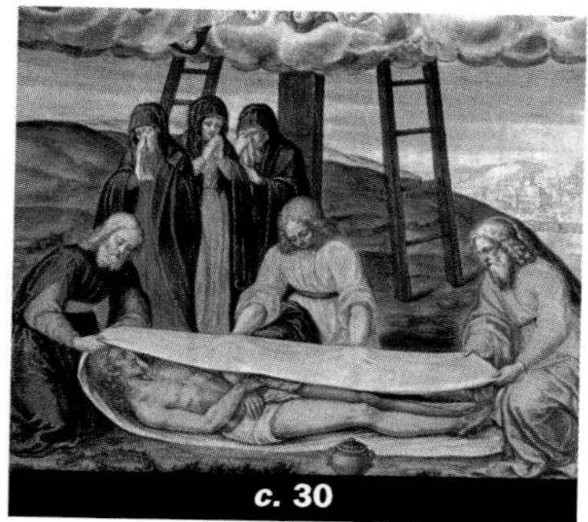
c. 30

177

525

c. 30 Death of Jesus by crucifixion in Jerusalem, and his burial by wrapping in a *sindon* or shroud. According to the Christian gospels, some thirty-six hours later this shroud is found abandoned and the tomb empty. According to later sources, a cloth imprinted with Jesus' likeness is taken from Jerusalem to Edessa (the present-day Urfa in eastern Turkey), where it is instrumental in converting Edessa's King Abgar V (reigned 13–50) to Christianity. But following a later reversion to paganism, this cloth's whereabouts become lost.

177 Accession of Edessa's King Abgar VIII, the Great. During his reign a flood in Edessa in 201 is reported to have damaged an apparently purpose-built 'church of the Christians', one of several indications of this Abgar's toleration of Christianity at this very early period. This causes some historians to favour him as the true Abgar of the 'conversion' story.

216 Four years after Abgar VIII's death, Edessa's full absorption into the Roman Empire, ending its monarchy and therefore the period within which the Jesus-imprinted cloth could have been brought to the city.

375 A version of the story of Edessa's conversion, the *Doctrine of Addai*, referred to the 'portrait' of Jesus brought from Jerusalem to Abgar as having been 'painted'. But from pilgrims' descriptions of the city from the same time, it is clear that there is no knowledge of this object's whereabouts, or even of its existence.

525 Edessa is again seriously flooded. Probably during the major repair operation which followed, a cloth imprinted with Jesus' likeness is found sealed in a niche above one of the city's gates. This is immediately hailed as the cloth which five centuries before had been brought from Jerusalem to Abgar V. Its imprint of Jesus is unequivocally described as 'not the work of human hands'. Some accounts describe it as a *sindon*, also as a *tetradiplon*, doubled in four, indicating it to be a large cloth folded considerably smaller than its full size. In Christian art there immediately emerges the distinctive likeness associated with Jesus' human appearance to this day.

569 A poem of this year likens the marble of Edessa's Hagia Sophia cathedral, which has been rebuilt after the flood, to 'the image not the work of [human] hands', i.e. the Jesus-imprinted cloth being housed in this cathedral.

944

723 Outbreak of iconoclasm. As part of a vogue for religious purity which will continue for the next 120 years, man-made likenesses of Jesus are destroyed throughout the Byzantine and Muslim empires. But the Jesus-imprinted cloth in Edessa (which has fallen under Muslim rule), survives unscathed.

943 An army sent by the Byzantine emperor Romanus arrives at still Muslim-held Edessa. Its general promises to leave Edessa untouched, to pay a large sum of money, and to release 200 Muslim prisoners, all in return for the Jesus-imprinted cloth. After much negotiation a deal is struck and the cloth is taken to Constantinople, where on 15 August 944 it is received in the city amid great celebrations. It is accorded its own feast day, 16 August. Because of the awe in which the cloth is held in Eastern Orthodox thought, there is no public showing. However, among the high dignitaries accorded special private showings one, Gregory Referendarius, mentions being able to see on the cloth the wound in Jesus' side. The cloth is installed in the Pharos Chapel of Constantinople's Imperial Palace, the repository of other most sacred relics of Jesus.

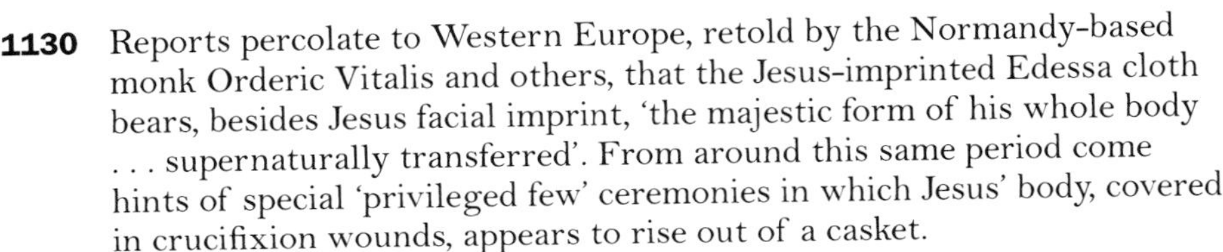

1130 Reports percolate to Western Europe, retold by the Normandy-based monk Orderic Vitalis and others, that the Jesus-imprinted Edessa cloth bears, besides Jesus facial imprint, 'the majestic form of his whole body . . . supernaturally transferred'. From around this same period come hints of special 'privileged few' ceremonies in which Jesus' body, covered in crucifixion wounds, appears to rise out of a casket.

1204

***c.* 1192** Hungary's 'Pray Manuscript', created about this year by an artist strongly influenced by Constantinople, shows the body of Jesus laid out totally naked in identical 'crossed hands' style to the Shroud. The shroud depicted in the same drawings exhibits what appear to be the mysterious poker holes still visible on the Shroud to this day.

1203 The French Crusader Robert de Clari, viewing Constantinople at a time when he and his fellow-Crusaders are guests in the city, reports seeing in the Church of St Mary at Blachernae, Constantinople's rallying place in times of crisis, 'the shroud in which our Lord had been wrapped'. He adds: 'On every Friday this raised itself upright so that one could see the figure of our Lord on it.'

1204 The French-led Fourth Crusade captures and sacks Constantinople. Many of the city's treasures are looted. Whatever the identity of the cloth of Edessa, it disappears in the confusion. Robert de Clari writes of the 'shroud' he saw: 'Neither Greek nor Frenchman knew what became of this shroud when the city was taken.'

1205–1306

1205–1306
A century of silence concerning the Shroud's possible whereabouts, except for reports of the Crusader Order of Knights Templar worshipping a mysterious bearded male head at secret chapter meetings. A very Shroud-like Templar panel painting found in the environs of an English Templar preceptory at Templecombe, England, suggests that this head may have been the Shroud.

1314

1307 13 October. On the orders of the French King Philippe the Fair, every Templar in France is arrested at dawn on a series of heresy charges, including worship of the 'head', an object which, despite the surprise nature of the arrests, is never found.

1314 19 March. The Templar Order's highest dignitaries, Jacques de Molay and Geoffrey de Charny, are burnt at the stake in Paris, protesting their order's innocence.

1355 According to the later 'd'Arcis Memorandum' (see below), held at around this time are western Europe's first known expositions of the Shroud as we know it today. The location is the tiny church of Lirey near Troyes, founded by a local knight, Geoffrey I de Charny. The Shroud's first known European owner, this Geoffrey is killed at the battle of Poitiers on 19 September 1356, leaving a widow, Jeanne de Vergy, a young son, Geoffrey II de Charny – and the Shroud . . .

1355

1389 15 August. Royal officers arrive in Lirey, where reportedly Geoffrey II de Charny has been displaying the Shroud as if the true shroud of Jesus. They are foiled from seizing it on the grounds that the key is not available. Later in this same year Bishop Pierre d'Arcis of Troyes writes a forceful memorandum to the French anti-pope, Clement VII, claiming the Shroud to have been 'cunningly painted' and asking for showings of it to be stopped, a request which is declined.

1398 22 May. Death of Geoffrey II de Charny, ownership of the Shroud passing to his daughter Margaret, who despite two marriages, appears to have been unable to bear children.

1418 6 July. Because of security risks arising from the wars with England, the Shroud is moved from Lirey to the castle of Montfort, owned by Margaret de Charny's second husband, Humbert, Count de la Roche, then later to St Hippolyte sur Doubs, in Alsace-Lorraine, close to Switzerland.

1418

1453 22 March. Elderly and still childless, Margaret de Charny receives a castle and an estate from Duke Louis of Savoy, in return for 'valuable services'. The 'valuable services' are understood to have been the hand-over of the Shroud to the Savoy family, who will be the Shroud's owners for the next five centuries.

1464 6 February. Margaret de Charny having died four years earlier, Duke Louis of Savoy agrees to pay the Lirey clergy a rent as compensation for their loss of the Shroud, clearly indicating the Shroud's derivation from the de Charnys of Lirey.

1502 11 June. Inauguration of a new 'permanent' home for the Shroud, the Sainte Chapelle, specially built for it at Chambéry.

1506 21 April. Pope Julius II accords the Shroud its own feast day, May 4. This will be the day of the year on which many subsequent public showings of the Shroud will take place.

1509 10 August. The Shroud is installed in a magnificent silver casket specially commissioned for it by the Dowager Duchess of Savoy Margaret of Austria, regent of the Netherlands.

1532

1532 4 December. A major fire breaks out at the Sainte Chapelle, Chambéry. With no time to summon the key-holders to unlock the Shroud from its iron-grilled repository, it is rescued by the skill and heroism of a local blacksmith, though not without serious damage. Molten silver from Margaret of Austria's ruined casket is found to have seared through one corner of the multi-folded cloth, scarring it with a patchwork of burns. Yet much to people's amazement the all-important image has hardly been touched.

1534 16 April–2 May. Four Poor Clare nuns carry out repairs to the Shroud, stitching it onto a strong Holland-cloth backing, and sewing triangular-shaped patches over the more disfiguring burnmarks

1535 Invasion by French troops necessitates the Shroud being moved from Chambéry. Its subsequent travels during the next few years include Turin, Milan, Vercelli and Nice.

1534

1578 The Shroud is moved to Turin, ostensibly to save saintly Cardinal Charles Borromeo the rigours of crossing the Alps to Chambéry, after he vowed to venerate it following Milan being spared a terrible plague. Except in times of war or similar danger, Turin Cathedral will be the Shroud's new home, a special repository being built for it at the high altar end.

1694 After conservation measures by the Blessed Sebastian Valfré, including sewing on a new black lining cloth, the Shroud is transferred to the newly completed Royal Chapel, linking Turin Cathedral and the Royal Palace, as designed by Guarino Guarini. It is deposited in a specially constructed repository, above the chapel altar (designed by Antonio Bertola) that will be its home for most of the next three centuries.

1706 The Shroud is temporarily moved to Genoa.

1737

1737 4 May. Before huge crowds, the Shroud is displayed from a balcony of Turin's Royal Palace to mark the marriage of Duke Charles-Emmanuel III of Savoy.

1868 24–27 April. A public exposition of the Shroud in Turin Cathedral, the first ever in which it is displayed statically in a frame, as distinct from being held up by clergy. Princess Clotilde of Savoy personally replaces Valfré's black silk lining cloth with a red one for this occasion.

1898 25 May–2 June. A public exposition of the Shroud in Turin Cathedral to mark the Savoy family's fiftieth anniversary as rulers of all Italy.

28 May. The Shroud is photographed by local councillor and proficient amateur photographer Secondo Pia, revealing for the first time the extraordinary, life-like 'photograph' when it is viewed in negative.

1973

1902 21 April. Anatomy professor Yves Delage, an agnostic, presents a paper to the French Academy of Sciences arguing that the Shroud is too medically convincing not to have wrapped a genuine, crucified human body.

1931 3–24 May. A public exposition of the Shroud in Turin Cathedral as part of the marriage celebrations for Prince Umberto of Savoy, later to become King Umberto II.

23 May. Turin photographer Giuseppe Enrie takes a series of black-and-white photographs of the Shroud, including the face life-sized. These will be the definitive photographs for the next half-century.

1933 24 September–15 October. A public exposition of the Shroud in Turin Cathedral as part of the celebrations for the Holy Year.

1939 September. For safety, following the outbreak of World War II, the Shroud is secretly moved from Turin to the Benedictine Abbey of Montevergine.

1946 The Shroud is returned to Turin.

1978

1973 22 November. In a specially prepared room in Turin's Royal Palace, the Shroud is exhibited before a limited gathering of journalists and others. This is the only known occasion of its being displayed vertically rather than horizontally.

23 November. The Shroud is filmed for the first time for colour television.

24 November. A commission of experts secretly studies the Shroud, and a sample of its linen is snipped from one corner for Belgian textile expert Professor Gilbert Raes.

1978 26 August–8 October. A public exposition of the Shroud in Turin Cathedral. This is attended by some 3 million pilgrims.

8–13 October. Intensive scientific examination of the Shroud in a specially prepared suite in the Royal Palace. Some twenty-four American scientists and specialists, the STURP team, participate and take samples.

1988

1979 24–5 March. STURP announces preliminary findings that the Shroud's image was not created by an artist, a conclusion subsequently challenged by Dr Walter McCrone.

1983 18 March. Following the death of Umberto II of Savoy, the Shroud is bequeathed to the Pope and his successors, thereby, for the first time in its known history, becoming formally owned by the Catholic Church.

1988 21 April. In the presence of the heads of the Arizona, Oxford and Zurich radiocarbon-dating laboratories, Prof. Giovanni Riggi snips a sliver from the top left-hand corner of the Shroud. This is then carefully

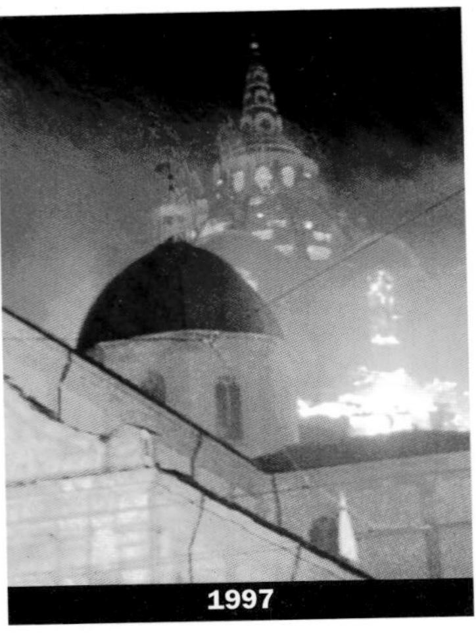
1997

1988 (cont'd)
divided up so that each laboratory receives the agreed amount of Shroud sample.

6 May. The Arizona laboratory's Shroud sample produces a date of 1350. In the ensuing months the Zurich and Oxford laboratories arrive at similar dates.

13 October. The radiocarbon dates of 1260–1390 are announced to the world via press conferences in London and Turin.

1993 24 February. The Shroud, still in its traditional casket, is removed from its normal home in the Royal Chapel and installed in a new, temporary display case behind Turin Cathedral's high altar.

1997 11 April. Fire breaks out in the Royal Chapel, where the Shroud had been kept for three centuries prior to 1993. With the Chapel ablaze, the Shroud is in danger even in its temporary showcase, which has to be smashed by firemen in order to remove it to safety.

14 April The Shroud's condition is checked by a hastily assembled team of experts. It is found to have been unharmed by the fire, and is taken to a secret location.

25 June. New, high-definition photographs of the Shroud are taken by Giancarlo Durante.

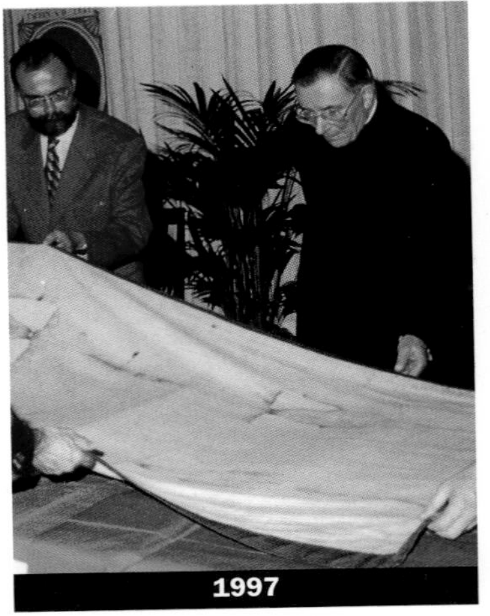
1997

1998 15 April. The Shroud is brought from its secret location to temporary sacristy in Turin Cathedral. Mechthild Flury-Lemberg and Sister Maria Clara Antonini remove its blue satin surround and sew it onto a new white cloth.

17 April. The Shroud is installed in its new conservation case.

18 April. Commencement of a public exposition of the Shroud, commemorating the centenary of Secondo Pia's discovery of its photographic properties.

24 May. Pope John Paul II visits Turin Cathedral, prays before the Shroud, and delivers a homily on it.

4 June. The conclusion of the public expositions. The Shroud's conservation case is switched to off-display mode.

2000

2000 2–5 March. A symposium is held in Turin with delegates invited to 'identify and examine in depth . . . any questions which may become the subject of future research . . . in view of a possible future campaign of studies and research'.

BIBLIOGRAPHY AND GUIDE TO SHROUD RESOURCES ON THE WORLD WIDE WEB

ADLER, ALAN D., 'Updating Recent Studies on the Shroud of Turin', in ACS Symposium Series no. 625, *Archaeological Chemistry: Organic, Inorganic and Biochemical Analysis*, Mary Virginia Orna (ed.), American Chemical Society, 1996, pp. 223–8

ALLEN, NICHOLAS P., 'Verification of the Nature and Causes of the Photo-negative Images on the Shroud of Lirey-Chambéry-Turin', *De Arte*, 51, Pretoria, UNISA, 1995

BULST, WERNER *Betrug am Turiner Grabtuch: Der manipulierte Carbontest*, Frankfurt, Knecht, 1990

– and HEINRICH PFEIFFER *Das Turiner Grabtuch und das Christusbild*, Frankfurt, Knecht, 1987

CAMERON, AVERIL, *The Sceptic and the Shroud. An Inaugural Lecture in the Departments of Classics and History delivered at King's College, London, on 19 April 1980*, London, 1980

CAMERON, J. M., 'A pathologist looks at the Shroud' In P. Jennings (ed.) *Face to Face with the Turin Shroud*, Oxford, Mowbray, 1978, pp. 57–9

CARTER, GILES F., 'Formation of the Image on the Shroud of Turin by X-Rays: A New Hypothesis' *ACS Advances in Chemistry No. 205, Archaeological Chemistry*, pp. 425–446

CRAIG, EMILY and RANDALL R. BRESEE, 'Image Formation and the Shroud of Turin', *Journal of Imaging Science and Technology*, vol 34, no. 1, January–February 1994

DAMON, P. E. et al., 'Radiocarbon dating of the shroud of Turin', *Nature*, vol 337, no. 6208, 16 February 1989, pp. 611–15

DANIN, AVINOAM, ALAN D. WHANGER, URI BARUCH and MARY WHANGER, *Flora of the Shroud of Turin*, St. Louis, Missouri Botanical Garden Press, 1999

DE CLARI, R., *The Conquest of Constantinople*, trans E. H. McNeal, New York, Columbia University Press, 1936

DREWS, ROBERT, *In Search of the Shroud of Turin*, New Jersey, Roman & Allanheld, 1984

DUBARLE, A. M., *Histoire ancienne du linceul de Turin jusqu'au XIIIe siècle*, Paris, O. E. I. L., 1985

FINALDI, GABRIELE, *The Image of Christ: The catalogue of the exhibition 'Seeing Salvation'*, London, National Gallery Co. Ltd., 2000

GARZA-VALDES, LEONCIO A., *The DNA of God?* New York, Doubleday, 1999

GILBERT, R., and M. M. GILBERT, 'Ultra-violet visible reflectance and fluorescence spectra of the Shroud of Turin', *Applied Optics* 19, pp1930–36

GOVE, HARRY E., *Relic, Icon or Hoax: Carbon dating the Turin shroud*, Bristol (England) and Philadelphia, Institute of Physics Publishing, 1996

– and S. J., MATTINGLY, A. R. DAVID, L. A. GARZA-VALDES, 'A problematic source of organic contamination of linen' in *Nuclear Instruments and Methods in Physics Research – Section B*, Amsterdam, Elsevier, 1997, pp. 504–7

GRABAR, ANDRÉ, 'La Sainte Face de Laon et le Mandylion dans l'art orthodoxe', *Seminarium Kondakovianum*, Prague, 1935, pp. 5–37

GUSCIN, MARK, *The Oviedo Cloth*, Cambridge, Lutterworth Press, 1998

HAAS, NICU, 'Anthropological Observations on the Skeletal Remains from Giv'at ha-Mivtar', *Israel Exploration Journal*, vol 20, nos 1–2, 1970

HELLER, JOHN H., *Report on the Shroud of Turin*, Boston, Houghton Mifflin, 1983

– and A. D. ADLER, 'Blood on the Shroud of Turin', *Applied Optics* vol 19, no. 16, August 1980, pp. 2742–4

– 'A Chemical Investigation of the Shroud of Turin', *Journal of the Canadian Society of Forensic Science*, vol 14, no. 3. 1981, pp. 81–103

IANNONE, JOHN C., *The Mystery of the Shroud of Turin*, New York, Alba, 1998

JUMPER, E. J, A. D. ADLER, J. P. JACKSON, S. F. PELLICORI, J. H. HELLER, J. R. DRUZIK, 'A comprehensive examination of the various stains and images of the Shroud of Turin' in J. B. Lambert (ed.), *Archaeological Chemistry III, Advances in Chemistry Series*, no. 205, American Chemical Society, 1984, pp. 446–76

KAEUPER, RICHARD W., and ELSPETH KENNEDY, *The Book of Chivalry of Geoffroi de Charny: Text, Context and Translation*, Philadelphia, University of Philadelphia Press, 1996

KERSTEN, HOLGER and ELMAR GRUBER, *The Jesus Conspiracy: The Turin Shroud and the Truth about the Resurrection*, Shaftesbury (Dorset), Element, 1994

KOHLBECK, JOSEPH A. and EUGENIA L. NITOWSKI, 'New Evidence May Explain Image on Shroud of Turin', *Biblical Archaeology Review*, July/August 1986, pp. 18–29

LAVOIE, GILBERT R., *Unlocking the Secrets of the Shroud*, Allen (Texas), Thomas More, 1998

MCCRONE, WALTER, *Judgement Day for the Turin Shroud*, Chicago (Illinois), Microscope Publications, 1996

MEACHAM, W., 'The Authentication of the Turin Shroud; An Issue in Archaeological Epistemology', *Current Anthropology*, 24, 3, June 1983, pp. 283–312

– (ed.) *Turin Shroud – Image of Christ? Proceedings of a Symposium held in Hong Kong, March 1986*, Hong Kong, Turin Shroud Photographic Exhibition Organizing Committee, 1987

MILLER, V. D., and S. F. PELLICORI, 'Ultraviolet Fluorescence Investigation of the Shroud of Turin', *Journal of Biological Photography*, vol. 49, no. 3, July 1981, pp. 71–85

MILLS, ALAN A., 'Image Formation on the Shroud of Turin: the reactive oxidation intermediates hypothesis', *Interdisciplinary Science Reviews*, vol 20, no. 4, December 1995, pp. 319–27

MORETTO, GINO, *Sindone, La Guida*, Turin, Editrice Elle di Ci, 1996

MORRIS, R. A., L. A. SCHWALBE and J. R. LONDON, 'X-Ray Fluorescence Investigation of the Shroud of Turin', *X-Ray Spectrometry*, vol 9, no. 2, 1980, pp. 40–47

MOTTERN, R. W., R. J. LONDON and R. A. MORRIS, 'Radiographic Examination of the Shroud of Turin – A Preliminary report', *Materials Evaluation* vol 38, no. 12, 1979, pp. 39–44

NICKELL, JOE, *Inquest on the Shroud of Turin*, New York, Prometheus, 1983

– 'Pollens on the "Shroud": A Study in Deception', *Skeptical Inquirer*, vol 18, summer 1994, pp. 379–85

PELLICORI, S., and M. EVANS, 'The Shroud of Turin through the Microscope', *Archaeology* Jan–Feb 1981, pp. 35–53

PERRET, M., 'Essai sur l'histoire du S. Suaire du XIVe au XVIe siècle,' *Mémoires de l'Académie des Sciences, Belles Lettres et Arts de Savoie*, IV, 1960, pp. 49–121

PETROSILLO, ORAZIO and EMANUELA MARINELLI, *The Enigma of the Shroud: A Challenge to Science*, Malta, Publishers Enterprises Group, 1996

PICKNETT, LYNN and CLIVE PRINCE, *Turin Shroud: In Whose Image? The Shocking Truth Unveiled*, London, Bloomsbury, 1994

RINALDI, PETER M., *It is the Lord: A Study of the Shroud of Christ*, New York, Vantage, 1972

SCAVONE, DANIEL C., 'The Shroud of Turin in Constantinople: The Documentary Evidence', *Daidalikon: Studies in Memory of Raymond V. Schroder*, S. J. Raymond F. Sutton Jr. (ed.), Wauconda (Ill.), Bolchazy-Carducci, 1989

'The Turin Shroud from 1200 to 1400', *Alpha to Omega: Studies in honor of George John Szelmer on his Sixty-Fifth Birthday*, W. J. Cherf (ed.) Chicago, Ares, 1993

SCHILLER, GERTRUD, *Iconography of Christian Art, vol 2, The Passion of Jesus Christ*, trans Janet Seligman, London, Lund Humphries, 1972

SCHWALBE, L. A. and R. N. ROGERS, 'Physics and Chemistry of the Shroud of Turin', *Analytica Chimica Acta* 135, 1982, pp. 3–49

SCOTT, JOHN BELDON, 'Seeing the Shroud: Guarini's Reliquary Chapel in Turin and the Ostension of a Dynastic Relic', *Art Bulletin*, vol 77, no. 4 (December 1995), pp. 609–37

SOX, DAVID, *The Shroud Unmasked: Uncovering the Greatest Forgery of all Time*, Basingstoke, Lamp, 1988

STEVENSON, KENNETH E., and GARY R. HABERMAS, *Verdict on the Shroud: Evidence for the Death and Resurrection of Jesus Christ*, Ann Arbor (Michigan), Servant, 1981

TRIBBE, FRANK C., *Portrait of Jesus? The Illustrated Story of the Shroud of Turin*, New York, Stein & Day, 1983

UPINSKY A. A. (ed.), *L'Identification Scientifique de l'Homme du Linceul Jésus de Nazareth: Actes de Symposium Scientifique International, Rome 1993*, Paris, François-Xavier de Guibert, 1995

VIGNON, PAUL, *Le Saint Suaire devant la science, l'archéologie, l'histoire, l'iconographie, la logique*, Paris, Masson, 1939

VOLCKRINGER, JEAN, *The Holy Shroud: Science Confronts the Imprints*, trans Victoria Harper, Manly, Runciman,1991

WALSH, JOHN, *The Shroud*, New York, Random House, 1963

WHANGER, ALAN, 'Polarized Overlay Technique; A New Image Comparison Method and its Application', *Applied Optics*, 24, np. 16, 15 March 1985, pp. 766–72

WHANGER, MARY and ALAN, *The Shroud of Turin: An Adventure of Discovery*, Franklin (Tennessee), Providence House, 1998

WILCOX, ROBERT K., *Shroud*, New York, Macmillan, 1977

WILSON, IAN, *The Shroud of Turin*, New York, Doubleday, 1978 (also published as *The Turin Shroud*, London, Gollancz, 1978)

– *The Mysterious Shroud*, New York, Doubleday 1986 (also published as *The Evidence of the Shroud*, London, O'Mara, 1986)

– *The Blood and the Shroud*, London, Weidenfeld & Nicolson, 1998

ZIAS, JOSEPH and ELIEZER SEKELES, 'The Crucified man from Giv'at ha-Mivtar: A Reappraisal', *Israel Exploration Journal* vol 35, no. 1, 1985.

ZIAS, JOSEPH and ELIEZER SEKELES, 'The Crucified man from Giv'at ha-Mivtar: A Reappraisal', *Biblical Archaeologist*, September 1985

ZUGIBE, FREDERICK T., *The Cross and the Shroud: A Medical Examiner Interprets the Turin Shroud*, New York, Exposition Press, 1982

The following is just a small sampling of the Shroud resources that are now available on the Internet:

www.shroud.com – The Shroud of Turin Website (English) – Presented by Barrie Schwortz.

www.sindone.torino.chiesacattolica.it – Archdiocese of Turin Official Shroud Website (Italian, French and English)

www.ctv.es/USERS/linteum – Centro Español de Sindonología's (CES) Website (Spanish, French & English) – Official site of the organization formed to investigate the Sudarium of Oviedo

www.di.unito.it/sindon/ – Centro Internazionale de Sindonologia (International Center of Sindonology) Website (English and Italian) – Official site of the major Turin organization formed to investigate the Shroud

http://.space.tin.it/scienza/bachm/ – Collegamento pro Sindone Home Page (Italian & English) – Official site of one of the major Rome organizations formed to investigate the Shroud hosted by Emanuela & Maurizio Marinelli

www.shroud.com/bstsmain.htm – Gateway page to the British Society for the Turin Shroud section of the Shroud of Turin Website – Official site of the British organization formed to study the Shroud.

www.shroudcouncil.org – Council for the Study of Shroud of Turin (CSST) Website (English) – Official site of the organization formed by Dr Alan Whanger to study the Shroud

http://asso.itbs.fr/mntw/ – Montre-Nous Ton Visage (Show Us Your Face) Website (French) – Presented by one of the major Shroud organizations in France

http://www.petech.ac.za/shroud – Shroud of Lirey-Chambéry-Turin Home Page (English) – Presented by Dr Nicholas P. L. Allen, who concludes that the Shroud is a photograph produced in the Middle Ages.

http://humanist.net/shroud/ – The Skeptical Shroud of Turin Website (English) – Hosted by the Committee for the Scientific Investigation of Claims of the Paranormal (CSICOP).

INDEX